Going Steady

Anna Blake

Going Steady

More Relationship Advice from Your Horse

Cover design and formatting by JD Smith

Published by Prairie Moon Press

All enquiries to annamarieblake@gmail.com

First published 2019

ISBN: 978-1-7328258-2-6 (ebook)
978-1-7328258-1-9 (paperback)

Dedication

For the Faraway horses and the Transient
horses, those who shared fleeting hours,
showed how to listen to an unspoken language.
I remember you.
A flash of brilliance or an instant of hard-won
honesty. You linger, traveling on with me,
staying in my mind until I find the words.

Winter Solstice

"Should I get a Horse?"

February 2, 10 p.m., 12 degrees. There was dense fog all day. We didn't see the sun and the temperature stayed in the teens. My barn is full now, with three fosters visiting, on top of the usual herd of boarded horses and my family horses.

It's time for the night feeding; I'm wearing double socks in my muck boots, sweats over my pajama bottoms, coat zipped to the very top, and two layers of hats and gloves. The dogs come with me as I carry two buckets of warm mush; one for the fosters who could use just a bit extra on such a bitter night, one for the elderly toothless donkey who can't stay warm by chewing hay all night like the others. There's some of her supper frozen in her feed-pan; she's a slow eater. Everyone else gets extra hay, a flake of alfalfa, and a visual once-over.

I've fallen hard enough on icy ground that I've had to catch my breath and then crawl to a safe place to stand again; I swear, icy winter nights are more dangerous than horses. So, it's small steps, testing my boot cleats as I go around the barn to throw hay in the back pen. I want to put eyes on everyone, but my headlamp is flickering. A bit of whacking and head-shaking works and when I'm finally satisfied everyone is okay, I head back to the house to un-peel. My boots and coat are off when I remember the water. There's one tank that I should have topped off. The layers come back on and I waddle out the back door again, but no dogs volunteer to come along this time.

My barn hydrant has been frozen all week, so I've rolled out hose from the far side of the house. I can't stand the thought of hose-wrangling on this night, when the frost is as thick as snow, so I walk a pair of five-gallon buckets instead.

Here's why you should particularly feel no sympathy for me. Right about now, I set the buckets down, pull my phone out, and take my gloves off. It's so beautiful that, even in the dark, I take a few shots. It all looks night-vision green in my view finder and my eyes are too cold to focus. Then as I deliver the water, Edgar Rice Burro exhales a staccato series of heavy breaths, his precursor to braying, and I give him an extra scratch before going in for the night. Then, because Thursday is blog night, these last seven years, the dogs and I go to my studio to start writing. If there's anything less romantic than below-freezing trips to the barn, it's pounding out a blog past bedtime. Again, no sympathy for me; I'm hooked.

Tonight, I've been thinking about an email I received from a reader. The subject line asked, "Should I get a horse?" What a silly question.

The email was from a woman of a certain age, who has taken riding lessons every week for a couple of years but dreams of having horses at her home. Her husband and family think she shouldn't; she thinks I might be impartial since I don't know her. Really? I'm not sure I'm the right person to ask. Even now, I'm driven by the compulsion to have a horse.

It was a serious question and I gave her a serious answer. Keeping a horse at home is ugly work, and not just for the weather. It's constant fence repair and mucking and less time to ride than you imagine. I reeled off the numbers: cost of care, feed, vets, farriers, and all the rest. But the money is the easiest part.

Horses are somehow both accident-prone and dangerous. They get hurt or sick and it isn't always obvious until it's bad. It takes years to gain the required knowledge and methods to keep them well. Then, she'll need two; it's cruel to own one. Horses need the company of their own kind. And she'll need a truck and trailer and a safe place to ride. Or if she hauls to ride or have lessons, the horse left home might have anxiety, so maybe three horses are a better number. It gets complicated fast.

The heartfelt wish to have a horse is the selfish and easy part. I tell her it isn't so simple to just get rid of them if it doesn't work out. I give her the commitment talk. And of course, she must include them in her will to avoid them landing in rescue or on a truck to Mexico if they outlive her. Then I urge her to make a list of what she'd be willing to give up if she needed more money in the worst-case scenario.

Sometimes parents ask me about a horse for their kid (and none of us are much more mature than that) and I always say no, don't do it. Instead, lease a horse at a barn. When we get it wrong, it's the horse that suffers.

If the kid (you) can't eat or sleep, and begs relentlessly for at least a year, then consider getting a horse. Only do this thing if you think you'll die without one. Know that you will see ugly things that will haunt you forever and you'll be terrified a good part of the time. Then, take the leap, if you must. But, it's a lot to go through for the view of a horse outside your window.

I never candy-coat horse ownership, but what I don't say (and what I really believe) is that there's too much cheap talk about loving horses. I never think the answer to the question 'Should I get a horse?' is about owning one specific horse. I think we need to own all of them–each one of us literally owning each one of them.

Loving horses is not restricted to the conditional love of a personal horse or a breed of horses, but means accepting the old crippled ones, the babies that need care and training, and the ones destroyed by abuse and neglect, track horses and plow horses and horses past any kind of work. It's volunteering at a local rescue or therapeutic program when you're done at home. It's taking in an elder in the name of a heart-horse you've lost. And when your barn is full, then get out the checkbook and spend whatever is left there to support local riding programs and rescues. Show up and witness abuse cases in court; call your elected officials on horses' behalf. Then hope to encourage others by your example.

Should you get a horse? No. You should get all of them.

How to Ride Creatively

Riding a horse is the simplest thing in the world. Just point 'em and kick. What's so hard about that? As long as you don't care where you go or how you get there, no worries.

But we're humans, prone to having expectations and goals. And horses are sentient with thoughts and emotions of their own. Perhaps the first thing that horses and humans have in common is a dislike of random chaos, like wild turkeys falling out of trees or ice coming off the roof of indoor arenas.

Then the horse or rider might decide some sort of leadership is needed. You ask for something simple: Go away from the barn. Walk on the rail. Canter. But they don't.

About this time, it occurs to us there might be more to riding than we previously thought. Seeing others ride happy horses with finesse and relaxation, you might even start to think there's an *art* to riding. That's when training starts.

Because a horse has in-the-moment awareness, if you're in the saddle, you're the trainer. In other words, you're the *artist*. Creativity is your fuel.

But have you ever tried sculpting? Eye/hand coordination isn't as easy as you'd think. Tried painting? Paint-by-number exists because a paint brush is hard to control. Now lay down the paint brush and add a live horse to the mix. The worst part is self-judgment, seeing what's wrong in a picture is always the easy part.

But being an artist in the saddle means proposing a question with creativity, while floating in the realm of possibility. Is this the kind of nebulous idea that makes your head want to explode?

Start here: Any work of art starts with a foundation of technique. In this case, find balance in your seat, be aware of what your body is doing, especially your hands. Most importantly, relax. Creativity doesn't respond well to tension or force, any more than a horse does. So how do you ride creatively?

Step one: Let go of expectations and judgment. They only make your mind run like a rat on a wheel. Checking your mental list for mistakes doesn't help, but even worse, the deafening clatter of self-doubt makes it hard to hear your horse. Breathe; go silent and listen.

Step two: Have an idea about what you are asking for; it might be lateral work or trotting a box or making a water crossing. Then let it go and repeat step one.

Step three: Lower your expectations for perfection. Know you'll both get it wrong, but since you aren't judging, you don't care. Training something new is like you and your horse feeling around for each other in a dark room. He doesn't know what you want, and you don't know what he'll respond to. Lighten up, not because you are a patient saint, but because the most important thing is that your horse gets encouragement to try. Be positive. If he feels like everything he does is wrong, he'll stop trying. Sound familiar at all?

All animal training systems begin with rewarding a good basic response. The word dog trainers use is "shaping," meaning the progressive building of a response, step by step. In behavioral science they call it "successive approximation" or implying an *approximate* answer, not the correct one. It's a technique you learned early. Remember playing Hide 'N Seek as a kid and calling out "warmer, warmer, HOT" to help the seeker?

In the saddle it means that you think of a logical cue and ask for something. Then when he gives you the wrong answer, believe him because making him wrong ends the conversation.

Reward him, not to affirm the wrong answer but because he responded. A responsive horse is the foundation goal.

Here's where the creative part comes in: Because asking the wrong way louder never works, ask the same question using a slightly different cue. Let his first answer inform the next cue. If he gave you an answer that was more sideways than forward, for instance, take him at his word and ask again politely, but with a bit more forward. It's a short ask and a quick reward.

A horse learns what he did was right *after* you reward him for it.

Teaching an impatient horse to stand still can be a challenge. Ask for the halt and if you get anything kind of like slowing down, reward him. Walk on and ask again. If the halt is just a bit closer, reward that and walk off. Collect good tries and ignore the ones that don't happen. If you lose sight of the goal and start correcting him for moving, before he knows what *halt* means, then it's not fair. It's scribbling on the *Mona Lisa* with a sharpie pen. Take a breath and don't kill his try with correction. Get open-minded and find a cue that he can succeed with. Most likely a smaller cue.

A couple of years ago, I was training a mini-mule to drive. Focus was erratic and we had a time finding our rhythm. Our halts were a nasty combination of distraction and anxiety. The usual exhale/butt-scratch did nothing, and even as she spun around in the long lines, I had to stay behind her in the driver's position. Her anxiety was getting louder.

Is the leadership being questioned? By either you or your horse? Wonderful. Take a breath. Do you want to inspire your horse to confidence and partnership? Now is a good time to remember training is an art. And you are an artist. Exhale again.

So rather than increase the mule's stress, I found another place to scratch. It's that hairless place on the underside of the top of their tail. Do you know the spot? Horses love it too. Sure, passing cars wonder what you're up to; another reason to be glad that you gave up judgment of both you and your partner. Meanwhile, the mule got quiet and still, loving that gentle touch on the downside of her tail. She cocked her hip and we let time pass in this positive place, even if my hand wasn't thrilled at the location.

Beyond that, we waited long enough that she had some time to assimilate the whole interchange into the big picture. It involved her seeing me differently. Soon an exhale and hand on her hind was a reward enough, and from there, just my exhale brought the relaxation of a reward.

(Just in case you think what works with a mule is different that what works with a horse, you are totally correct. If it works with a mule, it works at least *twice* as well with a horse.)

One training technique will not work on every horse; they're individuals who respond individually. Looking at training this way, isn't creativity a greater asset than a huge, expensive box of harsh aids? Now it boils down to the confidence you feel in your own creativity.

The bad news: you can't buy creativity. The good news: we are born with infinite creativity. So it follows that we can all be genius trainers like Nuno or Klimke or Dorrance…at least in our own minds, but that's exactly where it matters to a horse.

Halt, Rein-back, Cha-cha-cha.

This is how a resistance-free trot feels: your horse glides with rhythmic relaxed strides. At first you think he might be moving slowly, but no, it's that his strides are longer. He has time to push from behind. Every vertebra in his back is loose. His movement is fluid and soft, like riding a wave.

His poll is relaxed without fear or tension, knowing there will be no pain in his mouth. Your elbows and hands float on the reins with no pull and no slack. You can trust him to keep his head steady because he's balanced by the forward movement. True "forward" relaxes the poll and his spine, all the way to a soft S movement to the end of his tail.

You're sitting the trot. You're not posting, and this is no western pleasure jog. With every stride you feel his hind legs push underneath you and lift your sit bone, one and then the other. Instead of trying to drive your seat back into the saddle, you lift just enough. You ride the up-stride. Lift, lift, lift. Light, light, light. And his stride gets a bit longer because your sit bone has created a space for him to step into. His back lifts and there's a magnetic quality between your seat and his back. This is where the conversation happens. It's small and quiet, but his movement is so much more than that.

As you finish the long side of the arena and come through the corner of the short end, toward C at the centerline, you give your good horse a half-halt. It's an inhale, your shoulders straighten a tad, with a light pulse of the thighs, you release quickly enough to feel the tiniest pause as he lifts his shoulders. He's ready. Then one, two, three strides and your seat melts.

If following his stride with your sit bones continues the trot, then allowing your seat to soften and rest, along with a squeeze of your thighs, means he will come to a halt, right at C. Let a five-second eternity pass. Breathe in, exhale. Let your body be soft, your hands quiet. He is immobile at the halt, standing square, but you both maintain a forward attitude; the shared awareness that you are not done. Inhale and allow your calves just an inch forward with light energy, and as he takes his first stride back, release a sit bone and move with the backward stride in the same way as a walk. One, two, three, four. Exactly four strides back, and a halt from a thigh pulse. Immobile.

Notice that you've done nothing with your hands. Continue doing that.

Especially now, do not rush your good horse. Inhale and cue his trot confidently with both calves. Go with him on the first stride, light and connected.

Exist together inside every stride; feel freedom and cooperation as equals. As you approach the corner, think about your outside aids as you turn your waist. Feel the inside hand open while the outside hand and leg close on his shoulder. Feel him turn underneath you, bending softly through his body. Because it's natural.

As you begin the long side, let your legs stretch down and your shoulder blades come closer. Inhale, let your legs ask for longer strides as you extend your elastic elbows just an inch so he can reach forward to the bit and carry you effortlessly on, dancing cheek to cheek.

I believe the halt/rein-back movement is as beautiful as any upper level dressage movement, piaffe or canter half-pass included. Some version of this movement has existed in dressage tests, from Second Level on up, forever. One clue about its difficulty is that a gait is skipped; from rein-back to trot without walk steps. It's deceptive in its simplicity.

The first thing I love about this movement is that it clearly reveals the quality of communication between the horse and rider. Are the steps diagonal? Is the horse's mouth relaxed? If your horse's head and neck can stay soft, if the rider can hold a neutral position, and if your horse can do the movements without bracing, your partnership will shine. This movement is relentlessly honest about your riding.

The other thing I love about this movement is that a Warmblood doesn't necessarily do it better than a backyard horse. A trot is a subjective thing but the halt/rein-back is not abstract. It isn't about gaits or breed or athleticism. Tack doesn't matter, and any rider is capable. It's about cooperation and oneness, as challenging as any upper level party tricks.

Ride the transitions without a horse. Imagine it in slow motion, training your brain to relax and notice details. Become so familiar with the movement that when you're in the saddle you can let your brain rest and focus on your seat.

The easiest way to ruin your rein-back? Use it as punishment, pulling the reins, see-sawing hands, using hyperflexion or pulling your horse behind the vertical. Betray the trust your horse has in you by slamming that bit, metal on bone, against the bars of his jaw. Shame on you.

How to train it? Like everything, start with small pieces and do them separately. Remember the top half of your leg cues half-halts, halts, and downward transitions. It might feel more like your knee than your thigh, but it definitely feels different from your lower leg, calf, ankle, and foot, which are used for forward cues. Learn to use upper and lower halves of the leg independently.

Start with the halt, give him time to get past not feeling the bit in his mouth, but feel your leg instead. Even if he just slows a stride, reward approximation. Be aware of your seat in every step. Ask for longer strides melting to stillness. He is on contact but you aren't pulling. Not an ounce, so your seat is the only cue he feels.

Be clear, ask for his best effort, and reward generously. Then give a long rein and be cheerful. Don't think too much. Instead, look for any opportunity to say, "Good boy." When you have a soft peaceful halt with no rein, followed by an easy walk-off, then begin schooling a rein-back of the same quality. Expect it to take time to become habit. Like piecing a patchwork quilt, stitch one square at a time.

In riding, don't be fooled by smoke and lights. Anyone can spur a horse into speed and jerk them to a halt. If you want to know true connection, look for partnership between the movements. Because the art is always in the transition.

Winterizing the Compassion Fatigue. Again.

There was ice in the water troughs this week. It's dark early now, and the sun is cooling. The flies are slow and stupid, and more aggravating every day. The horses and donkeys have grown their winter coats and just like usual, I haven't added a single hair.

Are there flies in heaven? Just tell me now because I blow my animal-lover status with late season fly-hate.

I cleaned the tack room, almost too well. Then I updated the first aid kit, and pulled out the winter blankets, just in case. Meanwhile, I mucked out my own mind. It was sorely needed. I've been busy at the rescue, we have more than our share of frail elders here with us, and I'm as mentally tired as I am physically exhausted. When my resources run low, I get testy. I even rant at flies.

There's a term used in the caregiving world: Compassion Fatigue. The physical expression of that term is a long deep sigh.

It isn't an accidental condition, like getting a cold. It's a term we first heard of in medical caregiving professions, but it soon spread to animal welfare workers and many other helping professions. The shoe fits a lot of us.

I like The American Bar Association definition of the term. It's broad and it includes real life: "Compassion fatigue is the cumulative physical, emotional and psychological effect of exposure to traumatic stories or events when working in a helping capacity, combined with the strain and stress of every-day life."

It's when a few layers of normal things like work and financial responsibilities and world events meet up with fear and loss and exhaustion, along with the awareness that you aren't getting younger. It feels a bit like doubt, only sticky and dark. Your horse might be the first one to notice. He's stoic so he recognizes the change. He likes it better when you laugh.

There's always a fence to mend before the weather changes, and in that quiet work, I indulge my voices. Yes, I hear voices. It's my parents, both gone for decades now, who come back to nag me for my foolishness.

My father did not suffer idiots. Well into my adulthood, he wanted me to "grow up," which always meant act like him. After all, the world is cruel and no place for ridiculous idealists. Idealist is my word for it; like most bullies, his terminology was more coarse.

My mother's approach was practical; she pleaded with me to be more "normal"; to keep my head down. Always reminding me that life was a veil of tears. My mother knew the safe comfort of giving in and suffering silently.

Here's what I like about replaying the old tapes–I remember who I am. I remember my particular rebellion–it hasn't changed. I choose to care. In their eyes, I cared about things that were like gravity; things that weren't worth fighting because they were never going to change. You can't save them all, so don't even try.

My steadfast response: For the ones I help, like this relic of a donkey, one is enough.

Now I'm preparing for my hay delivery by pulling out pallets to clean out the musty hay underneath. Time passes. That's a given, but the passing of a season is like an arm around your shoulder, urging you to scurry along.

Okay, I admit it. It's been a rough summer. I don't think of myself as a worrier, but I do keep my mind busy with positive tasks. It's a choice to be aware; choosing to care is a kind of prayer to the world. What some people see as a weakness, I am certain is our greatest strength: To stay vulnerable in the face of darkness. To hold a vision, against the odds is our superpower.

Perhaps compassion fatigue isn't the worst thing. Having compassion as a pre-requisite, and that requires a special kind of strength in the first place. You know that you have enough to spare and then taking a step forward when a door to possibility opens. Compassion is the best part of us. Against skeptics, fly that flag high and proud.

I drag the tank heaters to the barn with a smile. Hail damage got us a new roof and I upgraded to metal. I know the animals will be a bit more snug this winter. Everyone's weight is good, the llamas are in full fleece, and I'm considering growing some hair between my toes. It seems to work well for the dogs.

Experts say that the remedy for compassion fatigue is self-care. It's the art of showing yourself the same compassion you have for rescue horses, stray dogs, and your dear ones. It means letting yourself be the stray dog that you welcome into your own heart. To come in out of the cold, welcomed by the person you were meant to be.

My spiritual beliefs rest with nature. It's my test of truth; I'm comforted that gravity works on all of us. I trust the natural laws. I trust that the monochromatic prairie is just resting and that the sun's warmth will return. Nothing dies; it transforms. And if we are butterfly-vulnerable as we can be, more compassion and strength are possible.

The new foster dog has some issues and so do I, but we'll chew our way through because sometimes there is a sunset like tonight. Just one beret-shaped cloud perched on Pikes Peak, Jupiter is alone in the southern sky, and a peachy pink and orange gloaming soaks down to the tall grasses; the world is filled with unbearably precious beauty. This dusk coats good things and bad things as equals, as we choose. Being vulnerable means that I can have this infinite moment of perfection.

You're a Timid Rider?

What if it isn't a bad thing?

I have a "big picture" thing I want to say and it's going to take some explaining. Just food for thought, really, but there's some defining of terms that has to happen first, with full knowledge that making generalizations is always a bad idea. Here goes.

Some riders fall into the category of timid. Another word for that is cautious. They may compete or trail ride or participate in any number of other horse-related activities, but they are always aware of a certain voice in their heads that's a bit reluctant, concerned about possible injury or just not having control. And they ride anyway. My thesaurus adds these synonyms for timid: apprehensive, demure, modest, nervous, browbeaten, yellow, milquetoast, mousy, fainthearted. Is it just me or do the words run to name-calling near the end?

There is a level of fear that runs deeper than timid. It's a rider who is truly unable to breathe or smile. They are almost pathologically tense and then when something happens, like a horse looking to the side, they react more than respond. They might jerk the reins or grab in some other way. It's a level of fear that is nearly disabling. The thesaurus seems to respect fear more with these synonyms: angst, despair, dread, horror, panic, terror, abhorrence, phobia.

Then there are riders who demand obedience from their horses; riders who are boss. Domineering riders who *appear* fearless and strong. They'll make their horse do anything, and many times, crowds cheer them on. Again, I find the thesaurus associates interesting words with domineering: arrogant, autocratic, dictatorial, tyrannical, coercive, insolent, iron-handed. (I have to say, seeing that last term made me blink hard; its second meaning, when applied to riding, hurts my ears as much as seeing it acted out on a horse hurts my eyes.)

These are obviously over-generalizations, and people are individuals. Putting riders into piles is a bad thing because most of us are in the middle of change every day.

In my tiny corner of the horse world, most of the riders I work with would refer to themselves as timid. They apologize for it like it's a bad thing. They tell me it's hard to remember to breathe and that they don't ride like they did when they were younger. They see being timid as a flaw.

I have a confession: I like timid riders.

There's probably at least one time that every rider has fit into each of these categories. Whatever kind of rider you think you are doesn't matter. The only thing that matters is what kind of rider your horse thinks you are. They're truth tellers. A horse will tell you that a domineering rider is afraid or that a fearful rider can get through it. A horse will say, "Enough already!" putting an end to saddle time for a rider who can't be trusted, or show patience and tolerance to a rider with good intention, or just shut down to a rider's rude barrage of noise and cues.

True, I'm no fan of domineering riders. I won't work with them. I consider respect for horses fundamental. Still, these riders do have a certain success because horses will succumb to intimidation. For a while. But their horses rat them out, from their sad eyes and tense poll, all the way to the tip of their clamped tail.

What I love about timid riders is their willingness to go slow. They're sensitive and they want to really listen to their horse. Half of the time, I think the anxiety that they feel is a message from their horse in the first place, and they are the kind of partner who will take the blame for a friend. They have the honesty to admit how they feel and it makes their judgment of how their horses feel just a bit more compassionate.

Now is when I have to say that not everyone who claims to listen to horses actually does. In fact, it's a pretty rare occurrence when any of us truly put horses first. Once you do that you're insuring yourself a life of change and learning. You'll have to give up your ego, but then ego never works with horses anyway.

Finally, there are a few riders who aspire to redefine leadership in a more nuanced way. They're kind leaders who are irresistible to horses who crave safety over fear. And all horses do. Even sour horses become calm partners. Insecure horses start blowing and never stop, as if they've been holding their breath forever. A kind leader doesn't stand out in a crowd, unless it's a crowd of horses. I suppose they do something like whisper, but it's not a joke or a movie title to them.

Maybe the big picture looks like this: There is a long continuum and at one end is violent dominance and the other end is total submission. We all start with horses someplace on this continuum. Some of us started hard-hearted and horses taught us that fighting doesn't work. Some of us started soft and lost patience and got callus. Some of us look like deer in headlights, confused by the unsolicited opinions of people who think they know our horses best.

And there's a tiny place on the continuum, a sweet spot, that has balance and respect and safety. If it was easy to find, everyone would be there.

Dear Timid Rider, please don't apologize for being sensitive. It's the language of compassion and honesty. Be proud of this underrated strength.

The Truth Behind Bit Drama

Do you know how your bit works? Not the sales pitch from a catalog or a romantic story about a tradition told by a cowboy on YouTube. Not some English rider's justification for a twisted-wire snaffle in his horse's mouth or an opinion from a railbird that the answer to all issues is a stronger bit.

I'm still stewing about this: A new rider explained that his horse had been professionally trained and successfully shown before he bought him. His horse was *finished* and as such, wore a *finished horse bit.* (It was a spade bit, with a port so high that it was capable of doing equine brain surgery the slow, excruciating way. No one debates that spade bits are the harshest bits made, not even those who use them.)

This was the second time he had instructed me about how this soul-killing bit works. Maybe he thought that I was just not bright enough to understand. Or if he repeated his misguided explanation a few more times, I'd palm my forehead and giggle like a school girl. Instead I held eye contact and told him it's an illegal competition bit in most disciplines and not allowed on my farm. The look on his face tells me that he has no more respect for my profession than he does for his horse.

Yes, I require my clients to use legal bits. It gets worse, I mean legal dressage bits, which boils down to snaffles for the most part.

Then it dawns on me: There's a stinky part of me that envies trainers who promote harsh bits. It's easier to put a severe bit in a horse's mouth so the new owner can force a "frame" and everyone can pretend the horse is *finished*. Anything is easier than teaching a rider the feel of good contact on a gentle bit. Anything is easier than learning to ride force-free to fluid, soft contact.

Contact is like holding hands with someone you are so comfortable with that there's overlap where they begin an you end.

For all my professional years training, I can't say I've ever met a *finished* horse. I have met horses so shut down from bit pain that they have dead eyes and no will to go forward. Does that term actually refer to a horse who's finished with people?

But let's go with the fantasy of buying a *finished* horse in the way that he meant it. Does having the purchase price make you a *finished* rider?

Here's where someone says that a bit is only as kind or cruel as the hands on the reins. Sure, I've seen horses totally brutalized by a snaffle bit in the hands of a monster. At the same time, having slack reins on a shank or spade bit doesn't impress me; an extreme bit causes a threat of pain, even if no reins are attached. A harsh bit that hearkens to a cultural tradition still isn't good horsemanship if the horse suffers. There is no beauty in domination. Control is a cheap substitute for partnership.

What if the goal was to ride in such a way that the horse moves with the same liberty he does while not under saddle?

I was talking with another client about their bit. The horse was tense in her jaw and had a nervous habit of kind of chattering the bit in her mouth. We were talking about other options for the mare, and after I described how a comfort snaffle (a three-piece bit) worked versus a mullen mouth (a solid bar), my client asked which I liked best. I said, "My preference doesn't matter in the least. Instead, let's ask your horse."

Saddle up like usual, put your helmet on like usual, but skip the bridle. Use a neck ring or clip reins on a web halter. Go to a safe arena and begin your ride, as usual and be ready to learn something.

If your horse moves more freely; if his neck is longer and he blows, that's a message you need to hear. Has your bit been working like a passive parking brake? Does the mere existence of a gentle bit in his mouth back him off? That's pretty common. As you feel his stride lengthen, his back lifting, and a lightness to his hooves, be happy. It means you can do better for him.

Humans who feel out of control tend to get grab anything that will give them a quick submissive result. Does riding without a bit make you feel unarmed, with no means to punish your horse? Are you perhaps using your bit almost like a weapon? If riding without a bit proves you ride more with your hands than your legs, that isn't a bit problem at all.

It's time to challenge ourselves to pursue the art of riding, instead of asking our horses to tolerate our poor horsemanship.

Just in case you could possibly think that there has never been a day in my life that I dropped to my knees and begged for a stronger bit, you're wrong. Or that there were times that I hoped that the issue was a broken, abscessed tooth and not my hands? Back then, his head flipping around made me look bad and I lusted after a cruel bit. But I never worked with the sort of trainer that allowed stronger bits. And that was back when I was still riding in a saddle with a horn. Instead of a stronger bit, I was told my hands needed *finishing*, along with the mentality behind them. I'm still grateful for that clarity and I pass it on.

If you listen to your horse, he'd say there's a problem underneath the bit problem and behind the hand problem. He'd say that a cruel bit is the sign of a fearful rider and the real problem is trust.

The Passion to Punish

First, last, and always, this is the truth about communication with animals: Punishment is the lowest form of expression.

I don't write about all the animals we foster here. A couple of months ago, Jack, a Corgi-Jack Russell cross, was here for a foster/evaluation visit. He was a riot. I'm not sure why he was relinquished, but he was a dog's dog. Maybe his owners wanted a people-dog. I suppose depending on how you see things, his problem could have been his "bad" half. He was the personification of both breeds, loud and proud.

A great dog-woman adopted him and they are busy living happily ever after. She keeps me posted on the battle to see who gets under the covers first. It was a simple foster to a happy ending. They should all be this easy.

I'm working with a new foster dog now who's more of a challenge. He's got his problems but rescues deserve to be written about as much as beloved companions. It's bittersweet but I find the biggest feeling I have about this dog is that I'm mad. Really mad.

This new dog has big ears and quiet eyes. See how cute he is sleeping, white belly exposed, toes in the air? He came to rescue with his shock collar and his meds; he's on canine Prozac. Oh, and he's just thirteen months old.

His people were first-time dog owners. I think they did their best but got the very worst advice available. As much as it pains me to talk badly about an animal, this pup has a list of problems that are destructive, or scary, or both. The fancy term is resource guarding, but it's complicated. He isn't just quirky. He's a mess. And still very cute belly-up.

He went to an obedience class. The pup sits and shakes hands and goes in his crate. But somehow while learning tricks, the conversation must have changed, because someone thought a shock collar was a good idea. Who uses a shock collar on a puppy?

I agree with what Lara Wilber, from the positive dog training blog, Rubicon Days, has to say about shock collars: *"The argument is not that they are not or cannot be effective. The argument is that the potential fallouts of training with these devices can be increased aggression, shutting down, and confused associations. Aside from not wanting to deliberately hurt or scare my dogs, these risks are too great."*

And if that wasn't enough, what kind of vet prescribes Prozac for a puppy? A Corgi puppy? Did he even weigh twenty pounds? I remember back in the day that people used Prozac as a murder defense, claiming aggression was a side effect.

Most days, I want to scream at the top of my lungs, "Stop taking advice from idiots!" I always recommend that people ask for help. Just be sure it's the right help. As if there was an easy way to spot idiots–even professional idiots. Like any trainer would admit to being an idiot, even if they were. At the same time, when I hear people say that all trainers are idiots, I want to raise my hand and say, "not me." It's a dilemma.

The first day, this little foster destroyed a couple of toys, stole most of my socks, unloaded some shelves, and shredded a cardboard box into small bits. He was frantic out of his crate, but he's been crated so much I want to give him a chance. He had no recall and he wanted to play with the other dogs so hard that he pushed them relentlessly. Now they don't like him much.

Then he ate one of my Crocs. A few minutes later, he got another Croc from a different pair. I lifted what was left up and looked at him. He stopped chewing and sat dead still, his brow furrowed, braced for something bad. I still hadn't made a peep, but he was worried and put his head in a corner. My stomach got tight. How many people have failed this dog in his short life? That's what I'm mad about. Not him.

Right now, my plan is to let him breathe. He needs time. I called a moratorium on punishment. He's had enough discipline for a lifetime. So, for now, this little guy is in detox. His meds certainly weren't helping. He's still waiting for that *sting* that makes his head want to explode, but it isn't going to come. Instead, he gets to chew sticks in the yard and I hid my shoes. Sometimes, he comes now, if you say good boy first. Sometimes he flashes his temper and starts a fight. Then he falls asleep with his pasty white belly turned up to the world, as vulnerable as a baby. Sometimes he won't let me touch his neck. He's afraid of flyswatters. Other times he crawls into my chair and lays his big, flat head on my chest and looks into my eyes.

As concerned as I am for him, I might be more concerned for us. Are we so intolerant that we have to legitimize torture for puppies? It's profanity; dogs are our best animal friends. If humans truly have a passion for punishment, then it's us that need to learn to get along.

Ride Shorter, Progress Farther.

If I were to write a training book entitled *Less is More*, it would be hundreds of pages long. The irony is not lost on me. At the same time, it's an idea that I defend constantly. We humans can be like rats on a wheel sometimes.

We've all seen the rider I'm talking about. Maybe she starts by lunging her horse in tight side-reins. He can't breathe and gets a bit panicky, confirming her opinion that he needs lunging to take the edge off. Most misunderstandings start this way with a simple mistake.

Then it's like dominoes. She wants to get it right. Her horse tries in the beginning. She's so focused, she pushes too hard, for too long. She doesn't notice that she's talking to herself, about her horse, but not talking to him. Each try, she wants just one more effort a bit better, but by now her horse has lost heart. He's just getting the same cue again and again and he has no idea what it means anymore.

Wake-up call: If you find yourself in a hole, stop digging.

And by the way, how did things go at work today? (Like your horse even needs to ask. He could tell by the difference in how you greeted him, before you even tacked up.)

Part of the challenge of riding well doesn't have a thing to do with the barn. It's just being who we are. That usually means having a full-time job, maybe a couple of kids. Those responsibilities are enough for a twenty-four-hour day right there. Being retired is just as busy, dealing with health issues, technology, and family. Not to mention, navigating changing relationships. Is that a strange man in the house or do you recognize him as the guy in your wedding photos? Then there's book club and maybe a random thought about climate change and horse rescue. Balancing responsibilities and obligations with your passions and bank account ends up being a recipe for guilt. At the very least, it's a lot of extra weight for a horse to carry.

Then some idiot trainer like me climbs on your horse, and with no fanfare or angst, your horse does that elusive movement for a few strides, as I smile and throw down the reins, like it's no big deal. Ouch, apparently it's easy for your horse.

And then my client says to me, "Know what your problem is? You don't want it bad enough." There's an instant where the words hang in the air… and then we howl. A sense of humor will always be the very best training aid.

And she's right. There's an art to riding *as if* you don't care. Sure, it's an "untruth" and we should care about our riding technique. But I also hope we find a way to not torment our horses any more than we have to along the way. It's pretty easy to get that *Night of the Living Dead* appearance in the saddle from just trying too hard. Your effort shows in your horse's stilted gait and tense back.

So, your life is busy and you don't have much time to ride? *Good.* Ride less. Ride lighter, and trust your horse. He doesn't forget how to be ridden and he doesn't need to be drilled. His memory is strong; he remembers his training as clearly as he remembers your frustration.

Since we humans think in hour-sized hunks of time, start when the big hand is on the twelve. First, curry too long. Use one arm and then the other. Feel his skin warm as his blood flow increases. Then feel your shoulders relax and do the same. Forget the stupid clock; tune in to horse time.

Bridle him with slow hands and lots of deep breaths. Pause on the mounting block and let your guilt and stress drain out into a dark, sticky pool under your boots. Then lightly mount.

Once in the saddle, take a moment to feel your sit bones go soft and the weight of your heels sink low. Acknowledge you have a partner and not an adversary.

Take all the time you need to allow your horse a warm-up on a long rein without correction. Just rhythm and stride. Never doubt this is the most important part of the ride. Feel his body with your seat and legs. Use time freely because quality matters.

Now is a good time to get off. Yes, so soon. Quit early, while you want more and your horse is happy. Finish by taking too much time brushing him down, give him a snack, and still have time to run an errand on the way home.

If you want to train just a little longer, be serious enough about your riding to remember the best work happens when it feels like play. Successive approximation is that happy path of bread crumbs. We reward a horse for trying, even imperfectly. If you get one good effort, quit right there. Jump down immediately. Then trust your horse's intelligence, even if you don't quite trust your own. If your trainer releases you early, or your ride was only thirty minutes long, give yourself chocolate. *You* deserve a treat!

Current opinions about training have changed. Three days a week of actually schooling is plenty for most competition horses. Keep your horse fit with hacks or arena games or cross-training. Or anything else that doesn't feel like boot camp. You know the two cardinal rules in training: Be consistent. Change things up.

If you still want to tell me that your horse is that hot kind of horse that needs to be ridden hard every day, well, ask yourself the hard question. "How can I help his anxiety?"

Then in an instant, another summer's gone, the days are getting shorter. The world has a way of twisting things sideways. If we don't slow down and pay attention, blessings start to feel like poverty. It isn't true. What you have to offer is more than enough and your horse is just as magical as he ever was.

Bite Your Tongue

I tied a client up last week.

Let me start at the very beginning. As a riding instructor, I'm always trying to encourage the horse and rider build to a positive tendency in their work. It isn't about being perfect; it's about a peaceful process with good effort and affirmative rewards.

Unless it isn't. When things spiral downward, and frustration or fear are on the rise, good intention is easy to forget. Some trainers might yell, "Don't be so tense!" or worse, "Stop being scared." Not helpful. Being told to *not* do something isn't a cue a horse or rider can take. Really, it's more like name calling than instructing.

Meanwhile, my client is trying so hard that even her eyebrows are stiff. There's no bucking; it's more of a grudge match. By now the frustrated rider is over-thinking and over-pulling and over-kicking. The horse is over-stimulated and can't even remember how it started. Maybe, he recognizes a corner of a cue to try, but just as he is about to do it, the rider gives a bigger cue that feels like a correction, so he doesn't do what he was just about to do... which was try. It seems like the uproar and noise in the saddle is un-answerable, so he gets the deer in the headlights look–tense poll, hollow back, tight lips. Identical to his rider.

Can we all take a collective breath and admit we've been there?

Years ago, I developed this technique to counter this kind of downward spiral, not that I recommend it. It's what I do in a lesson, after I've suggested breathing and going slow and a few hundred other things, and nothing seems to get through. Then I try something creative. (Others might call it something absurd.)

Did I mention this particular client was ramrod straight, her heels pushed down and her hands immobile? Her position was perhaps too good, meaning she tended toward stiffness. So, I suggested to her that she do an impression of me riding. I'm guessing that she'd say I ride a bit like a boneless chicken sometimes. Her eyebrows became a straight line across her forehead. She wasn't amused. Clearly, mimicking me is a stupid idea, so stupid that she makes a face. Now she's more frustrated with me than her horse. See? There's an improvement already.

But then she slid down deeper in the saddle and pouched her tiny belly out. She was doing it to poke me back, but in the instant that her back released, her horse blew and went soft. She melted into his rhythm rather than trying to fight it. Sometimes drawing the attention away from the horse is all the help a rider needs, along with a self-deprecating giggle.

"The biggest enemy to the partnership of dressage is impatience and the human nature to dominate other creatures." –Walter Zettl

Be clear on this: It's our instinct to pick a fight or throw a tantrum. It's as natural as a filly spooking when a plastic bag careens across the arena. As natural as a Labrador chasing a ball all day and then, all night. Riding well means training ourselves to go against our instinct. Riding well requires that we put the horse first. And to do that we have to use their language; not ours. Best to just lay down whatever shred of ego you have left now.

And the hardest thing to do in the saddle is to do less. When things start to come apart we instinctively speed up and get louder with our cues. Feeling unheard, we really can't shut up now; we repeat and nag and chatter. Our hands are busy and our feet bang away on the horses' flanks. As if the harder we communicate, the more sense it will make.

It's my goal to interrupt the negative spiral when I use this kind of creative ploy to distract a rider from fighting. I might ask an obscure question or tell a story. Sounding ridiculous is fine; I'm just trying to buy the horse a moment of quiet.

So, there we were doing groundwork, a different client and a different day. I was helping with a trailer loading issue. I'm not saying my client was over-cuing, but I started to imagine those flashlights with the long red cones that they use at the airport. She'd worked up a head of steam and tied her sweatshirt around her waist. I was reminding her about breathing as much as she was flinging her rope. Her sensitive horse was getting taller by the minute. That was when I tied her up. I re-tied her sweatshirt to her waist, pinning her elbows under it. I was going for a version of Temple Grandin's famous squeeze chute for humans.

My client didn't get mad; that's a good sign. Instead, she decided to ridicule the idea by doing a penguin impression. She said it wouldn't work, demonstrating by barely flailing her hands, to exaggerate how much she couldn't move. Mid-rant, her horse dropped his head and blew. Then, she does even less, even slower, but with a surprised smile. He stepped quietly toward the trailer.

She was dead certain he'd never do it. But that thought needed a release, too, didn't it?

It's natural to try to dominate. We're loud, even if we're passive-aggressive about it. It's our instinct. But in our laser focus on the task at hand, we forget that a horse's awareness is much keener than ours. It isn't that they can't hear us; it's the exact opposite. Time to hush the brain. When we whisper, they lean in to listen.

I just love it when a bad attitude teaches a good lesson. Having a sense of humor might be the best cue we can give a horse.

The Best Reasons to Stop Riding

I think I've heard all the clichés about change that I can stand. At a certain age, we don't need to be reminded how hard change is. But fall is all about change, I notice. Most of us get poked by the passing of time, in one way or another, right about this time of the year. Falling leaves and all that.

Every now and then, I read an article declaring that riding horses is cruel, any horse. That it's just too demeaning for horses; that ethics require that all horses be freed from their slavery to humans. I might be imagining the righteous tone. Return them all to the wild, I guess is what they'd have us do.

On the other hand, I get notes from riders in their nineties, riding horses in their thirties, with an arthritic shell of bravado. Good for you, really. So pleased that your horse has avoided injuries that long, and the same for you. What luck.

Then there are the rest of us, pushing the muck cart and casually wondering which hip will be replaced first. We have horses that had long careers or got hurt in turnout or weren't born with perfect conformation. Or maybe we just aren't lucky. Is it time for someone to be turned out to pasture?

Has it crossed your mind that your horse is slowing down? Maybe more than once? Is it really hard to push him to the canter and then he breaks right away? Or maybe he's reluctant about being caught. After a sluggish warm-up, he seems depressed and you kick him a little more all the time. Or maybe he drops his head lower and lower in defeat. If he's stoic, of course. Not every horse has that patience.

So you check with the vet, try some stronger supplements, and that buys you another year. Then you start negotiating. No more steep trails, or maybe you get new arena footing. But now you're asking yourself again if it's time.

I'm sorry it hurts, but listen to him. Good horses don't randomly start lying. And if your horse really is asking for the break, I know it breaks you even more, but let him rest. In this light, a career-ending injury has the clarity that slow-motion decline lacks. Maybe he'll feel better in the spring and maybe not, but for now, let him be and tell him he's a *good boy*. A horse's riding life isn't a race where the last one standing wins. Don't make him feel he's failed you.

Love him enough.

Maybe it's you that is having a hard time; your past injuries are catching up and it's hard to get comfortable in the saddle. Maybe you are a certain age and your courage hormones have abandoned you. They do that, you know.

Or time makes you rush too much. You have a list of all your lists and so many people depending on you. You burst into the barn and ride fast, but you're still late. Your horse behaves like the victim of a drive-by assault. It's an honest response and you'll deal with it when you have more time.

Or maybe your fear has just grown an inch at a time until it became disabling. It isn't that you aren't as brave as you once were; it's an actual full-blown anxiety attack that you're trying to fight but it never goes away. It's a fear that paralyzes your lungs and you can't control your limbs. It isn't the usual common sense alert that something might happen. It's an air raid siren that never goes silent. Never. You know your horse feels it, too. Would it be different on another horse?

So, you get the help of a kind trainer and you do your very best. Still, you dread the worst, every stride, and fear never lets you breathe. It happens every time, but you don't admit the truth. Months pass, you know you're safe, but there's no logic or relief when it comes to fear. It's possessed you.

You feel obligated. You feel like a loser. You're too old or too busy or too frightened. You'd hate to think what people might say. You'd be letting your horse down. But in the quiet, when you listen to your heart, you know.

Love yourself enough.

We all have dry spells and going into winter is a great time to take a break. Nothing bad will happen. Your horse won't miss your holiday stress. He won't forget his training and neither will you. I promise. Come spring, you'll be back in the saddle or you won't and that's okay, too. It's the way change works; you can depend on it.

If you know it's bigger than a season, take a breath and try to tell the truth. You might have to say it a few times to get through it. Integrity matters because secrets, or the illusion of them, are poison. Besides, your horse knows.

What if it isn't wrong?

I have a barn half-full of retired horses; some have been retired longer than they were ridden. They let me know every day that they are no less for it. We should have that confidence.

Humans allow so much self-judgment on whether they ride or not. I see it every day, as an instructor. Riding is wonderful; I'm glad I'm still in the saddle. But the longer I'm around horses, the more I believe that they don't care if we ride or not. Relationship, as it relates to herd dynamics, is what matters to horses, and that isn't defined by our altitude. Maybe it's time to re-invent ourselves and up the conversation. Wouldn't it be ironic if no longer riding meant that our horsemanship improved?

The scary question: If it's the end of the world, what will you do instead of riding? Love them, just like you always have. That never changes.

What To Do When Your
Horse Is Wrong

It started small. It started the way it usually starts; the rider pulled on her horse's face. It's a fundamental disagreement: the rider thinks it's her right to control the horse and the horse doesn't like having metal jammed on his jaw bone. They weren't even on the same subject.

So, the gelding got fussy. The rider kicked and steered, trying to make him go. But the horse heard more whoa than go; all the steering happened by pulling the rein back, not that it was ever the rider's intention to give the horse conflicting cues. There was head-tossing and mouth-gaping. It started small.

The next part was tough. Maybe it's because we're predators or maybe it's our ego about having our way, or maybe we've been taught that we must show them who's boss in some Neanderthal version of dominance, but it's as if the rider had blinders on, unable to see (hear) her horse. The horse noticed the beginning of a fight immediately. It takes the rider longer, of course. It isn't that the rider is mean or belligerent; she just believes she's right.

It was just about then that things started to come apart quickly. It's like we have a snowball theory of disaster that says if the horse hesitates a second, or gives just one thought of resistance, then all is lost. That one small action will necessarily gain speed and size, like a snowball rolling down a hill, and so we panic and accelerate. Which, by the way, works like a cue for the horse, too.

The horse is frantic, the ride is coming apart badly, and it's all happening faster and faster. If you are capable of a thought, know that the horse isn't wrong. You cued the acceleration, whether you meant to or not. Getting mad or holding a grudge will do no good.

Horses are never wrong.

Right now, I hope that the rider is frustrated. If the rider paused before throwing a temper tantrum, she might actually feel that frustration and anxiety, and take it as a cue to go slow. Hooray! It's a huge win to recognize an internal feeling and stop the snowball race long enough to become self-aware.

In that tiny pause that feels almost like surrender to the rider, the horse can take that cue, too, and things begin to decompress immediately. It seems like an accident at first, almost a kind of butt-fall into better leadership, but it counts. Your horse just confirmed it and rewarded you for better behavior. If you're smart, you accept the invitation to partnership and start the ride again.

First, let a moment or two pass. It'll feel like forever, but you're teaching yourself patience. When you label it that way, it should feel slow. Learn to enjoy it.

Now the game begins. Training is a creative process. It should feel a bit like the two of you trying to slowly find each other in an unfamiliar place. You are directing your horse toward something he might not know or have the confidence to try. And if the only answer you accept is perfection, then it's you that's failed. Instead, you are negotiating a better answer each time, by rewarding him as he tries to find the right answer.

It feels different. The tone of the ride has changed. You have evolved away from being someone focused on failure who makes serial corrections; nagging the horse about what he's done wrong, again and again, making each ride a punishment. Now training becomes more like a game of habitual rewards for the efforts your horse puts into the work. The more he offers, the happier everyone is. Now it's as if you nag him about being a smart horse.

Here's where creativity matters the most. Knowing that your horse is never wrong, that it's the rider's challenge to ask a better question and then accept and reward the answer she gets, and to continue patiently and cheerfully until the best answer is consistent. Training is nothing more than the "serious work" of playing a game of collecting and rewarding good experiences for your horse.

A moment for the cynics in every discipline that will say that affirmative training is fine for trail horses or amateur horses, but if they're asking for really hard advanced work, then pushing the horse hard is justified, whether it's reining or dressage or jumping. Moving in fear and tension is just not how horses learn. Adding anxiety to the process will not result in a responsive horse.

Maybe you did make a small mistake, but you are in the middle of your ride and it isn't too late. Take a breath and remember the best ride you ever saw. It doesn't matter what riding discipline, but the horse's ears weren't pinned and his tail wasn't clamped. He lifted his feet and his body looked strong and soft at the same time. It was freedom and partnership and trust, and most of all, you could tell it was art because it lifted your heart.

Whether you are a beginning trail rider or an ambitious competitor, begin by asking your horse if he wants to play a game. Let the question change you. Then start where your horse is at right now. Ask for just a stride of walk, and reward him generously. Let it be enough, as you set about helping your horse be totally right.

Judging Dressage

Dressage isn't perfect, but what part is baby and what part is bath water?

Watching the Dressage competition at the Olympics was inspirational and horrific. There were impeccable riders with fluid bodies and invisible cues, and riders who were brutal, with hard hands and cruel methods. There were horses who were light and brilliant; who moved with such freedom and elegance that it took my breath away. There were horses whose bodies were so filled with tension and resistance that I choked just watching.

In other words, pretty much the way I feel when I see any riding competition. There have always been two ways to train and ride, and those methods, harsh or kind, are written in the horse's every stride.

Social media chimed in from all sides: Some people deny horse abuse happens and some defend it. Some believe all training is abusive, refusing to admit there is such a thing as affirmative training. Others just like to pour gasoline on the fire, leaving horses and riders tainted with rumors, guilt by association, and out-and-out lies. It's the easiest thing in the world to be critical. Ranting can have a value if enough of us do it, perhaps horses will benefit. Still, tearing the entire sport down from the cheap seats is too easy.

But let's be clear. The problem is not dressage. Or eventing or racing or reining. The problem is that we lose sight of the thing every horse-crazy girl knows. You always have to put your horse first. Obviously, the biggest challenge going up the levels in dressage is to lift our own humanity, along with our horse's movements, to a more balanced and beautiful place.

A few weeks back, I got a call from my local dressage chapter looking for volunteers to scribe at a show the next Friday morning. A scribe sits next to the judge during the rides and writes down the comments and scores for every movement in each competitor's dressage test. It's like taking dictation but there isn't much room to write and tests move along quickly. I've scribed for famous international judges and starting-out learner judges and I always come away with something valuable to take back to my clients.

Friday morning is bright and cool. One at a time, each rider comes into the indoor arena for a brief warm-up, greets the judge, and when the bell rings, enters the dressage school to begin her test. Some of the rides are smooth and sweet. Some come apart and we've all been there. Some of the riders are cool and relaxed with lots of experience. Some are new and giddy to be out with their horses. There were pre-teens and women of a certain age and everyone in between. Some horses are fancy with lively dramatic gaits and some are steady and kind partners of no particular bloodline.

There were no cruel bits or bloody spurs. I saw no horses behind the bit and each rider did their best to keep quiet hands and soft legs. Everyone wore helmets. The horses were well-groomed and well-loved, and the riders polished their boots. Pride of appearance is the first way we show respect to the discipline we love.

We shared pizza for lunch and people congratulated each other. This judge was somewhat quirky, which I don't have to tell you is totally normal for the horse world, but her comments were consistent; she didn't give away any free marks, and if a rider was unhappy but they were good sports about it. In the afternoon the judge showed me photos of her own horses back home. I think she was missing them.

Toward the end of the day, during the obligatory afternoon thunderstorm, a young woman finished her test with the usual salute and released her reins. Her smile was as bright as the tall stockings on her horse. It was her second test that day and an improvement over the first. Instead of turning to leave, she trotted toward us, blurting out with so much wild enthusiasm that it bordered on shrill, "Thank you! Thank you for coming!" We almost flinched at the howl of good will.

Driving home I thought, "This is my dressage."

Dressage isn't owned by millionaires or elite breeders or any particular nationality. The clear majority of dressage riders in this country are happy amateurs riding horses they'll keep forever. They own this sport as much as anyone.

Some years I have clients who compete and I'm on the other side of the judge's table. Sometimes the horses I work with never compete but practice dressage, working to gain strength and suppleness and balance. Riders might ride in a western saddle or not always wear tall boots, but they all agree that riding a twenty-meter circle is a lot harder than it looks.

Dressage literally means training; that's our commitment. We try to improve, not to please a judge but to help our horses.

I don't mean to sound biblical, but doesn't most disagreement boil down to good and evil? Isn't the challenge always how to live up to our best potential? I don't deny the dark side of dressage. I hate hyperflexion and cruelty; horses never stand a chance against human ego and greed. At the same time, watching a young woman and her horse quietly navigate a dressage test is a fine and beautiful thing.

Dressage will change for the good of horses. We'll demand it. Change comes slowly, but I hold hope because of days like this one. Amateur riders with a horse and a dream are the reason I refuse to hand my beautiful sport over to the haters.

On the world stage, the rider who won the Olympic individual gold medal in dressage, two consecutive times, wore a helmet, setting a fine example. She and her horse didn't have an easy start early in their partnership; she needed courage and wits to match his fire and sensitivity. They forged a partnership out of chaos. Sound familiar? For their final test, she acknowledged she was nervous, aware of the distance they'd come and her desire to finish their last ride together well. But once they started moving, she said, *it was as if her horse held her hand.*

An Olympic gold medal rider talking like a horse-crazy girl. That's my dressage, too.

Safety and Being a Spoil Sport

Wanna see me ruin your simple, carefree ride in one sentence? I'm a riding instructor. Wait, it's worse than that. A riding instructor who has read the small print of her liability insurance, as if I didn't feel responsible enough before. Horses are dangerous because they're flight animals. Beyond that, I'm certain that if one of my horses hurt someone, it wouldn't be his fault and it would break my heart. Maybe literally.

Or how about this? My barn isn't safe for kids. Wait, it's worse than that. My barn isn't safe for adults, whether they are city slickers or old hands. Come to think of it, it's not even safe for the horses. And I don't mean to sound judgmental, but I don't think your barn is safe either.

A while back, the director of a riding program invited me to give a talk on safety to a group of good men who volunteered to help with handyman work on her farm. The director didn't feel the men were taking her requests seriously. Among other things, they were bringing the horses in using an ATV, moving them at a breakneck speed. When the director asked them to slow down, they all looked at her like she was a whiny spoil sport.

I gave a strong presentation. I used examples and spoke intelligently from experience. Rules exist for reasons and I actually know those reasons. I made eye contact and sprinkled my talk with humor. They looked at me, the ones who stayed awake, like I was a whiny spoil sport. I get it.

Why is being around horses so complicated and tiresome? It's the same look I get when I recommend that every rider wear a helmet, every ride. The look I get when I ask if a rider's horse might have ulcers or if they've had a saddle fit recently. They tell me it's just a horse, after all. I get it.

These things are inconvenient when we have time constraints and it all costs money that would be better spent on a vacation. Then, it's my fault for being difficult when all they want to do is just ride. Oh, I really do get that.

It's time for the annual reminder that horses are not dirt bikes. Or more poetically:

"The animals of the world exist for their own reasons. They were not made for humans any more than black people were made for white, or women created for men." –Alice Walker

Horses are creatures of intelligence, great sensitivity, and instinct that has insured their very survival for centuries. Horses have physical requirements as complicated as any other wild animal, but are social and generally kind to humans. It makes horses appear more docile than they actually are –kind of like big stuffed toys.

Things come apart when a horse has a normal equine response that frightens or injures us humans. Then horses pay the price for our complacency, when it's our responsibility to keep ourselves safe, and in that way, ensure our horses' safety and security, as well. Yes, I just said if we get hurt, it's our fault.

I want you safe because I've been around long enough to know too many sad stories. I want you around to care for your horse into his old age, and maybe a couple of horses past that. I want you safe because our bodies are frail and standing around with that *deer in headlights* reality with a frightened thousand-pound horse will always be a losing proposition, even if you have to admit it in hindsight. And most of all, because there will never be a guaranteed kid-safe horse, or flawlessly secure barn, or totally predictable outcome.

And because sadly, we humans need to feel safe and

sometimes we over-compensate, using bravado as a kind of false courage. Horses aren't fooled.

It isn't that we mean harm; we all love our horses. But we also like to show off or we fall into the habit of taking shortcuts. We get distracted and lose sight of the big picture. Complacency is like gravity; it settles on us and makes us dumb to our surroundings, dulling our senses. That's when most injuries happen.

I understand how cool it is to stand next to a draft horse and call him *Baby*. Sometimes it can seem like throwing a leg around a saddle horn, laying on a horse bareback, or encouraging a horse to come close and mug you makes it look like you're a horse whisperer in tune with the equine heart. I have to tell you –it's the exact opposite.

Call me a whiny spoil sport. It's my professional responsibility to look at a situation and imagine every horrible, crippling possibility for the horse and rider, while holding a light, affirmative thought for the best. But really, isn't not allowing ourselves to become complacent just good horsemanship? Too many horses go to rescue or worse because we don't hold up our end.

So a reminder to stay focused and listen to your horse. If you don't do groundwork, it's time to start. If you do, it's time to freshen your focus. Know that your horse wants safe leadership most of all. Begin when you halter him, speak his language. Use your peripheral vision, your horse eyes, and be aware of your surroundings. Encourage good manners and reward him lavishly for every effort. Horsemanship boils down to what we give our horses, even more than what they give us.

Some of us are rule breakers by nature. We don't like to do was we're told. I'm at the head of that line myself. And some rules are meant to break. Common sense will tell you that when it comes to requiring dirt-magnet white breeches for dressage. But too many people are more concerned with the respect a horse shows them in the saddle, than the respect they show the horse the rest of the time.

Perhaps consider rules as an affirmative way of demonstrating love for horses; a constant awareness of their dignity and a method for showing them respect for who they are and how they think.

When we see them galloping with ears sharp, tails flagged, and hooves churning up the soil, they are the epitome of strength and sensitivity, intelligence and timeless beauty. Even the most cynical people pause and stand a bit taller, just existing in the same world with horses.

In that light, treating horses carelessly or like a fuzzy teddy bear seems outlandishly demeaning, doesn't it?

Talking Animals at Midnight

I've just come in from the night feed. It's long-john weather, my head is bandaged with layers of hats and a muffler. I'm wearing thick boots and a winter barn coat that makes me look like one of those inflatable lawn ornaments folks have in town. It's ten degrees on a particularly black night, when the stars are the starkest white. There's a silent dusting of snow.

The night is so quiet that animals aren't hunkered down in their stalls. Instead, they are standing in friendly groups, playing nose games. When they hear the backyard gate, there is a round of nickers, each voice recognizable. Edgar Rice Burro takes a few wheezing gasps warming up for his full-out bray.

Winter Solstice is the longest night of the year. I love this night for its supernatural quality. You can half-see every horse you ever loved in the periphery, never really gone at all. Throw some extra hay for the long darkness tonight. Extra hay for the horses who have walked on, for those yet to arrive, and for those who have none. Throw extra hay as an affirmation that it'll all be okay.

European countries have traditional stories about animals talking at midnight. Some say it starts with the Feast of Santa Lucia, others say Solstice or others, Christmas Eve. It's oxen and donkeys mainly. One fable says oxen knelt and welcomed the baby Jesus verbally. Like many folktales, they have pagan roots as well. In those stories, animals talk at midnight, but not always kindly. Some animals take revenge and owners get their due for poor care or over-work. Which does sound like something to celebrate.

So, I drag my feet, considering the variations on this folktale, as I finish in the barn, nod to the ghosts, and start back to the house. On a sacred night like this, I hear voices. Oh, that's a lie. I always hear voices. Animals are chatterboxes if you listen to their body-voice and even the most stoic horse over-talks when he thinks he's being heard.

What would animals say? No shortage of human opinions out there. I must hear my father's voice loudest, also a ghost now, but still insisting that dumb animals, beasts of burden, can't think or feel. A traditional majority agrees with him. Science says differently and more of us are curious. That's a partial win.

The other extreme? A touchy subject. I'll call them Romanticizers. They love horses so much that they have a barn full of skinny rescues with long hooves. Some rally behind the term "no kill" and sometimes that means suffering. Some believe horses are divine spiritual teachers. They put human words into equine mouths to support their goals or politics, and then feel superiorly-humble about it. It's okay. Horses don't seem to take that seriously.

I have my own opinions, not any more popular. I don't think horses consider us the center of their lives, no matter how much we wish they did. They have full sentient lives, more connected with the herd than the humans who visit a few hours a day. Some of us are pretty interesting to them, but we are other.

I'm interested in those of us in the middle of these two thought extremes, trying to listen and be perceptive, while not over-humanizing horses. It's challenging because we only have our human experience to compare with theirs. Kind of a dilemma, if you follow. It means pushing our love and passion aside, using our human language to describe them, while respecting their equine nature and instinct primarily.

On this solstice night, what might horses say about us?

Some would say humans are a warlike species, angry and

cruel, to be avoided and never trusted. Other equines would wonder if humans might be a sentient species. Some might think we seem to read their minds from time to time. Other times they might say humans are flighty and spook easily. They may wonder if humans are capable of communication, so they come close and try to listen. Beyond the din of our words, they notice that many humans give conflicting messages. Many humans are timid or ill-tempered.

So, they give us calming signals to let us know that they mean us no ill will. That we don't have to be so emotional; that we don't have to try so hard. They share breath with us, suggesting peace as an alternative to our incomprehensible mental chatter. Some horses think humans might even have souls.

Riding a Suspension… of Disbelief

Some of us are okay with who we are in the saddle. We don't question the ride, or if we do, we put it on the horse and he's fine with that. It is what it is, and it works for lots of horses and riders.

Some of us pause in the saddle; it starts with a small moment of awareness that there might be more possible. Maybe you are crossing a log and you feel your horse lift his back. Maybe in a canter, there's a moment of body-to-body unison that hooks you in the heart. Or maybe in a blind or uncertain moment, your horse moves under you and offers more, when he didn't have to. And then the air feels richer.

It's a wake-up call and in that instant, there's a shift in perception; a teasing glimpse into a hidden place. Horses call us there, but it's our choice to listen or not. We teeter at the threshold of a desire so hot that we fight and try to dominate a horse's magic and a whiny envy without action; a fierce fairy-tale prayer that our horse will do it all for us, if we just give them treats.

I'm particularly interested in what it takes for riders to progress; what we have to do mentally to go from being a passenger to a true partner. In the best sense, it's the transition, beyond fighting or dreaming, to an honest connection.

For a novice rider, even one who's ridden for years, the reality is that we get the ride we ask for. If we want something more, we are the ones who have to change. So we try to do more–we kick and pull and things get immediately worse.

The harder we think the work is, the harder we ask. Not always with force; more often with micro-managing doubt. We think too much. Even if we know that somehow *less is more*, we try so willfully hard to do less, that our horses wish for a whip... just for clarity. Our desire just looks like dense fog to them.

We are limited by the extra layer of false gravity that we create; we make it harder to accept our own worth because we are always looking at what's wrong with us. What if the real meaning of improvement was letting go of being our worst critic in our own mind?

We are a species who thinks we can control outcome. We like to focus on what's wrong, immerse in those problems, and then *make* them right. Even with good intentions, it's a negative approach.

But if I could give riders a gift, it would be a suspension of disbelief.

The reason to suspend disbelief is simple. Disbelief is the sarcastic voice in your head that says, "Who do you think you are? Your horse is nothing special. You aren't good enough; you don't deserve what you want."

Suspension of disbelief is a cue to your inner demons to just shut up; a half-halt to give us a chance to prove to ourselves that we are enough–until we believe it.

A suspension of disbelief would be a perfect moment when your rider to-do list gets extinguished by a dance where your horse freely lifts you and holds you in the light. Oneness is not a destination you can chase down. It's something your horse has already, but you have to quiet your thoughts and actions enough to notice and then claim for yourself.

Maybe when riding, the best thing to straddle is that line of possibility, with one foot deeply grateful for all that the two of you have shared together, and the other foot holding a space of absolute wonder. Good riding is naturally uncertain ground; that's why riding is an art.

How can you tell you're on the right path? It becomes forever less about you and more about doing the best for your horse. To truly put your horse first is much harder than it sounds; it requires a humbling level of honesty that will be fact-checked by your horse.

He'll let you know that humility and insecurity are not the same thing at all. Humility is a place of openness where a horse and rider find balance. The other word for that is grace.

Negotiating, not Fighting.

It was last spring when this ancient donkey came to the farm. In the beginning, we thought she might not make it. She wasn't eating, a sign that she wasn't really adjusting to her new life. Nobody likes change but we couldn't tell if it was a hunger strike or her organs shutting down.

Then she nibbled and sipped and gave us a chance. Eventually she began gaining weight. She was likely in her upper-thirties. She had no teeth; she couldn't graze. Her big old ears were mostly deaf and her eyesight was poor. We called her Lilith.

And I'm not saying Lilith was quirky, but the only friend she made was the goat. And that only happened after she managed to kick him in the head.

Some days her walk was almost fluid, all things considered. But by fall, she took a bad step sometimes, and it devolved into a limp. After a few months of actual nutrition, her hooves started changing. I thought I saw a crack, and I wanted to check it out, not that she would let me near her hooves.

Let's be clear; she was alive for a reason and it wasn't being stupid about her feet. That's how predators kill donkeys out on the prairie; they clamp down a leg and it's all over.

Lilith had developed a new habit of coming up to strangers for a scratch. It almost created the illusion that she'd surrendered, that I could just reach down... I knew better. If my hand snuck a few inches too far south of her spine, her hind end came my way fast.

That dance must have been strange looking to outsiders; Me reaching down and Lilith teetering her butt around stiffly, her hind hooves twitching up and down fast enough to send me scurrying out of her way. Is this what all my years of dressage training have come to? A war of wits with a relic of a donkey. Well, yes.

Choosing to not pick a fight is always the right answer. But it doesn't mean giving in either. I like to call it peaceful persistence.

Our process had to speed up now that it was clear she was hurting. I set a date with my farrier, and came up with a plan.

I rigged up makeshift stocks by dragging an old gate into the corner of a pen. I secured the front of the gate to the fence panel at a corner using twine. It isn't that twine worked all that well, but it's a tradition at this point. Sometimes I even think twine's good luck. The gate was angled wide, with a friend with a bowl of feed at the ready.

Then I led her in and slowly lifted the gate, bringing it parallel to the fence panel, but not tight enough to squeeze Lilith. My friend offered her a snack which was apparently an insult. Lilith pulled back. I held onto the lead rope, and began slowly touching her shoulder. She was mad, nipping at me while I sweet-talked her.

Finally, I lifted the first foot. *Good girl.* For all the thousands of times I've cleaned hooves and never seen a rock, this time there is a sharp one wedged deep by her frog, and I went for it. There's no telling how long it had been there; years maybe.

It probably would have been good to stop right there, but I worried about what I might find in her other front hoof. She was stomping mad when I got to her other side; meaning stomping quick enough that I couldn't catch her hoof. Now would have been the time to get frustrated or even just more forceful. But I moved extra slow to reach for her hoof, then quickly picked it clean. After that, we let her go, let her hind feet wait to have their turn. She paused to glare at me good and hard before walking away, assuring me she would never forget this offense. Never underestimate a donkey's memory.

The next week, all I saw was her backside. Instead of our usual scratch-fests, she only seemed to remember the atrocity, and spun gingerly around, kicking at me as she left. If her hooves felt better, she didn't say so. I went to work melting her new grudge, and just when she was almost accepting scratches again, the farrier came again.

We used the same chute set-up, except that I thought she'd had probably stressed her neck pulling back, so this time her head was loose at the front of the chute and I had a rope behind her rump. The farrier began slowly touching her leg, until finally, Lilith released a foot. My friend stood at Lilith's head with the feed pan again; this time Lilith ate a few bites. Or rather, she was so mad she bit her feed, the way she wanted to bite us.

The trimming took a few minutes but Lilith stood well. It was a long time to stand on one front foot. After a rest and more sweet talk, lifting the second foot seemed much harder. It would have been the time most people would have doubled down to push on through. She's little and frail; the three of us could have manhandled her easily.

Instead, my farrier started humming softly, and Lilith lost the will to attack her feed pan or any of us. We all praised her, grumpy as she was. When we finished, she limped away sore and unhappy. I wasn't sure I felt any better than Lilith did.

I began wondering about her quality of life again. It didn't help that the weather turned cold. Now she seemed all-over uncomfortable: Still sore in front and her hind seemed worse as well. I gave her a couple more weeks to recover from the trimming. Everything goes slower with elders.

Then I had the rescue's vet come out to check her. She perked right up and walked toward the vet with curiosity. No way was she standing still for that stethoscope, though, I knew. I got the halter slowly over her nose before it occurred to her what that might mean. She walked off while I was trying to clasp the buckle. She kept on marching and I kept on struggling. Think slow-motion bull-dogging, only now I'm fussing trying to get my gloves off so I could do the buckle, too. Negotiating; not fighting.

Eventually I talked her into coming back over with me. The vet gave her ears a scratch. Lilith stood quietly in the stocks, picked up her feet fairly peacefully, though she still passively tried to bite the vet, as a matter of pride. That's how negotiation works; you refuse to escalate. In time, everyone gets to have their way. Just not all at once.

Lilith's diagnosis: Not bad for her age; let's try some Previcox for the pain, and see if she can be more comfortable. Probably a decent diagnosis for me, too.

Mental Focus Means Not Trying Too Hard

My friend and I took yoga while we were in high school. It was 1971 or so, and I can't remember if the group met in a church basement or at the "Y", but I will never forget my red leotard. It had long sleeves and was a garish scarlet color, with matching semi-transparent tights–think Red Snapper.

When class began, we were asked to close our eyes, and take some deep breaths. I didn't bother because trying to breathe made my chest tight, so I squinted my eyes open just enough to critically compare myself to everyone around me. As the class continued, I evaluated my limberness, strained muscles pushing for the most extreme position in each pose, all the while squinting to see who was watching me. It wasn't because I thought I was so good; it was the exact opposite. When it was time for *savasana,* that meditative time at the end, I fell immediately asleep, probably due to a lack of oxygen and relentlessly judging myself.

My keen ability to let my mind run like a rat-on-a-wheel was even less helpful when I began riding seriously–something I had actual passion about. Stilling my mind was the biggest change I had to make in myself in order to partner with a horse. I get reminded of my *Time of Red Leotards* sometimes when I'm giving riding lessons.

The most common trait I see in clients who want to improve

their riding is a misunderstanding about what it means to be focused in the saddle; to be mentally strong. Can we even tell when we're trying too hard?

You climb on your horse, and with great diligence, pick up the reins, clamp your body into a position, and set your jaw for the work at hand. The horse takes the cue and does the same. Then, you set about correcting every answer your horse offers for the next hour because you want to be really good at this.

It degenerates to a rat-on-a-wheel death spiral: The worse it goes, the harder you try; the harder you try the worse it goes. About now, you hear a Neanderthal voice in your head saying, "You can't give in and let your horse win. He will never *respect* you again; he will be ruined." Because you have passion and it feels true that riding is about the hardest thing in the world, you double down, choking on loud emotions, and ride harder. Things don't improve but you clutch desperately because you think you're being tough.

Have you checked in with your horse through this? He's the one who actually decides what good riding is, after all. Beneath appearances, he is the one who knows who you are–a mess. And as kind as he may be, he won't give you the benefit of the doubt forever.

Still, there you two are; you've wrestled him into a hole by trying too hard. You have good intentions, and you're both trying to get it right, but your horse is tense. Is he belligerent, or confused, or does it even matter? Now what?

Is it too late to remind you that the first runaway is usually the one inside our own head? Riding isn't about putting up a huge fight; it's about having the mental control not to. It's about behaving like a leader instead of a petulant child in the saddle. Do not take the bait. As tempting as it is to throw a fit, don't lose control of what matters to your horse.

Be still. Start by breathing deep and letting him hear you exhale. He might not mimic you on the first try, so in a clear soft voice, say "Good boy." Not because he is being good right now;

throw it to him like a lifeline in the ocean of confusion. Then slack some rein, ask for something simple, like a step forward, and reward him for that. Not because it's a complicated task, but because you want to remind him that you are capable of not complaining about everything he does. The priority here is to change the tendency of behavior. Yours.

Mental strength, or the ability to focus, is at the very core of who we are as riders, at any level. It sounds counter intuitive but in order to become a more advanced rider, you have to find a way to do less, do it sooner, smaller, and confidently. In other words, you have to behave as if you have character.

If we become blinded by the goal; if a task–like cantering exactly at a certain letter, or doing a certain obstacle–becomes more important than our connection with our horse, we lose sight of who we are and our character suffers. That's the moment a horse loses trust in his rider. And he is right to do it.

Riding technique is necessary, but it isn't enough. Horses respond to our character first. Our temperament matters most. It's their nature to seek a leader who makes them feel safe. It's the real and true meaning of respect.

Instead, ask your brain to think less and feel more. It will take discipline to train your mind in the beginning. Humans are burdened with self-awareness; the place where our egos live. It's our nature to over-think; it isn't a crime. But if you're on a horse at the time, it creates a separation. It's selfish.

Start again. Embrace this new moment. Bring yourself back to stillness within his movement. Be calm and receptive. Have the strength to not jump to conclusions, to not react with emotion, but rather respond with acceptance, keeping your body soft and your cues small. Patiently maintain a quiet mental place, free of anxiety, where you can feel your horse and he can come to trust you.

This mental place is the only part of riding that you will ever be capable of controlling. The good news is that it's all the control you'll need.

Remembrance:
Someone's Always Dying

It's that weird week between the holidays. I never know what day it is so I mess up scheduling around Christmas, only to follow through and mess up the same exact way one week later for New Years. Squinting at the calendar doesn't help tether me and everyone seems immersed on a remembrance vacation. There are the *best of* lists of movies and books and anything else we give awards for. Those achievements are followed with a memorial for the famous people we've lost. It's a long list this year and it's all that anyone talks about. It's like an end of the year emotional profit-loss statement.

I do the same thing here on the farm, with less fanfare and more wonder. This year the *Best Geriatric Come Back* goes to Lilith, the carbon-dated donkey. She gained weight, shed out years of steel wool and grew a soft coat, and went on Previcox for major lameness. Her physical quality of life is a complicated question, but she's loud, cantankerous, and she can land a decent kick now. Her life had been fighting coyotes before her rescue; sometimes I wonder if she just can't find a way to rest. Either that or her warm mush diet rocks.

Most Improved Dog goes to Seamus, the corgi, also a foster. He came off his puppy Prozac, his collar still frightens him, even though we stopped the electroshock therapy, and he's detoxing from his strong meds and over-correcting people. The darkness is slowly getting lighter. I no longer have to lock myself in the bathroom to put my socks on. Rehab continues; he was doing well but then relapsed when we had workers in the house for a couple of weeks. He tore the linoleum off the bathroom floor. That was fair. They made me crazy enough to have a relapse myself. Far from okay, he hasn't gotten worse and sometimes that counts as a win.

It was a hard year for losses to our home herd. We said goodbye to Hank, the elderly toothless cat who fought vermin and intimidated dogs well past his prime. And Walter, the Corgi rescue with an operatic bark and a lure coursing title, whose short life was surrendered to chronic liver ailments. And the most loving farewell to the Grandfather Horse after thirty years of excellence, carrying me over rough ground until I had my footing. It's easy to see how fortunate we are here, isn't it?

It's common sense that with so many animals, we'd have more frequent passings, as well. You'd think that it would get easier to say goodbye. I can remember a time, a perfect summer, when every animal on the farm was young and strong, and I had a season of almost invincible confidence. Even then, I was aware of the fragility of life and grateful for every sunset.

In truth, I think the process of dying is a constant and not a special occasion in any way. I'd do better to make friends with it. After all, there's a twenty-two-year-old llama in the south pasture that's bound to slow down one of these years and a fifteen-year-old dog sleeping under my desk as I write.

Most of us are linear thinkers trained to see time as a beginning, a middle, and an end with a straight flat precision. I prefer Vonnegut's concept of being unstuck in time. I want to think all the moments happen simultaneously, so that even as the Grandfather Horse drew his last breath, we were galloping the old airstrip when he was five. It doesn't take a fleck of the pain away, but I do it for selfish reasons. This way the last moment has less power.

Yes, mourning is a good thing. Our beloveds deserve that

affirmation that they're loved and missed and worthy of our tears. And after the cards and condolences, after our friends forget, the beloved memory lingers. There's a hang-time for loss. It can circle around and ambush us when we least expect it and then the smart thing to do is just give in and have a good screaming cry. Nap during the day. Feel sorry for yourself. But beware: it's just in this moment that we must be the most careful.

Because if we let that moment of loss have too much power, then death gets as loud as an overbearing house-guest and we can become afraid of having an open heart. Afraid of rescue puppies and cranky old donkeys and our own mortality.

"What good are they if they're just going to die on us?" Cynics abound.

What a stupid question. What good are your parents, then, or great philosophers or authors or artists? Religions can debate terminology but the spiritual truth is undeniable: Life is a continuum and even when the landscape appears barren there is life everywhere.

Most animals do have shorter lives than humans, but what if that isn't wrong? Not just that the design of this Circle of Life isn't wrong, but also that death isn't the villain. It's like railing against gravity. Then, by adjusting your perspective and making a conscious choice, experiencing loss can be a path to insight and even inspiration. Wouldn't that give purpose to the lost life as well as our own?

So now I reserve the warmest run in my barn for a lost elder who needs a soft place to land. I do it in memory of my Grandfather Horse but I'm the one who benefits by staring down death and loss. When you screw together your courage and look it straight in the eye, death just doesn't deserve the same respect that a toothless old donkey does.

Maybe the problem is that we've lost our sense of perspective. None of us humans are getting out alive either. There is nothing remarkable about death. It's sad and ordinary and as common as dirt.

Yes, it's been a rough year. Winter encourages us to contemplate the dark and the landscape chimes in with agreement. But even now the days are getting longer and the sun is coming back to us. Death will always be a part of life, but we can put it on *stall-rest* and get about living life in a way that honors those who have gone ahead.

As long as we breathe, there's promise in a New Year and that's worth celebrating.

Serenity NOW! A Cue for Calmness

"I struggle with him to stand still. I suspect he recognizes I'm nervous," she wrote. I'm answering an email question from a novice rider whose horse doesn't always stand quietly. She thinks that she might be part of the problem. Naturally, I love her, even without meeting her.

Dear Rider, thank you for your honesty. Yes, your horse feels your nervousness. If it was easy to snap your fingers and make the fear evaporate, I'm sure you would have done it. So you "struggle with him" to stand. Is it possible to cue him to relax; cue him to come to rest instead?

First let's ask, what is fair to expect from a horse? If you think your horse should stand flat on a loose rein while the rest of the horses leave for the barn at a high gallop, well, you're in for a disappointing and fast ride home. If you think that a halt should hold for an hour without moving, or during a dust-devil attack, again, not really fair. If you believe you should be able to control your ride totally, then I recommend riding something with an ignition.

We can begin only with a horse when you're willing to negotiate. The other word for that is train. Suppose you are sitting in the saddle and want your horse to park quietly. Your horse takes a step to the right, so your right foot corrects him. But he steps forward a stride, so you use your reins to pull him back. Then he tosses his head to one side, so you use the opposite rein to straighten him, and then he backs up. You put enough leg on him to stop him but he continues to jig. You're too nervous to notice you're tense, but your reins are tight and your cues have an edge of panic to them.

Right about now, some railbird will tell you that you need a stronger bit. It would be fine with me if you tell them they're an idiot.

It's hard to not accelerate one correction after another if all either of you know is that everything you do is wrong. The more corrections you make, the deeper the hole the two of you are in. If you stop to think about it, he actually is being responsive to the cues you give him. And if it feels like you're training your horse to be fussy, well, you are.

Take a breath. You're in a rut of nagging and correcting. Some horses will shut down just to make the barrage of cues stop, and some will get reactive. Either way, your horse isn't learning anything by having his past behaviors corrected. Change the tone of the conversation by asking him *to do something*, rather than correcting what he has already done.

Here's where some trainers will tell you to circle your horse, with the idea being that eventually he'll want to rest. But circling can become a kind of emotional evasion for the horse; a way to disconnect. Pretty soon anxiety seems to become part of his personality, and yours, too.

If you are emotionally active in the saddle... he will reflect that.

First, before you address your horse, take an internal inventory. Do a literal scan of your body for tension. What do you feel? Is your seat tense in the saddle or are your knees tight on his flanks? Consciously soften your seat and let your knees feel light enough that an egg wouldn't break under them. Grasping him with your legs is a cue to go forward, so take a moment and breathe looseness all the way to your ankles. Then check your shoulders–do they belong up by your ears? Release them soft with your breath, let your elbows become kind and elastic, and your wrists be free and open. Finally, how's your jaw? If you can't do a human version of *a lick and chew*, neither can your horse.

Become conscious of your own body but don't judge. Thank yourself for the awareness. When you feel anxiety, train yourself to exhale slowly. The process takes time and practice. It runs counter to our instincts, but keep at it. Fear is something that gets stronger in the dark, so drag it into broad daylight and invite it along for the ride. Pretty soon fear will behave like a sullen teenager because you've ruined its fun.

Now that you've addressed the tension in yourself, you can start learning to stand. Pick an easy day because training a new behavior in the middle of a rodeo isn't the best choice for either of you. Now you and your horse are walking together. Feel your body move in unison with his, and his body move in unison with yours. Say whoa, melt into the saddle and rest your sit bones. Slack your reins and trust him. If he slows to an almost-stop, you win. He isn't sure what you want, let him think about what your seat is telling him. Then count to one, reward him profusely, and ask him to walk on. Muster a laugh. Horses like us to laugh because it releases tension in the body.

Repeat this simple walk-halt transition. Don't hang yourselves out to dry by wanting too much. Keep the halts short and walk again before either of you get too anxious. Good boy! You'll notice that your horse likes *not* being corrected all the time and reward yourself for that. Gradually add trots and canters, and let the halts last longer. Take forever, and say thank you every time.

During the process losing awareness of your breath is natural. No guilt, just start again at the walk. Count three strides on the inhale. Hold it one stride. Count to three strides on the exhale. Breathing will slow everything down. You'll know when you get it right because your horse will exhale with you.

This re-training will take time. Reward his effort every time he gives you *approximately* what you want. Then run your body scan again. It's possible neither of you is perfect just yet. Give your horse time to notice how nice it is being calm together. Give yourself some credit for that and feel your own confidence grow.

Then comes that perfect day, you'll find yourself and your horse with a group of other riders, when someone stops breathing and grabs their reins a little too hard. The other horses will sense a tussle of panic in the air.

Without thinking, you will exhale and your horse will stand still. In hindsight, the idea of training a cue for calmness doesn't feel impossible at all.

Going the Full Heart Distance:
Saying So Long

It's deep fall here on our farm. Most of the leaves are gone; Canada geese are on the wing. Each morning there's a thin shell of ice on the water tanks. Local horse-people know the season change in Colorado can be extreme. The barometer goes nuts for a few weeks, temperatures dance wildly, and we keep a special eye on the elders. My Grandfather Horse usually has a veterinary emergency every fall, but not this year.

Trigger warning: This next story is about the peaceful passing of a well-loved horse.

Our story started with a foolish decision: I bought a colt who wouldn't let me touch him. In my lifetime of horses, I have no explanation for why this scruffy Appaloosa colt hooked me as deep and true as he did. From breed shows, to trail riding, to reining, to jumping, and finally dressage, we had a good thirty-year run; all of his life and half of mine. Maybe it was giving him such an infinite name; there was no telling where my *spirit* stopped and his began.

This Grandfather Horse had a rough summer. Chronic arthritis controlled his movements even on warm days. His knees wobbled and even collapsed on him sometimes. He had a collection of tumors; the largest one had grown to ten inches. I asked a kind vet for a consult; I didn't need a diagnosis. It isn't a crime to get old.

I was told that the thing most likely to kill him wasn't even the condition that caused him the most daily pain. The management options were exhausted. Of the three possible outcomes, two were brutal. The vet left and I languished in selfish thoughts, intense memories, and the inability to verbalize anything.

Then I practiced saying the words out loud, like a spoonful of poison a day. A week later I called for the appointment to euthanize Spirit. I got some of the words out and found a day at the end of September; far enough off that I could torture myself with doubt, screw up my courage, and say a last, best, thank you. For half of my life, he was my only constant. I wanted to hold steady for him now.

Then he made it easier for me. Don't you hate that? There was a strange incident that left him disoriented and out of balance. A stroke, perhaps? After that day, his eyes were dimmer but we doddered on.

Thirty years; closer than kin. Readers and clients sometimes tell me that they wish, for the sake of their horses, they'd known me thirty years ago. Spirit would be the first to tell you I was no prize. He was always the brains of our partnership.

As our horses age, we continually lower the bar when thinking about their quality of life. We know they're flight animals but we mitigate their lameness with supplements and injections. We want to believe they don't miss running. As teeth are lost, we make mush for creatures designed to graze twenty-four hours a day. We keep them safe from younger, stronger horses in turnout. When they can't move enough to stay warm in winter, there are waterproof quilted blankets. With the Grandfather Horse, eventually, the bar got so low that he was a shadow of the beautiful gelding who changed my life.

If I look at this objectively, through the magic of hindsight, Nature would have taken my Grandfather Horse a decade ago. By the end, I had become more afraid of a painful midnight blizzard emergency than I was of losing him. There were no better days ahead. I knew he'd given me everything he had, and

I'd done the same; now there was only this one final kindness.

The day before our appointment, I stayed in the pen with Spirit and our family horses. It was a golden day. Spirit reeked of Showsheen, and the curry was as warm as his old heart when I finished. I took hundreds of photos. He looked miserable in most of them; his eyes were almost closed and he only moved a few steps all day. But we were all together.

There's nothing special about death. What matters is how we live.

On the last morning, the family horses had breakfast together like usual. Spirit wandered away from the herd, stood in the sun, and dozed. I stayed close, not that he noticed, and kept my breath matched with his, treasuring each inhale.

We'd been thrown some curve balls over the years, but I will never regret a single moment with that horse. Not even this one.

Spirit had no fear of vets or needles; I didn't need to hold him. So we shared an apple, in the way that we always did. I bit off a piece, sweet in my mouth, and gave it to him. The vet began the procedure and an instant later, Spirit was free. My first feeling was relief. It went well. No fear or suffering. I felt like I'd saved him.

"Let the pain wash over you. Don't fight it, feel it. Let your tears free. Cry without judgment; it's just a different kind of breathing." I wrote that years ago; horses taught me to believe in emotional honesty.

I brought the family herd into the pen after the vet left. Nubè was curious and quiet, while Clara was frightened, flagging her tail and galloping arcs around Spirit. Edgar and Bhim were stoic. Eventually, everyone made their peace. Little Arthur, Spirit's goat, stayed longest. He laid down by Spirit's back leg, as I sat by his head, holding vigil until the truck came for his body.

A cut this deep has a purity about it.

I'm sorry to share this; there's no shortage of sad news. My voice has an aching squeak; it's taken a month to write this eulogy. Everything I say sounds trite and superficial. The words feel insignificant, like an out-of-focus snapshot. I'll live in the shadow of this horse for the rest of my life. If I'm lucky.

Personally, I'm not a fan of the Rainbow Bridge. If it gives you comfort for loss, take it to heart. As for me, I hate the idea of all my animals waiting for me. Besides, I think horses might be Buddhist. I hope he's gamboling through a pasture, on brand *new* wobbly legs, catching the eye of another horse crazy girl who has a lot to learn. I'd wish him another life just like this one.

Mostly, I'm overwhelmed with bittersweet gratitude. I knew he never belonged to me. He was always part of something bigger than my tiny, conflicted life. I had to leave my puny-sad-self behind to keep up with him. It was the best trade of my life.

Vernal Equinox

Release, the Unflattering Truth

A few weeks ago, I was standing, talking with a client at the end of her lesson. She was at her horse's shoulder, close enough that her sleeve touched him, and he had his head curved toward her. He wasn't mugging her; just standing. My client said, "I suppose you don't think I should let him be this close, do you?"

It's a well-known fact that all riding instructors live for the sole reason of ruining any good moment a rider might be having. And it's a common event that we talk about horses when they are standing right there, so the answer was clear. "Let's ask your horse."

I was about six feet away and I asked my client to step back as well, out of his space, and let the lead rope rest on the ground. That last detail is important. If we hold the rope, even loosely, the rope moves as our bodies do, but if it's resting on the ground, it's a clear, undeniable message. It's the difference between waiting on hold and hanging up the phone.

My client and I continued talking about the lesson and a minute–just a minute–later, he dropped his head low. He exhaled a long slow breath and loosened his jaw. His body got softer and quieter. His eyes closed part way. Neither of us had seen stress in him before but he was clearly and obviously more relaxed. This good gelding is a stoic sort of horse; sometimes you learn more in hindsight than in the moment.

In this example, let's define release as ending the conversation (whatever training or work you were doing) and letting the horse be. The physical part of that is easy. My client had dismounted, taken off the horse's bridle, and put his halter on, all the while standing within a few inches of him.

The mental release is a good deal more complicated for us humans because it involves ego and desire and horse-crazy girl fantasies. In other words, it involves putting the horse first. We all like to *say* we put our horses first.

And we want to give a reward. There's no doubt that a horse responds to a kind word, a warm touch, or even a physical treat. Humans like that interchange, too. We revel in that moment of connection and gratitude. I don't want to negate that in any way, but this sweet gelding told the truth. He was still, at the very least, wary of us. And if taking a step farther away releases that feeling, why wouldn't we do it?

The easy answer is that it isn't flattering to us humans. I remember the first time I heard that the best reward for a horse was release. No, it couldn't be true. I confess joy in mugging a horse, but even more than that I just hated the thought that my horse didn't appreciate my cloying affection. Like a first boyfriend, I wanted my horse to hang on my every word and want to cuddle and coo. And for the horse, just like a first boyfriend, he'd rather have the relationship than talk about it. Ouch. Just ouch.

In order to progress in an equine partnership, it's important to learn to truly release a horse, both on the ground and in the saddle. If it's possible to cue a horse to have anxiety, (who hasn't done that?) then it must also be possible to cue a horse to relax.

A horse who mugs a human isn't being affectionate. When he searches your pockets for treats isn't cute; it's a moment of anxiety. It's the insecure kind of behavior a weanling in a herd might exhibit, but not a confident adult.

Gaining the confidence to *hold his own self up* may not be easy at first. If his lacks confidence, you might have to shake your lead a bit, almost like asking him to back, before letting the rope hit the ground. But if you ask him to step back, then you do the same. Demonstrate what you want from him; create space. It might take more than one try and he'll need time to understand. Help him find that distance easier. Say "Good boy." Rest. Then watch his honest release response.

The ability to cleanly release your horse from your mental expectations, no matter if you are fearful or bold, might be the highest sort of leadership, but we must get our emotions out of the way to do it. Engendering an experience of safety and consistency is the basis of a bond with a horse. It's the comradery of standing together, confident, with no need to prove anything on either side. Autonomy.

Back in my martial arts days, we were taught that a human had a personal space that was about three feet in all directions and it was considered an aggression to enter that space uninvited. I was an introvert and sometimes confused with social parameters. I appreciated that this three-foot rule gave me a kind of line of demarcation; I could choose to hug someone, or if I felt uncomfortable, I could step back, and use any number of the same calming signals I saw horses exhibit. If we recognize that we are similar animals to horses, it was easier to understand the confidence he could feel from an honest release.

Yes, the exact word is confidence. Isn't that the elusive goal?

So try this experiment: Give your horse a complete and honest release. Start by standing a few feet farther away than you want to. Still your body, drop your weight, soften your shoulders, and cock a hip. Let Sting's *Set Them Free* play in your head.

Inhale. Pause. Exhale. Finally and most importantly, let go– free as a bird—and release any expectation and judgment of him that you're holding in your mind. When you have done it for him, then do it for yourself as well. Be the kind of leader he needs.

Inhale. Pause. Exhale. Be partners in peace.

Energetic Tidiness in the Saddle.

Some of us climb into the saddle and have all kinds of crazy dangerous things happen …right out of the blue. We didn't do anything at all, and for no good reason, the horse came apart.

Some of us are almost okay in the saddle, carefully moving along until it happens; the horse jerks, we lose balance, and jerk back. It happens so quickly that we scare each other half to death.

Some of us think of our horses as therapists. When we're cross or out of sorts, all we have to do is go to the barn, climb into the saddle, and in no time at all, we're feeling better.

Finally, some of us, the very luckiest ones, have horses especially interested in teaching their riders some *energetic tidiness.*

Right about here, I'm going to stick up for horses. They don't come apart "for no good reason"; they don't have some sort of vendetta to hurt people. Short of a bee sting, or some other sharp pain, they give us a series of warnings that things aren't right. About the time we notice them, we flinch and get defensive. It's just human nature that losing confidence makes us insecure. So we ride with timidity or bravado and not all horses, especially those with confidence problems of their own, tolerate us well.

It's an unpopular thought but just because some horses seem good at dissolving our negativity, is it fair to expect it of them? How does the therapist part of your horse's job affect the other work he does?

Too often the rider's mental awareness limits the horse's behavior options. We all acknowledge that the most challenging horses are the ones who teach us the most, but can we articulate how they do it?

As a riding instructor, I think about it a lot: What does it take for a rider to improve? Sure, we can always improve technique with our hands. Balance and communication in the saddle is crucial. Small corrections in our riding position can make a big difference in our horse's willingness to go forward. On the mental side, it's all about energetic balance. If a horse is nervous, do we get tense or can we aid their confidence by breathing. If the horse is dull, can we lift our energy a bit to aid them? The bottom line is we must admit the impact our mental state has on our horse at any time.

We all know that horses sense our fear but it's more than that. They sense confusion, distraction, and all sorts of lesser emotions. They can even mistake anticipation for anxicty. It might be happy anticipation to be riding with a new group, but your horse reads it as anxiety. Or we might read their anticipation as fear.

If our thoughts and emotions are swinging from one extreme to another, we aren't much of a leader. The difference between riders who continue to have the same tense ride year after year and those riders able to progress with their horses boils down to maintaining a consistent positive state of mind. It might be as simple as recognizing a concern and saying, "We're just fine, good boy." It's an affirmation for both of you.

No, I'm not suggesting you can exert mental control over your horse. You can't control the environment, either. The only thing that will ever be within our control are our own thoughts and emotions.

The first thing to know is that a good rider doesn't just ignore her fears and concerns. Denial is how most of us became nervous with our horses in the first place. Is there a way to acknowledge our nervousness without giving in to it?

It's an affirmative action to choose your state of mind; to discipline your thoughts to stillness. Think of it like picking up your bedroom. Put your fear and drama away in your underwear drawer with your flimsy doubt. Close it. Check the floor for stray socks, expectations, over-wrought dreams, and thoughts about aging; those all belong in the hamper. You can do the laundry later. Might be time to get rid of that Megadeath poster...

Now straighten your shoulders as if they're sheets on your bed. Smooth yourself out. Then open the closet and take out a clean outfit of calm-listening. Accessorize with sparkling intention. Settle your intelligence and awareness inside a helmet and breathe. *This is energetic tidiness.* You're ready to ride.

It's hard in the beginning. Giving our horses only our best parts takes focus. Use kindness to spur yourself to understanding. When a bit of doubt crops up, kick it under the bed, and take another breath. Let your horse see your peace. Even if it's fragile right now, hold it to the light and let him reflect it back to you. It's no different from learning to keep your heels down. Repetition builds habit.

Being committed to listening to your inner stillness is wildly attractive to a horse. Horses recognize it because it's how they are, too. There is strength in vulnerability.

When I look back to my own *furious* efforts to improve, I'm sure I drove my horses nuts. I wonder at their tolerance. Trying too hard, even to improve, looks exactly like anxiety and pressure. Luckily, horses read the quality of our intentions as clearly as our fear. It's here that affirmative change begins.

Soon enough the rider begins to find a tidy and still place inside her horse, too. It's the place we always dreamed of, that we obliterated searching for, and now we find it, in plain sight. Self-criticism that made it harder to discover than need be.

I'm not saying that horses or people will ever be perfect. Every relationship is a negotiation: some days they carry us and some days we carry them. The goal is to improve your overall tendency of confidence in the saddle by working to build a quiet internal focus on affirmative thought.

Eventually a day comes when your energy becomes an aid to your horse. You can share your energy if his is lagging. You can comfort his pain with breath instead of worrying him with baby-talk. You can lift him with compassionate strength that you didn't know you were capable of, for all the times he as lifted you by just looking in his eye.

Horses inspire us to be better people. Better people make better horses.

A Trailer of One's Own

Do you remember your first horse trailer? Mine was a navy blue two-horse straight load. It was the late '80s and no one I knew wanted to show their horse but me. I'd been preparing for years, buying spare buckets and hay nets and trailer gadgets. Finally, I talked a friend into buying one together. It weighed a bit more than my truck–without horses in it. The inside had rust that you couldn't really see because it had been spray painted silver. There was a tiny dressing room up front with saddle racks at an impossible angle. I could not believe my wild luck.

Then came the day *I grew up*. I loaded my horse and my gear and headed off alone with Jerry Lee Lewis roaring from my tape deck. Driving with all the tense earnestness of a high school student with a learner's permit, I made my way carefully to the fairgrounds in the next county. It might as well have been another country; I knew no one but it was my first Appaloosa show and I was sure it would be perfect.

There was also a goat show at the fairgrounds that weekend. Have you ever heard a few hundred goats bleating? No? Neither had my young horse. He visibly quivered–out and out vibrated– as I tacked him up. It was contagious. I'm always saying goats are the remedy for Type-A personalities, and this is where I learned it. Lucky we were a day early.

I wanted to quit and go home, but I'm no quitter. So we worked for a while, both of us spooking the other. The best I can say about the ride was that I managed to stay on. Before dark I was laying on a camp cot in my trailer and wishing it all was over. By morning my horse was a little better; neither of us can hold that level of adrenaline forever. I hosed off my head and felt awkward in my show clothes.

Naturally I'd entered every class I could because I didn't know any better. It was probably more about persistence then riding well, but by the trail class Sunday afternoon, we counter-cantered just on the other side of the fence from the goat pens. *Intentionally* counter-cantered. We didn't win any blue ribbons, but I did win the reserve high-point award, I think just by sheer numbers. My prize was a purple plastic spray bottle–like the $1.29 ones at the drugstore. I was insufferable. After spending thousands of dollars on board, training, this trailer, and a truck to pull it, *I won a prize!*

In my years since that first haul, I've honed my skills. There have been sunny days at horse shows and trail rides with friends, but much more important trips, too. I've pulled horses from auctions in the nick of time and picked up rescues from people heartbroken to surrender them. I've hauled foals to vet schools for surgery and made midnight emergency colic runs with sick horses. A trailer buys safety for your own horse, but also the ability to help others. We've had some fires in recent years and I've gotten choked up seeing lines of trailers ready to help evacuate. It makes me proud.

A horsewoman told me that, at sixty-three, she was the proud owner of her very first horse trailer. I let out a congratulatory yell and I've been smiling all day. Trailers add a layer of independence to the freedom we feel with horses.

The new trailer owner's husband asked that the trailer be *her* responsibility. That's good news. Husbands and wives tend to agree about trailering about as much as they do driving, I suspect. Beyond that, no one prioritizes horses like an owner does and the ability to *not be dependent* on others is priceless. With no objection, she soon hired a trainer to help sort out the details of hooking up and loading. Backing up was the most challenging part. She had to overcome some beginner's nervousness, but she's feeling pretty proud of herself now.

Owning a hauling rig is expensive, in ways you can't imagine in the beginning. But at the same time, it isn't really a luxury, either. Keeping horses at home means lives do actually depend on it. Consider starting with a simple, affordable stock trailer.

If fear has been holding you back from hauling, maybe now is a good time to step up to the challenge. It wouldn't be the first time you've been stretched out of shape for your horse. Take a ride in back and figure out how slowly you should corner the thing. Spend some time pulling it empty at first. Head to a parking lot and take your time. Make a mess of backing until it gets easier because having people direct you is just crazy-making. Now head for a gas station and work on steering through narrow places. Notice that slight swagger as you walk back to check the latches? Take a breath; the whole thing is so much easier than learning to ride.

If owning a trailer just isn't possible, do you have an emergency plan for your horse? Does that trailer owner know she's your emergency plan? Now might be a good time to consider asking that person for hauling lessons. Offer to be a back-up driver and learn to hook up. Trailer knowledge shouldn't be limited to owners; in the worst-case scenario, you could save the day.

Owning a horse requires an unusual and ever-growing skill set. Hang around a barn long enough and there is nothing you won't be asked to do. It takes a fair range of courage out of the saddle, too, because horses depend on us in this messy world. We're lucky we're such hard-headed, relentlessly persevering folks.

And oh, one last thing. Practice your steering wheel wave. It's like our secret handshake. Traditionalists like a subtle one finger lift, an acknowledgment of solidarity to others pulling rigs. An acknowledgment that we share a sacred task; horses in our trailers. It's understated but the meaning is clear from one rig to another: I've got your back. You can count on me... and so can your horse.

Thin Horses, Body Scoring, and Inconvenience.

There is no rule that says when a horse's age goes up, his weight needs to come down. Age is no excuse for thin horses.

Take my Grandfather Horse. You could tell he was three-times the age of the other horses because he was sway-backed and sunken-eyed and the buckled-over state of his knees. His poor knees. He was thirty when he passed, with a list of maladies a mile long: nearly toothless, blown tendons, arthritis, heart murmur, cancer, and near the end, he had some sort of stroke... but his weight was just dandy.

I have a habit of attending horse abuse cases in court. On sunny days, when I could be giving lessons or working with my horses, I sit in rooms with no windows to listen to lies. If I was guaranteed convictions with real penalties, I'd call it a *guilty pleasure.*

The hard part of this dark hobby is listening to the evidence. Testimony on behalf of the horses includes the state of the facility; the quantity of manure, along with usual empty water tanks, and lack of feed. There are usually statements about the condition of the horse's feet and their teeth, but their weight is the most visible symptom. We use a body condition score (BCS) rating system to describe the physical state of the horse on a scale from one to nine.

The most common excuse that lousy horse owners use to

justify neglecting their horses is claiming that older horses are just naturally skinny. And yes, there are a million other flimsy excuses for how horses get to this sad state, but it's ridiculous how often you hear the "old horse" excuse. How many elders end up at auctions looking like the walking dead. It's ridiculous how little it takes for these same elders (without health issues) to regain a healthy weight.

Sometimes good horse-people get into trouble. There could be a death in the family or a job loss. Law enforcement doesn't want to seize horses; it's actually a complicated process. They would rather help the owner find a solution. By the time charges get filed, it generally means that the owner has refused a few ideas and horses have died.

How do you tell the difference between an owner who's trying and actual neglect? My personal rule is that if the water tanks are empty, it's a bad sign. Water is free, after all. Even if it is *inconvenient* to walk out to the pen.

Horses who lose weight with feed available probably have a dental problem. Equine teeth "erupt" through horse's lives; they continue to grow. Daily grazing wears the teeth down but as time passes, sometimes the teeth don't wear evenly, leaving sharp hooks and edges that result in painful ulcers inside the mouth and less effective mastication (chewing) means less of the nutrition in the hay is available to the horse and he loses weight. Teeth change as a horse ages, weight should not.

Good horse-people get dental care for their horses; "floating" is the process of filing the teeth level to improve the tooth surface for effective chewing.

Growing up, I don't remember seeing floats done. We were poor farmers and my father dispatched "useless" animals that were thin or old. Times change and when we know better, we can do better. But ignorance is no excuse. These days, checking teeth is part of a routine vet check. Unless, of course, a horse doesn't get consistent veterinary care, either.

Sometimes in a pen of horses, a few will be an okay weight

but others will be too thin. They are being under-fed. The more assertive horses are eating the hay while the more submissive ones are starving. That's still neglect; don't wait until they are all emaciated.

Sometimes I sit in court listening to a cloud of evidence: some combination of no hay, or no vet care, or just lies and excuses. The defendant always has friends in the court, ready to testify on behalf of the abuser. I always wonder if they were such good friends, why didn't they step in and offer help before things got so bad?

Last year in court, at the end of a full week of expert testimony about the horrific neglect that had resulted in the death of over half of her herd, I listened to a life-long horse-owner explain to the jury, in a perfectly reasonable way, that her horses weren't show horses and therefore they just didn't need the same level of care. I looked to the jury and no one's chin was on their chest. It sounded almost rational. Almost believable.

Don't be fooled. Neglect is failing to provide adequate care to any animal you possess and it's against the law.

Now for the rant: I know caring for animals is *inconvenient*. It's endless time and endless money. And as horses continue to age, you might have to soak mush or buy bags of senior feed. But still, the crime isn't getting old– it's lacking the compassion to *inconvenience* yourself.

If you feel you owe a debt to horses in your life, please participate in our legal system. Bear witness in court; let them know the community cares about animal welfare. Too many times people put their personal *convenience* above the needs of others, when it's our character at stake.

And if you see a thin horse, kindly ask the owner about floating. Make it easy; say that you didn't always know about it, either. Give them the chance to do the right thing.

Meanwhile, I'll keep an eye on our foster donkey. Lilith arrived in late spring, extremely elderly, rail thin, and with, in the equine dentist's words, "expired teeth." This fall, I had to cut back on her feed a bit, worried that too much weight would stress her old joints and make her move worse than she already does.

Part One:
The Strong Silent Type of Horse

While growing up, I saw the movie *She Wore a Yellow Ribbon* more often than I saw my relatives. My father controlled the TV and he liked real men like Henry Fonda, Robert Mitchum, and John Wayne. (I'm sure you can guess what he thought about James Dean.)

Later, like lots of us, I bought the notion of a strong, silent leading man when it came to movie star crushes. They had square jaws and walked with a swagger, always a little mysterious. I should stress here that they were acting. It was my mid-thirties before I made the connection between my taste in movie idols and my constant whining that the man I was dating wouldn't talk to me. Duh.

It took longer for it to dawn on me that my horse was stoic, too. His resistance wasn't easy to read. He hid lameness and acted tough. He did what I asked, even if it was too much. Neither of us wanted to admit that we probably held a grudge. We liked each other, so instead it was more like passive aggression on both sides. But you can't force a horse to talk to you anymore than you can a man. In hindsight, I think some of our training problems were more from ulcer pain than anything, but again, he didn't give me the usual signs that he was suffering that a more reactive horse might have. I'm still apologizing for not being more aware.

Trainers love to classify horses into personality types that over-simplify horses, so it's easier for novice horse owners to make assumptions. It's a mistake, none of us are that easy to pigeon-hole.

Instead, I consider most horses on a continuum, one end being stoic and the other end being demonstrative. I deliberately choose these vague words, give lots of room for individuality, and always remember that it isn't that some horses are more sensitive than others; they just express their emotions differently.

People like stoic horses because they seem quiet and easy on the surface. They're commonly lesson horses, therapy horses, and kid horses.

Dictionary.com defines Stoicism as "the endurance of pain or hardship without a display of feelings and without complaint. Synonyms: patience, forbearance, resignation, fortitude, endurance, acceptance, tolerance."

Does this definition make you a bit sad? What sounds heroic in a movie character is kind of soul-killing for a creature as beautiful as a horse. If you are a dominating rider, you might want that kind of hostage mentality, but if you are hoping for an equine partner, this is leadership without heart. Old timers had another word they used for stoic horses who seemed almost too easy to read: Counterfeit. They looked like the real thing, but there was something not quite right.

It isn't that stoic horses are dishonest; they're subtle communicators. If our cues get loud or inconsistent, he just tucks inside of himself. It isn't disobedience so much as self-defense. He looks well-trained, but his eyes are dead. You might want to think everything is fine, but as time passes, he gets more withdrawn. He might drop his head between his knees in submission; he might look like a push-button pleasure horse on the surface, but he gives you none of his heart. He doesn't want to try. Maybe you'll call him lazy and kick harder, but louder cues will just shut him down more. If you are honest, it feels more like coercion then partnership.

Then it happens, just like the big bloody shoot-out at the end of a western movie. After he's taken all he can, a stoic horse might explode with emotion. The rider says, "Everything was just fine but suddenly, for no good reason, my horse just started bucking." Or worse, all the light in the horse's eyes finally goes totally black and they just lose the will to live, looking years older than their age.

What's the best way to partner with a stoic horse? First, don't minimize his intelligence. Especially if he's a draft breed. Assume he hates being under-estimated and talked down to just as much as you do. Breathe yourself quiet. Show him respect and don't interrupt his thought process. Wait for him to volunteer. Listening will require better patience and effort; stoic horses aren't as blunt as demonstrative horses. Rather than bullying him through work, let him be who he is and answer in his own way. Yes, he will answer eventually, but you don't get to be the boss of that. Allowing that horse to volunteer is your single goal.

When he gets the answer right, or even partly right, reward him lavishly. Let him know that his input matters. He might act a bit like the shy kid who blushes when the teacher praises him in class. That's how you can tell it's working.

Now the tendency of your work together is starting to shift. Instead of being a robot, he might even offer something more than you ask for. Yay, and don't you dare correct him for trying too hard. See the big picture: He's learning, and shaping his behavior is much more important than demanding perfection.

Nurture this little sprig of confidence. Reward him with a big release. Like that same shy school kid, he doesn't want to be hugged until he faints; instead slack the reins or the lead. Let him stand on his own feet and feel pride in himself. Pause. Let his introverted bravado bask in the broad daylight. Then thank him for his honesty.

The day will come when the two of you will be together and you'll show him a challenge. Just reveal it; nothing more. In your quiet mind, you'll hear him say, "I got this." You'll feel him breathe; your legs expanding with his chest as he steps out.

Confidence is the greatest gift any rider can give their stoic horse.

Part Two: The Demonstrative/Reactive Type of Horse

Describing this horse sounds like reading the judge's comments on a marginal dressage test: *Tense in the back. Tight in the poll. Hollow. Too quick.* It doesn't stop there. He has twitchy eyes, a furrowed brow, and he clenches his jaw. Sometimes his head is so high you're almost unable to see around it and the muscle under his neck is stronger than the one on top. His flank feels rock hard and his breath is as shallow as yours.

And it isn't just physical. It's the way his mind works, as well. He reacts. When a different horse might reason it out, he jumps to conclusions, usually the worst. Everything seems like it's on the big screen; he's dramatic and impulsive. Sometimes he gets sullen, almost pouting, and a minute later, he's hysterical, jigging as if his hooves were on hot coals.

"He's just really sensitive," they say. Really? I see horses on a continuum; one end being stoic and the other end being reactive or demonstrative. It isn't that some horses are more sensitive than others; they're all sensitive. Some just express their emotions differently.

"My horse acts this way because he's hot-blooded," they say. Sure, some breeds are more energetic and athletic than others, but to my eye, many of these reactive horses look frightened or in pain. Can those riders truly tell the difference between breed traits and individual anxiety? Can this behavior be considered normal?

Does your horse make faces? Maybe he twists his neck and chews his tongue. He paws with impatience and pins his ears when it's supper time. Or he grinds his teeth, or flips his head, or you can routinely see white around his eyes.

Could your horse have ulcers? They are ridiculously common and practically all the behaviors I've listed so far could be symptoms. Think about it; no one denies the connection between ulcers and colic, still the number one killer of horses. On the high side, we didn't always know as much as we do now; it's actually great time to have ulcers. There's so much help available. Just to clarify, stoic horses have as many ulcers as reactive horses do, but worse, they just keep it to themselves.

What if these behaviors that we correct or punish are actually calls for help?

"She's just mare-y," they say. No, mares aren't just naturally cranky. Their hormones make them more like stallions than geldings and ovarian cysts are one of the most under-diagnosed conditions in horses. On top of that, the discomfort of that situation could cause a secondary condition of ulcers. So, lighten up on name-calling mares already.

"He's an alpha horse," they say. But just like humans, leadership isn't the same as dominance. The herd hierarchy has much more nuance than that. In my experience, alphas like a break from trying to control the universe and enjoy the peace that comes from affirmative training.

"He's never quite mean," they say. It's almost like he tries too hard. Exactly! Reactive horses are responsive, intuitive, and connected. They have contagious enthusiasm, backed by intellect. They are radiant and intense and luminous. And yes, their hearts burst with try. Don't believe me? Watch a thoroughbred run in slow motion.

More often, it's us that fails them. We think it takes courage to ride a reactive horse, but what if compassion is really what's needed?

Horses are fully dimensional sentient creatures. There's no

such thing as brain-dead plow-horses or ditzsy hotheads. They are individuals with complicated combinations of temperament, training, and past experience.

Anxiety is a different thing entirely, not necessary or permanent. There are positive solutions that will build partnership, and from that place of security, allow the horse to give you his most brilliant work. It's essential that a good rider listens to every horse with wide-open ears, accepts who the horse is, and then begins the conversation right there.

What's the best way to partner with a reactive horse? First, don't minimize his intelligence. And you might want to sharpen your own attention a bit. Now, if you want to dominate something, control your own self; make your seat soft. Breathe slowly, deep into your lungs. Keep your cues to him invisibly small. Most of all, don't pull on his face. Why make him feel claustrophobic when the responsibility for elastic, soft contact belongs with the rider?

Horses and humans both tend to speed up when they get nervous or think they're losing control. Resist the urge. Go slow. Runaways happen one step at a time and if it seems like the energy builds stride by stride, perhaps he's never been taught the joy of a downward transition. Reward him for doing less.

Walk for at least ten or fifteen minutes, then ask for a trot, but in just a few strides, before he accelerates, exhale back down to the walk. Repeat, and for now, always bring him back in a few strides before his anxiety grows. Some training methods would say that you're teaching your horse to quit by cuing a short trot, but nothing could be farther than the truth. Running a horse until he's tired isn't training. His trot will become more relaxed because the conversation continues. Teach half-halts and halts from your leg. Leave his face alone and let him breathe.

School lots of downward transitions, with immense praise. Let it be a slow dance.

Reward the least thing, so he understands that less is more. Let your mind be slow; he'll take the cue from you. Give him the confidence to let go of his fear and know he doesn't need to try so hard. Then, when his poll is its softest, shut-up, jump down, and step a few feet away from him. Watch him bask in the glow of being anxiety-free. See him stand quiet and still, let his eyes go soft, and droop that bottom lip.

Confidence is the greatest gift any rider can give their reactive horse.

The ultimate goal is riding well enough to help each horse find the center of this stoic/reactive continuum. When energy is balanced with trust, the horse is free to feel the dynamic strength and power of his own body, relaxed and forward.

Do You Communicate Like a Coyote?

Some of us baby-talk and cuddle our horses like they're twelve-hundred-pound teddy bears. Some of us enter the pen with enough flags and whips that we look like a lion-tamer at a circus. It's possible we're on a behavior continuum not so different from horses.

Human behavior runs from one extreme (very shut down) to the other extreme (overly reactionary). In other words, some of us are passive aggressive and some of us just plain aggressive. Too harsh? That's what the horses thought about the words stoic and demonstrative, too.

If you were the sort of screeching, hard-handed, bone-crushing, slimy-reptile Neanderthal who was brutal with horses, you would have put down my bliss-ninny positive training book ages ago.

That just leaves us passive aggressives. And it didn't start out being our fault. Most of us are women; we were raised to be polite and quiet. We were rewarded for being good girls.

I, myself, am a recovering good girl, so if I want some wine, for instance, I call the Dude Rancher, take a breath, and say, "Please bring some red wine home. Thanks, Sweetie."

A passive aggressive good girl might say, "Excuse me, Sweetie, if you have time and it's no trouble, perhaps you could detour on your way home, only if you want to, for some wine, if it isn't out of your way, but if it doesn't work out, it's no trouble for me to go later, Honey, even though my foot is swollen and

I'm a bit congested, I can limp out later after dinner, I was just thinking you might be able to get a nice Merlot, but it's fine, just fine, either way."

Just. Say. It. Already.

If you want to be passive aggressive out in the world, it's your choice. I'm just saying horses hate it at the barn

Horses are prey animals, and coyotes are their sworn enemies. Coyotes stalk them, passively aggressive, skulking around in the shadows, lurking and feinting. Circling their prey, just out of reach but relentless. People do this too. They might tip-toe with a halter partly hidden behind their back, or nag-nag-nag with their feet in the saddle, or be twitchy with their hand, or maybe just lurk on the stiff-side rein. They might give a cue, contradict that first cue, then give a different cue, and still not pause for an answer, busily talking to themselves, up there behind their horse's back.

Or worse yet, we might have so much compassion for our horses that we listen and listen, and never really say anything to them at all. We crane and squint and worry, wondering how they are responding. Is this the way he should behave? When a horse picks up on the doubt and confusion, they can do nothing but lose confidence. We chatter down to them, over them, beyond them, until nothing we say has meaning. In other words, if we stop and start, walk on eggshells to keep them calm, or over think everything in the saddle, we're stalking them.

Do you find this prattle confusing? Imagine you're a horse.

We lose our natural rhythm when we try too hard. We'd hate to consider ourselves abusive so we whisper, and even if we know horses are confused, we tend to commiserate with them about it and not clarify. They see a dog answer a sit command and get a cookie, and wonder why they have it so hard. It's enough to make a stoic horse shut down further or a reactive horse start to scream.

A horse will never confuse you for a horse. You will always be either a coyote or a human. Sorry for the bad news, but now let's set about being a better human. Honest and understandable communication is appreciated. Think short sentences with a thank you at the end.

Horses are looking for a quietly confident leader who respects their intelligence. Let your body be still. Listen without expectation of good, bad, or otherwise. Breathe. Plan ahead. Ask for a transition with awareness in your body. Then breathe again. Wait for his answer. Reward him.

If he's wrong, reward him for trying. Then re-phrase the question more simply. Go slow so that he can reason the answer. Slow yourself down so that you are sure to be clear. Be patient because there is nothing more important than a foundation of understanding. Speed is easy but real trust takes time.

Let him accept you for who you truly are, and if that's a bit of a mess, don't give him a whiny apology. Instead, smile, relax, and try to do better. Trust that he can tell your intention is good. Horses absolutely know honesty when they see it.

Horses are not looking for groupies and they don't want to be put up on a spiritual pedestal. They don't need adoring humans to give them purpose. They want a whole lot more from us than treats.

Scientists tell us that horses have feelings similar to humans, but that doesn't mean they share the same feeling exactly as we might in the same situation, and we'd be arrogant to think they did.

Horses are drawn to good people with calm leadership. They like a herd that feels safe; they appreciate emotional clarity. Try to leave your puny insecurities and your frail feelings in the house. No baby talk, no coyote stalking, no apologies.

Find your center. Feel your feet on the ground and stretch tall. Square your shoulders and speak with a kind, blunt body language. Horses would like us to be nothing less than their equal.

Trust: A Suspension of Disbelief.

You love horses. No, you really, really love horses. Because they are so amazing. We share videos of blind horses cared for by sighted ones. Ponies who tolerate wild kids and horses fulfilling last wishes of our own elders with gentle kindness. There are brilliant competitors dancing and racehorses running on heart. Trail horses who carry us to peace of mind. And don't forget mules fighting coyotes. We marvel at their intelligence and courage. Yay, equines!

Then there's a moment that happens. The instant when that "magical" horse does some small movement that looks normal, like something your horse does. Or the instant that your horse takes a couple of steps of piaffe for the fun of it. Or your horse does a beautiful liberty movement that you only notice you asked for in hindsight. It's noticeable. Maybe not identical but so close. The lights and mirrors go black and you have an inkling that your horse could do the same thing that previously looked like magic. And that what looked like magic was just being a horse.

It's a great moment. The line between magic and normal needs to be blurred. Horses are much more than beasts of burden. At the same time, believing some horses are mythical creatures with magical powers does a disservice to rescue horses and grade horses and most likely, the horse in your own barn.

I think the biggest challenge facing most horses is our own mental limitation on what we think they are capable of understanding. We have an innate us/them mentality. We think that other horses achieve a particular behavior because of some intangible circumstances not available to the average horse and rider. That's just not true.

But how much do we actually believe in their intelligence? Their ability to understand what's going on? How often do we act like they need training for common sense, and in that moment, seek to dumb horses down?

Some of it boils down to a question of trust, but when we think about trusting our horses, it usually involves our physical safety. We trust them to clear a jump, to come back after a gallop; we aspire to trust their responsiveness in some way we call normal.

Say you're asking for a simple in-hand obstacle like stepping onto a tarp on the ground. If he is standing with his hooves right next to it, do you feel you need to do more to explain, like lead him or cluck to him or teach it as if he's never seen it? Or do you trust that he recognizes the obvious?

Think of all the practical but lame reminders we give teen-agers, like to take a coat along on a rainy day. Of course, they roll their eyes. It's clear we don't trust them to come in out of the rain. You can say you're just being helpful, but the other side of that states a lack of trust that they can manage the basics. That's a horrible confidence builder. Would teens be different if we trusted they'd figure it out without us belaboring the obvious?

I recently read a brilliant article that said by demonstrating things to kids instead of letting them figure it out, we actually show them that we are capable, and they aren't. In other words, constantly bailing kids out of their situation creates a kind of learned helplessness –the opposite of our intended goal.

Horses are no different. The chronic habit of humans re-training or over-cueing is a kind of lack of trust in our horse's intellect.

The idea of allowing a horse autonomy, the freedom to volunteer, requires a suspension of disbelief. It means that you extend trust... not that they won't hurt you but trust that they are smart and can answer the question. Giving the cue louder doesn't make it more understandable. It just adds more anxiety. Ask quietly, with confidence in both of you. Then rather than doing the task, give him the time and support to figure it out. You get to pick the topic and he gets to pick the time.

Maybe trust is another word for patience.

If you believe that horses are sentient, then I challenge you to communicate with him that way. Mentor with your body, notice your own energy. Suggest rather than demand. And you know you should be breathing more.

Do your cues take on the urgency and size of semaphore signals on an aircraft carrier? Maybe a little less training enthusiasm and a little more confidence in your own ability and your horse's desire to align with your intention. Let it be easier.

It's possible they won't give us the answer we want immediately. It might be because of confusion or a lack of confidence but don't give into doubt. It's up to us to find a quiet way to ask, or cut the task into smaller pieces and be grateful for every tiny effort. Successive approximation again.

In that quiet moment, can you see a small change in his eye? Does his poll soften? In the past you may have thought he was dawdling or resisting the cue, but looking closer now, do you see his intelligence? Reward that; connect with the action of him using his mind.

Horses and riders get stuck in the same place for long periods of time because we don't hold ourselves to conscious creativity in our equine conversations. We don't progress because we unconsciously become repetitive naggers instead of scintillating conversationalists. If we believe that horses can read our minds in other situations, why would we have to resort to semaphore cues for something obvious and easy?

Trust your horse can be a true partner and not a minion. Let him rise to the occasion and feel pride in himself. Trust his intelligence because his species has survived for thousands of years. Celebrate that intellect as a thing that you both share.

The Mysterious Half-Halt

Ever notice how every definition you read of the half-halt starts with the disclaimer that it's the most misunderstood concept in riding? Not very encouraging. It goes on to say that it's a cue that combines both whoa and go. How hard could that be? There's squeezing and driving and pulling, but not too much. Eyebrow squint. WikiHow has an article about how to do the half-halt in twelve easy steps. Are you kidding me?

I love the discipline of dressage, but sometimes they make it sound a little harder than it is. It's okay, I'm sure they think I'm a little "simple" from time to time, too. Dressage uses complex concepts, described with intellectual precision. I learned half-halts this way, but it's enough to make a rider seize-up in the saddle with over-think-itis, a common dressage malady, especially if you're passionate about riding and try too hard, like I did.

The USDF definition says "The half-halt is the hardly visible, almost simultaneous, coordinated action of the seat, the legs and the hand of the rider, with the object of increasing the attention and balance of the horse before the execution of several movements or transitions between gaits or paces."

It's an okay set of words. I just wish they hadn't included hands. Riders tend to over-do with their hands, so why encourage it?

Not surprisingly, horses have a definition that's a bit more intuitive. I'm bilingual; let me translate for you.

A half-halt is a re-balancing. Can we all agree that balance is way more crucial for horses than we give credit? We want the horse to balance a bit of his weight back, but I hate to say "back" aloud because, again, we tend to use our hands too much to start with. Hands are over-rated; trust your body instead.

The mental part of the half-halt isn't always talked about but that's the mysterious part; the part beyond the physical cues. A half-halt is a mental re-balance as well. It's an instant that affirms the connection between horse and rider in that moment, but also in the near future. It's a blink of acknowledgment that the two of you are together, as well as a hint that something is coming, wait for it. The challenge is timing. By the time we remember to half-halt, it's usually too late, and the horse can't respond in time.

To further confuse the horse and rider, there is a long list of actions used to ask for a half-halt, some big and bold, some invisible. Riders tend to like a dramatic cue using several body parts, physical strength, and a few math skills, while horses like the soft, silent kind. They taught me to do it their way.

The first rule about half-halts is that you must be timely. Think of it as a discipline of preparation. You might half-halt to begin to prepare for a transition. One more half-halt to actually prepare, and then the transition. A half-halt asks for his attention but it should feel light and happy to him, like it will be fun. "Oh goody, a trot is coming..."

The physical part for the rider can be as simple as a breath because a breath resets the body. The inhale realigns your spine, your shoulders slide back as if you have a hanger in your shirt, which in turn realigns your arms and wrists. Let your hands rest. If anything, your hands slow an instant to feel the contact an extra split-second. Your seat straightens in the saddle. You can think of each of these things separately, because it's harder, or you can take a big inhale for an upward transition and your body will follow naturally.

An exhale softens your body, stills your seat, slightly deflates your horse's movement, and like a plane, you glide in for a soft landing. Use an exhale for relaxation or a downward transition, and melt any stray resistance.

If there is no response at all, ask again and perhaps add a slight tightening (upward) of your seat muscles or a loosening (downward). Does your horse respond? Praise him for his attention. Then breathe and cue small again, always trying for less. Think invisible.

I find a light pulse with my thighs backs up my breath and seat well if the horse needs it in the beginning. Inhale, and if needed, pulse your thighs for more energy, or an exhale and pulse your thighs for steadiness or relaxation.

At first your horse may have no idea what you are asking for. His response to you might feel like a dubious, "Huh?" Cheer his effort! This is about subtlety; a tiny half-cue that creates an energetic half-pause, lays the foundation for a relaxed transition. Give him time to figure that out.

Does your horse ever resist a cue from you because it seems abrupt to him? Perhaps he's trotting in a relaxed rhythm, when suddenly, out of nowhere, there's a canter cue –gasp, toss head, counter-bend, throw out a lead leg, and hope for the best. A well-timed half-halt is the antidote.

A few strides into the canter, he begins to speed up. Pull on his face if you want, but it won't help because he's probably tense in the poll already. Besides, you're trying to have better hands. Think about a better rhythm in his canter. Breathe. Focus your body. Reset his speed and steady him as your body realigns. Yay, you did a half-halt.

If this seems entirely too easy and you need to make it harder, may I suggest taking up chess? It's meant to be a war of the mind and there's an opponent. The half-halt is a nod between partners.

Regardless of the gait, and especially at the walk, if you half-halt kindly, with a generous reward when your horse responds, you might feel his back lift just a few millimeters. Reward him with a huge exhale and soft hands, because when he lifts his back a bit, your half-halt is on the way to becoming the cue to bring his head to the vertical without pulling. It's this instant that makes you really... no, really... believe that a half-halt has mystical properties.

Half-halts aren't trained in a day. Every horse is a slightly different individual. Every rider has a unique language. Rather than reading even more books about half-halts that eventually put both of you in a complete tense-halt about the topic, breathe and half-halt your own critical mind. Crank up the music, and while you and your horse are dancing, offer a half-halt. Ask your horse what he prefers, and then let yourself be trainable.

Are Your Legs Doing Too Much?

How are the half-halts coming? Does a breath and a light thigh pulse work or are your legs exhausted by the end of the ride? Is your horse ignoring your leg aids? And by that I mean, have you nagged him into a dullness?

Can you tell if your legs and seat are soft in the saddle? It isn't as easy as it sounds because it's instinct, once our feet have let go of the earth, to grab on with our legs, thighs tight, and calves tense. It's a reflex and if we're a bit timid, then even more so. Tense legs aren't a great idea, but we come by it honestly. Not that it matters to your horse.

The problem with tense legs is that it means that your sit bones aren't deep in the saddle, but rather, suspending you slightly above the saddle, making a disconnect between you and your horse. To maintain that position, your shoulders come forward and you want to hold on with your knees. As your balance changes, your horse might slow, thinking you have lost balance. He's right, but you might not be aware of much of this. You're busy using your horse as a Thigh Master. Rock hard thighs are not the message of lightness and relaxation you mean to send your horse.

You shouldn't be surprised when your horse doesn't want to go forward. But you are, and so you escalate. You've been taught to kick a slow horse. Or you're frustrated, so you kick. There's no response, because it all feels bad to your horse. So you kick harder; your leg never rests. If that doesn't work, you try spurs (not the real purpose of spurs, by the way) and a whip (not the real purpose for a whip, either.) So, you complain that your horse is lazy and won't go forward.

At least, you think, you have kind hands. Well, you probably don't. If the rest of your body is tense, your hands are probably tense, too, which means you might be unintentionally hard on his mouth. No wonder he isn't moving forward. And you aren't breathing in any more air than a chicken. But some jerk has told you that you can't lose this fight because if your horse doesn't respect you, all is lost. So, you double down.

What do I see from the ground? Your horse is mirroring you. His back is tense and his neck is stiff. As you kick, your thighs tense, pushing you farther out of the saddle. With that extra weight on his withers, he resists more. None of this is good, but worst of all, as your aids get stronger and bigger, I begin to see his ribs tense, and the muscle that runs from his armpit to his flank seizes up. Your horse is sensitive enough to be bothered by flies. He probably feels your legs more than you do. He's defending himself from your leg and your seat by tensing his ribs. He has no idea what you are asking now; he isn't breathing either.

Do your horse a favor and show some real leadership. Just stop. Release the reins. Say "Good boy," because you attacked him like a mountain lion and he had more patience for you, than you did for him.

Consider doing yin yoga. Become familiar with the Butterfly pose. Sitting or lying down, soles of feet together, and let your knees open; breathe and let gravity do the work. It will feel tight but just sit with that. Let an eternity pass. Like two whole minutes.

Your horse doesn't care about yoga, but if you were inadvertently giving him a halt cue with your thighs (you were), then you need to be introduced to the muscles he feels all the time.

Next ride, if your horse is safe, and naturally, you have your helmet on, begin your ride at the walk without stirrups. Feel your legs long and let your sit bones move with your horse's back. Let your hip flexor, or more specifically, your psoas muscle, become fluid and soft. The front of your body opens and your heels hang directly below your shoulder, perfect. Feel your feet heavy and your ankles soft.

As your horse walks, your legs flow with the movement of his flank. It's a slight sway that travels from your sit bones through your waist, up to your shoulders, and all the way down to your toenails. You could carry an egg under your knee without breaking it. You don't move more than your horse does, but most of all, you don't brace your legs against his movement.

When you finally do put your foot into your stirrup, you'll notice that it feels constrictive. Yes, a stirrup does make a foot brace a bit, but your job is to continue as if you weren't using a stirrup. Let your weight be on the outside edge of your foot, almost bow-legged. Your leg should feel as light and loose as a bird wing on his flank.

Now the process of asking your horse to respond to your leg can begin. He's gone dead on his sides because the pressure never stopped. Now use tiny cues. Inhale and ask him to walk on. If he moves one step and stops, reward him. Refuse to demean him, and yourself, by nagging.

Ask for a bit more. Jiggle your ankle but don't use muscles. Let the movement feel like a buzzing bug to him. Think energy, not force. Then reward him again, for giving you a chance to do better.

This is about successive approximation. He's still waiting for you to kick hard and that break of trust needs healing. So you reward anything that is an approximately the direction you want to go, while refusing to fight. Once he starts walking, follow his body naturally, but stop cuing. Trust him to do his job without nagging. Let him stride on; let your legs rest. In a few strides, just using your sit bones, ask for longer strides and when he does that, stop cuing again and let him carry it on. Now the two of you are conversing politely.

In order for a horse to be responsive to your leg, your leg

has to do less. It's counter intuitive –just like everything else about riding.

Circles: A Soft Bend

I'd led a sheltered life. I was thirty years old before I visited my first Saddlebred barn. I was just tagging along with a friend, standing flat-footed in the aisle, when I heard a yell, followed by a loud rattling noise. At the far end of an extremely long barn aisle, a tall horse with wide eyes was jangling toward me with a rider up. I backed against a stall as the noise got louder. He flew past me, knees high and chains clanging around his pastern, just above his hoof, in a tense march something like a trot.

They pulled up at the other far end of the aisle, awkwardly turned around and clip-clopped a walk back toward us, stilted and sweating. The rider stopped and exchanged greetings with my friend, while I did a squint-eyed stare at the gelding's long hooves wedged, weighted, and screwed together with metal strapping.

It was a lot to take in; I must have looked like a gaped-mouth tourist. Back in the truck, I grilled my friend who explained that they sprinted the horses up and down their barn aisles, keeping their horses straight because riding in circles "ruined horses."

Do you know the good reasons to circle a horse? No extremes, I don't mean tiny circles at a dead run, but the idea of walking or trotting a large arc? Imagine your horse's barrel; the inside ribs should compress a bit while the outside ribs stretch. Most of us will say that our horses are stiff one way and this is the peaceful antidote. It's common sense to want your horse supple and strong.

Here is the secret to riding a circle: Start by visualizing a circle on the ground. Then cut the circle into quarters and ride it one-quarter at a time. It's a way of staying fresh and mentally in the moment. If you want, count the steps in each quarter. Let the strides stay regular and keep your shoulders at the angle you want your horse's shoulder to be.

The more you think you need to steer with reins, the more "creative" your circle will be. Sometimes from the ground, I feel a need to clarify by saying round circle as a reminder. There is nothing easy about riding one.

Yes, horses have a stiff side in the beginning but the more you pull that side to make them bend, the more things come apart; shoulders dropping in all directions, over-correcting with reins, tense eyebrows and set jaws on riders, and confused ears on your horse. Scratch his withers for tolerating you.

Start again, care more about the track you see on the ground than the bend of your horse's neck. Ride that track. Sit squarely in the saddle and turn your waist, shoulders to the arc of the circle, one-quarter at a time. Ride with an energetic seat and legs, remember? And breathe. If that doesn't help your circle, don't be shy. Put some cones out. This is important for your horse.

Inside leg to outside rein.

It's an imaginary interior line from your horse's armpit (where your foot is) to his outside shoulder. Ignore his head for now. Every time his barrel sways to the outside, your calf will pulse lightly. No, lightly! Let it feel like a dancing cheek to cheek. The concept of bend must be in the ribs, meaning the whole body, as opposed to cranking his neck to the side.

Keep pulsing along at the walk and look down. If you are going his soft way, usually to the left, you will notice your inside rein slack as he softens to your gentle inside calf muscle. You want to see his withers being gently and rhythmically massaged to the outside of the circle. You want that outside arc of his body as sweet as a crescent moon, as soft as a peach.

After a while, reverse direction. He might counter bend a bit. Keep the inside leg massaging away but lower your expectations. It takes a good while; you can't make muscles release. Let your horse do that part. Remind yourself that a counter-bend isn't a disobedience; it's literally an under-developed muscle; his withers need time. Horses are born this way and if you create more resistance while asking him to bend his stiff way, that does defeat the purpose. Think long neck. Think of him stretching nose to tail. Pass the time breathing.

Remind yourself that curving or walking in an arc is a calming signal for a reason. This flexing of the horse's ribcage relaxes them. Wait for him to tell you it's working. He might blow out a snort, or lick and chew. Maybe his neck will get longer, maybe his stride will improve, his inside leg energized by your inside pulsing calf. These are all right answers. Say, Good Boy.

Once the circles are good, try a spiral. Start with a twenty-meter circle, carve it smaller with your outside leg pulsing (in rhythm as his barrel swings to the inside to move smaller) as you turn your waist a bit more, to a fifteen-meter circle, and adding energy to your sit bones, even smaller to a ten-meter circle. Once there, use your inside leg to gradually move out to twenty-meters again.

To begin just do a smaller circle inside of a larger one. Let this spiral have a chance to blossom as your horse gets more supple. If you are on the trail, plan a path using huge half-circle arcs instead of straight lines. Ride with your legs. Ask for slow, long strides, giving your horse time to step under. Stay mentally engaged; ride with energy and practice your own internal focus by feeling each step. Know that he is gaining strength from the inside out. Be patient. Think of coiling the spring, think T'ai Chi for horses.

If you find circles boring, reconsider. We don't ride them to please judges. There's a much better reason than that: *Supple bend equals longevity.*

Is there a better reason?

The Politics of Holiday Pie

Inconceivable: I'm going to share my pie recipe. This sort of thing could go either way.

There was that time years ago, that I had a date over for dinner. We hadn't known each other long and I always want to get off on the right foot. We were sipping wine in the living room when I went to check on dinner in the kitchen. I had rice on the stove. Lifting the lid, there was no water visible. I could see the beginning of a light golden color around the edges. So naturally, I turned up the heat and returned to the living room. I hate to cook and he might as well know that from the start.

For some people, cooking is a creative passion. I mean them no disrespect; I hope they invite me for dinner. Somehow cooking wound up being a political women's issue for me.

I was raised in a traditional home, meaning men and boys had all the fun and unhappy women cleaned up after them. My mother, who also hated cooking, tried to teach me right. She knew that ordinary girls, ones who couldn't get by just on their good looks, would need serious domestic skills if they were ever to find a husband. Especially an ordinary girl with a mouth like mine.

So yes, I sew beautifully but I used the concept of piecing fabric into clothing as a way of understanding how to hand-build gemstone settings, using tools like my oxy-acetylene torch, when I was a goldsmith. And it's only recently that I've admitted knowing how to type. It's been decades since a man has asked me to type their term paper, but now, after authoring a few books, I seem to have found good use for those "secretarial skills" they talked about in high school.

Truth be told, I'm a great cook but I hold that secret close. Excelling at the domestic arts wasn't the life I wanted. Once I left home, I shunned any traditional "women's work." Maybe I was afraid if I faltered once, I'd be doomed. Instead, I bit my tongue and pretended ignorance.

It was horses who made kitchens safe again. My pie recipe will make more sense now.

At first, I used to make my grandmother's crust recipe. It has a secret ingredient and is outlandishly good. Now, I buy the pre-rolled Pillsbury crusts. They're passable and easy, and my grandmother was always disappointed with me anyway.

Next, it must be understood that the pie is always made from fresh apples. Buy a huge bag of them and do the worst job of peeling them possible. Sure, I was born with the gene that allows me to create a paper-thin one-piece curl of apple skin, but that's just showing off and doesn't serve the big picture. I like to hack thick slabs of the peel off, so that when I'm done, the apple has a wonky octagon shape and is only two-thirds the size it was before I started. Then core the apple and slice what's left into the pie shell. Continue until the pie shell is heaping full. Quarter the rest of the apples and put them in with the peels.

Then I drag out my Betty Crocker cookbook with the red gingham cover. Mom gave it to me while I was still in high school and I certainly haven't bought another since. I turn to the Perfect Apple Pie recipe to remember how much flour, sugar, and cinnamon to sprinkle in. Then dab butter on top, but use more than they say. See? I've gone off recipe already. Put the lid on the pie, crinkle the edges together, and put it in the oven.

Now hurry. You only have an hour. Scoop the chunky apple peels into a bag and scurry out to the barn. Put a handful of peels in every feeder, while relaxing into the first equine thought that comes into your head. For me, it's always my Grandfather Horse; I miss him. This will be the first year in thirty that he and I haven't avoided the holidays together.

I made the pie early. I needed the apple-peel ritual that's part political, part spiritual, and part therapeutic. It's been a mean year and I'm behind on my breathing.

As the horses chew, my jaw softens. I sink down on a bale of hay. The barn feels like home and memories of all the good horses come galloping back. It's sweet to be reminded. If you're like me, you've been stronger than you ever thought possible. Some days you failed your horse, but you didn't quit. Other days, you've been lifted high and carried like treasure.

If you don't have a barn, it doesn't matter. Quietly remember the first horse you loved. Call him to you; let him star in his own movie. You know the plot by heart.

Through the manure and the mud, the horses saw something in us that had nothing to do with sex or career. It was beyond hair color or dress size or age. Horses treated us in a way that our own species struggles with. They treated us as equals.

An hour later, back in the house, the air is sweet with warm cinnamon and now you have a second apple treat to share with friends or family. They welcome you in with a hug that lasts longer than usual, and they hold eye contact. The pie is an afterthought.

There is something about a woman who knows horses. It's part apples and part muck boots, along with some stray white hairs on her sweatshirt. She's comfortable in her body because she knows acceptance; the glow that lingers from the barn.

At any age, we should know better than to confuse a silly pie with a woman's real worth. Never underestimate her. A heart filled with horses can accomplish anything.

When Your Horse Falls in a Hole

Horses fall into holes all the time. Metaphoric holes; the really tricky kind that jump up and surprise you when you least expect it.

Let's define falling in a hole as a simple mistake with the potential to blossom into a problem. Maybe you gave a confusing cue; you wanted to canter but instead found yourself flapping in the saddle, while your horse, against breed, was somehow in a road gait. Or maybe your horse spooks at a tarp that he's seen a million times that's in a whole new strip of sunlight, otherwise known as a leak in the space-time continuum. Or maybe somebody brought a baby goat to the barn and chain reaction chaos is going off like popcorn.

Sometimes your trainer is the cause. If a lesson is going well and a challenge is in order, I might announce loudly that I'm going to ask for something "really hard" or I'll literally say, "I'm about to throw you in a hole." Lots of times announcing it outloud is enough. Then, I usually ask for a transition requiring just a bit more finesse than usual, but since they're looking for the worst after my warning, it's easy to fall into a hole of over-thinking or over-hurrying or any other ordinary mental flop sweat.

The hole itself could be anything initially but the depth of the hole depends on what you do next. It's more of a challenge to your focus than anything. When given direction, can you maintain your rhythm and clarity? Can you catch a curve ball without disturbing your horse's energy?

During a lesson is a good time because if you're going to fall into a hole, doing it when the trainer is there is a smart thing. Your trainer can teach you something valuable; how to deepen the trust between you and your horse in the face of a challenge. It's the ability to turn a problem into an opportunity.

Rule number one when your horse falls into a hole, is to go right in with him. It isn't a problem unless the rider punishes their horse for making the wrong choice. If the rider assumes the worst first, rather than giving their horse the benefit of the doubt, and they punish and demand obedience, the hole is certain to get deeper. But by then the horse is upset, his mind shut down as his anxiety grows. Nothing good can happen now. Saying something like "You've seen that before, Silly" or "You should know how to do this by now" cannot possibly help. Standing at the edge of the hole and name-calling isn't a cue a horse can respond to and the rider has created a break in partnership.

Honestly, you were part of how he got into this mess, so embrace the bad. Stay present and connected. When your horse falls in a hole, go in there with him and help him find his way out.

The first thing to do when you get into the hole is take about three deep breaths to slow things down. Give him a scratch; you aren't so much rewarding him as reminding him that you are partners and you haven't abandoned him. It's what a good leader does to provide encouragement.

Now is a good time to lower your standards, so you can say thank you more often. Start by going back to something simple that you know he can succeed at, and as soon as he even thinks about doing it, reward him big. Be generous, so he will learn to be kind. When you are partners again and the trust bump has been smoothed, return to the original task and cut it into three or four tiny bites. Ask for one piece at a time with slow breaths and generous rewards. Take as much time as it takes. Then string a couple of the bites together, and eventually when he willingly does the whole task, pat your own self for remembering that going slow works every single time.

Remember trust is a fluid living thing; it grows and breaks down and is brand new every ride. Take nothing for granted. Trust is a gift that's volunteered. It's a sacred and rare prize that you can't buy with money, but it will grow and thrive when given a committed diet of respect and gratitude.

Eventually, challenges become a chance to shine. Even a trainer's warning that there's a hole up ahead becomes a cue to smile and maybe even show off just a bit; a time to be more consciously aware of working together and truly enjoy each challenge.

Then the experience of riding changes from defensively evading traps and possible land mines to strolling in an open green meadow; to perpetually enjoying an interesting conversation with your horse on a higher level, one of courtesy and confidence.

Of course, there are holes that riders fall into as well. It happens when we carry our day-trash into the saddle, or when a judge is watching us, or maybe when we have a gut-busting desire to relive the past, just one more canter depart as good as the one last week.

That's when, if you have been kind and fair, your horse gives you the benefit of the doubt and returns some of your generosity. Because he has had good manners modelled for him, he'll come into the hole and carry you out. He'll make you look better than you deserve, and in that moment, you'll be humbled by his heart.

Maybe the biggest challenge in being a partner with a horse is to adjust our thinking to see the world as a kinder place. The other word for that is optimism.

Touchy About Contact

The only thing harder than writing about contact is teaching it! Our brains immediately have a runaway. We call it a "frame" –that vision of a soft horse with its head on the vertical, but a "frame" is a hard-edged thing that hangs on the wall, and rule number one is that a horse's poll must be relaxed. As riders, we want round, soft horses. And horses, they want rhythm. The rest is negotiation.

One way to think about contact is the old car comparison. You use your legs and seat to ask the horse to go forward, like the gas pedal. You use reins and a bit too impede the horse from moving on, like brakes. Putting your foot on the gas pedal while still riding the brake sends a conflicting message, but many times when we ask for contact or a turn, that's just what we are doing. Bottom line: No matter what his head is doing, the answer is forward. The more we try to micromanage his head, the fussier his head gets. So, forward with quiet hands. Let the push from his behind straighten him out.

About now, people start thinking a bitless bridle might be the answer. No metal; hooray. But it doesn't correct your hand problem. A dead pull on the rein is still going to make a horse lose rhythm. I do like bitless bridles. You might be able to buy some tolerance from your horse if you don't use a bit. But again, if the hands get louder than your seat, it's still like riding the brakes.

Or if your hands are too light or you ride on a long rein,

when things come apart, you probably grab the reins. It's a common sense response for humans. So, your horse might go from no contact to harsh contact suddenly. In the end, the threat of being grabbed in the face by an otherwise soft-handed rider isn't much different from a rider with hard hands.

Most of us were warned early in our riding experience that our hands could hurt our horses. Truth. We learned to lightly rest our hands on the horse's withers, with the aim being that our hands would be quiet. First, do no harm. It's a good place to start.

The downside is that in fear of hurting our horses, we lose confidence and do something that translates to the horse as an incoherent mumble on the reins. We worry, do too much or too little, and they get confused. Tentative or inconsistent reins send a message, too.

If your horse has a fussy head, it's avoidance of the bit.

It's hard to have confidence on a green horse, but it's the thing they need from us the most. Let the horse walk out several steps before using any rein aid. Once that rhythm of his stride is established, your hands must follow the movement. And breathe. I know you aren't breathing right now.

Your seat follows the rhythm of his stride, the horse turns when you turn your waist, and your hands do nothing. It turns out that it's nearly impossible for a human to follow a horse's movement with their seat and have a thought. When we start thinking, somehow our seat stops following. Then the horse loses forward, or even slows to a stop, because we've cued it with our seat.

For the horse, avoidance of the bit happens just after a loss of rhythm or forward. Some horses twist their heads from side to side, some horses toss their head up, making their back hollow, and some horses evade by dropping their noses behind the vertical. It seems like something should be corrected in his face but the primary issue is that he lost forward, so leave the bit alone and ask him to go forward. Resist the impulse to correct with your hands, it's his feet that need your attention.

This is the reason I hate to talk hands. Riding is multitasking –like patting your head while rubbing circles on your belly. It must always be hand/seat together. So as you read words about hands, you must always hear a simultaneous loud chant: *Forward, forward, forward.*

Now we are at the part of contact that is really crazy-making for riders. Horses are individuals. Temperament and conformation matter. Some horses will tense to avoid inflexible contact. Some will do the opposite and actually kind of push out with their nose to complete the contact. They don't want their faces pulled on, but they seek a balance or connection. It gives them confidence. Keep an open mind and close your fingers on the reins and ask honestly for what you want. If you've been giving stalking "coyote" cues, stop being a sly predator, and just say what you mean. Use contact but listen closely and adjust yourself. Be ready for a full release if you get the answer you want.

The thing I recommend the most when learning contact, is to use a neck ring. Buy one or make one from old reins or a rope (usually about 70 inches long.) Hold the neck ring in your hands along with the reins, and let your horse feel the ring on his shoulders before the rein on the bit in his mouth. The neck ring can have a firm contact. It cues his shoulder –which is the part of his body that turns. It's genius.

If you ride with a bit, it must be left still and quiet in the horse's mouth, never used for correction, so the horse feels no anxiety from it.

Ride the entire body of the horse with your body, your seat cues his hind quarters, your shoulders cue the angle of his shoulders.

With energy, move forward! With elastic elbows and soft wrists, turn your waist and let your horse feel that turn through your body. Remind yourself again that we steer with our bodies and not reins.

If you feel resistance, release and ask again. The art of riding is always demonstrated in his rhythm of movement. If we break that rhythm with our hands, the horse loses balance. In the saddle, your seat should be elegant and energetic. Use forward cues to help his balance and your hands will be quiet.

If my answers about contact all sound too vague and abstract, that's because one size does not fit all. You shouldn't take control and dominate a horse with a bit, metal on bone, but rather find a happy medium between hard hands and mushy hands, by asking questions and listening to your individual and unique horse. Partnership was always meant to be a negotiation.

Then trust your horse to be the best judge of your contact.

Touchy About Bits.

There was a time that I would have sold my soul for a harsh leverage bit with twelve-inch shanks. My hands were thick and tense and I didn't breathe. Naturally, my horse was braced and tense and he didn't breathe, either. Teeth gritted as we struggled, I hoped my gelding would behave if I just had a stronger bit. Instead, my trainer took my bridle away. I think she just couldn't stand to watch me torment my stoic horse one moment longer. It's what good trainers do. A month later the bridle came back, along with a stick that I carried between my hands for the next nine months or so. And I'm still grateful.

It's spring. Passover and Easter are about forgiveness and I'm holding a grudge. It happened last summer and I'm still cranky. A cowboy 'splained to me (like I didn't know) how Spanish spade bits work. He had a certain tone as he explained the horse has to learn how to carry it (like the horse can't already tell that if he lifts his nose, he'll give himself a lobotomy.) In a situation like this I have world-class eye contact. His horse was in my arena in a halter because I don't allow illegal bits. The good gelding still refused to take even one step forward.

Later, I went online and googled a few videos by folks who looked like they'd won an extreme cowboy dressing challenge. I listened to them pontificate, candy-coat, and try to normalize how these bits work. I understood how a novice rider might even believe them. But I come by my skepticism honestly. Like the western trainer who took my bridle away, dressage riders use simple snaffles. All breeds, all ages, all snaffles, as horses are given time to figure out what "elastic" means where elbows are concerned.

I have no sense of humor about bits. I stopped going to the local donkey and mule show years ago because I couldn't stand to see the gaping mouths and pained eyes. Somehow it was harder to watch on long ears. Western rope reins and slobber straps are heavy, never releasing pressure on the horse's jaw. Bitless riders can end up pulling twice as hard. Others ride on a really long rein so they won't bump their horse's mouth, but then panic and grab the reins hard and fast, ending up being twice as brutal as riding on contact would have been in the first place. And some just try way too hard and wind up with a mental/physical death grip, like I did.

It's mainly the western world where people think that horses *grow out of* snaffles. Silly notion. It isn't true. I think what happens is about the time a horse gets tired of having his face banged on, like my gelding did, and starts tossing his head, all the "experts" standing around recommend a stronger bit. Then the pain gets ratcheted up until the horse shuts down. Some horses blow up instead, reacting to the pain with anxiety, and they "graduate" to an even more severe bit. Metal on bone.

Using a stronger bit is like winning an argument, not because you're right, but because you're holding a gun.

Now I'm the trainer, and listening to me, you'd think bits were my biggest complaint but that's ridiculous. I know a snaffle can be as much of a weapon as a leverage bit depending on the brutality of the rider.

In my fantasy world, we would all agree that bits are not the problem. We'd stop blaming our tack. We'd especially stop blaming our horses for their response to pain. Once and for all, we'd take responsibility for our hands. I believe hands are the biggest roadblock keeping long-time riders from becoming advanced riders. Poor contact delivers a stop/go message that's both confusing and crazy-making for a horse.

In defense, most riders can barely feel it happening. We hold our reins, threaded through our grasp from the pinky side of our hands, up through our palm, to the top or thumb side. As we start, our hands are slightly above the horse's withers and about shoulder's distance apart. Dandy. If they stayed there your horse wouldn't complain.

Maybe it's gravity or insecurity or frustration, but it starts with just a few ounces of pressure as the bottom, or pinky side, of our hands drops to rest on the rein. The horse feels it immediately and tightens a little to protect his mouth. The rider feels that tightness and adds a bit more weight to her hand, trying to control his initial anxiety.

Now the horse has lost some of his forward movement and all he knows is that it's more pressure on his mouth. The rider is getting more nervous, so the reins are actually being pulled, down and back. The horse receives the cue to brace from his rider and starts to feel claustrophobic. Doesn't his rider know that if his feet are moving, he has to move his head, too? He tosses his head to remind her. Now that the horse is tossing his head, the rider, well, you know…

If your horse asks you, either politely or not, to reconsider your hands, take the cue. I have a few suggestions.

First, and I know this for a fact, you have a clenched jaw. Your horse does, too. Take a breath and release your jaw. Repeat. Then repeat again. Forever, until both of you forget there was ever tension between you.

Did you try a neck ring, mentioned previous in the previous essay? If your experience with a neck ring leaves you frustrated, feeling out of control, and screaming in exasperation, it's a sure sign your hands are too hard. Take a break for your heart rate to return to normal and remember you have seat and legs for a reason.

Another illuminating exercise is reversing the direction the reins thread through your hands, meaning between your thumb and forefinger and then out on the pinky side of your hand. It will feel incredibly awkward, but better awkward for you than for your horse. The first thing you'll notice is that you can't push down on the rein, and in the same breath, as you feel vulnerable notice that your horse is quieter in his head.

It's impossible to forget that riding is an art. Our legs and spine work like shock absorbers, so the horse's motion moves through us instead of bouncing us like cinder blocks in the saddle. That same elasticity must continue through our shoulders, down past our elbows and wrists, and through sensitive reins to his fragile mouth. We must surrender our bodies to the horse's rhythm and learn the difference between control and cooperation. The thing that makes us feel vulnerable is the same thing that makes us feel free, even at the walk.

I'm slowly whittling away at my grudge about cowboy excuses. Horses appreciate me reminding riders about becoming too complacent about their hands and harsh bits. Horses tolerate more carrying us than they deserve, but they were always were the kinder and more forgiving half of the partnership.

A New Definition of Discipline

I am frequently asked, as an affirmative trainer, to talk about the specifics of correction. Riders find themselves struggling sometimes to know exactly what to do, not wanting to be too harsh but at the same time not wanting to be "a namby-pamby nag."

It's the dilemma, isn't it? Dominating a horse into terrified submission is always a bad idea. I'm not sure that nagging them into a stupor is any kinder. Finding the middle path with a horse, between these extremes, is the sweet spot where communication flows without stress and confusion. Name that place confidence.

First, I am always going to wonder why we feel such a need to punish or correct horses. The obvious answer is that they aren't doing what we want. Most of us feel some sort of nebulous voice warning us about respect or the danger of wild animals or the opinion that the natural world must bow to us because humans are superior. The voice has a slightly parental ring to it.

Most people tell me that they feel uncomfortable punishing animals, in spite of that traditional back chatter. It makes for an over-busy brain. Once and for all, pick a side. Dump the concept that correction or discipline is a necessary part of training. Tell those Neanderthal voices to shut up and correct the internal anxiety in your own mind. In that moment of peace, recognize that discipline is your friend.

Think about the idea of correction. The behavior that just

happened is already in the past, but we are choosing to drag it back into the present, so we can discipline our horse about something he thinks is finished. Sure, he does learn from being corrected but not what you want. Punishment damages the trust our horses have in us. Really think about that. Then, correct yourself; let go of your grudge and get back in the present moment. Reward your own discipline.

If something went wrong, on the ground or in the saddle, correct your judgment and take a breath. Hear the amen choir coming from your horse, who is now starting to love this new definition of discipline.

Did your horse swing his head too close or push into you? You're in his space. Discipline yourself to step back and let his anxiety cool. Watch for calming signals. If he licks or yawns or shakes his neck into a stretch, good job. You have listened to him. Real love means giving him autonomy.

Did your horse nip at your hand when he normally has wonderful ground manners? He's in pain; don't you dare correct that. Behavior is the only way horses have of telling us how they feel. Listen to where it hurts. If he doesn't stand still while saddling, think about ulcer issues. Correct your quickness. Slow down and pay attention any misbehavior, translated as discomfort. Listen to his body, regardless of your time constraints. Now that's real discipline; put your horse's needs above your ego. Good girl!

Let's say the thought that you might be a namby-pamby nag crosses your mind. Take the idea seriously. Have a no tolerance policy for muffling your own voice. Correct your mind-jumble. Pause, inhale and say exactly what you mean in a clear cue. Focus and don't apologize or let yourself be distracted.

Stay on task, don't repeat yourself. Watch his eye; his face. Is he thinking about it? Of course, especially if he's giving calming signals. Reward him right then. Reward him for thinking; build his try. Then trust your horse's intelligence. Let him figure it out. Discipline yourself to give him time to do it himself.

Is your horse listening? Is he trying? Train yourself to see the seeds of the right answer. Be generous in praise of all things heading the right direction. Discipline yourself to be ridiculously cheerful and positive. Now you're mentally looking forward for the next hint of positive response and your horse is looking forward to training. Yay! Winning!

Search your memory. Was there a time that being called out and humiliated taught you anything worthwhile? Did someone feeling sorry for you make you stronger? Have you ever felt betrayed by someone who under-estimated you? Then correct yourself when you say words like "rescue" and "problem with my horse."

If you don't like the plight of the horse, get off Facebook and into community government. Donate the money you otherwise might spend on manicures and hair dye and get ready for world transformation. Whining about it in front of a horse does more damage to how he relates to you, than it does good in the world.

Correct your definition of *training problem*; stop seeing horses as hapless children or dysfunctional victims. They are not stuffed toys who magically heal us. We must do our own work before we can help them. Discipline yourself to see horses in their full glory. Strong and intelligent. As perfectly capable of trust and partnership as humans are. Aspire to keep that promise.

Continue to cue cleanly, clearly, and consistently. The other word for that is honesty. It's a profound relief to just say what you mean. No longer biting your tongue, soon confidence seeps in because honesty just feels good. Nice correction, give yourself a pat. Most women have known enough confident asshats that confidence has gotten a bad name.

Redefine confidence is a sense of positive well-being based in honesty. Set about demonstrating that for your horse. Know that training a horse to have confidence, to feel peace and acceptance, is the resolution for every problem he will ever encounter. Leadership is giving a feeling of safety. Correct your stiff contradictions and anxiety about not being good enough. Recognize you're passing it on to your horse, causing the behaviors you want to correct in him. Discipline yourself to accept your shortcomings and promise to do better. Love yourself as much as you love horses.

Your horse doesn't care if you're always right; he just wants to trust himself through your partnership. Your confidence is his confidence. Train that.

Bend... Like a Crescent Moon

They were already mid-fight when I arrived at the barn where I boarded my horses. The barn manager was refereeing a dust-up between a trainer and a boarder. The trainer had tied his client's horse's head, snubbed down tight, to its girth by the stirrup and left the stall. Later, the boarder saw the horse tied in that harsh way and went into the stall to untied the horse. The trainer cried trespassing and the boarder cried cruelty. From over my shoulder, I heard the trainer growl, "Mind your own business!" at the boarder, an unapologetic older woman.

I have no excuse for this trainer but I know what he thought he was doing. Horses usually like to bend one way better than the other; they have a soft side and a stiff side. You could think of it kind of like being right-handed or left-handed, most horses are more willing to bend to the left. It means the horse would be weaker on one side which translates to a lack of balance. In other words, the horse is never straight. It's natural for the horse, but if we want the horse strong and balanced, we work both sides. Ambidextrous is the human version of straight.

The trainer's theory was that tying the horse around means the horse fights with himself, rather than a human. It's a common misunderstanding, like pulling a horse's head around to your foot while mounted. They say a rider should work the stiff side twice as much as the soft side, too. Common ideas, but that doesn't make them right.

I heard an anecdotal reason once, that a horse's bend

preference depends on which direction he was curled in utero. I don't know if it's true, but it stuck with me because it reminds me that bend is "natural" and it's an easy visual to understand.

Bend means a gentle arc from a horse's nose to his tail. That the inside rib-cage is slightly compressed and the outside rib-cage slightly expanded. Think riding a circle. It's why one direction is easier than the other.

The problem is that it gets adversarial quickly. It's the frustration of egg-shaped circles and wrong leads. We decide the horse is disobedient, so we kick more and pull our inside reins. We drill that stiff side repeatedly, trying to soften it, but our resistance creates even more stiffness. Some of us escalate to a physical fight while others set a hard hand and hold a grudge. And yes, resort to tying his head to his side and leaving. It gets personal.

That's the disconnect. Remember your mental image of a foal in utero. It's not disobedience. The horse isn't resisting you out of defiance. He's literally stiff. Think of how stiff feels; you would defend a sore shoulder. You'd lose balance and straightness just like they do. Only theirs isn't an injury or an attitude. They're born this way. It's natural.

I kindly want my horse balanced and strong and flexible, but wouldn't it be smarter to massage him into it and not pick a fight? And lucky me, I have the good use of an inside leg to do it.

Start over with new understanding. Walk a large circle his easy way, probably left. Feel your sit bones rise and fall with his stride, as your legs lightly follow the sway of his barrel. Begin by taking stock of your rib-cage. Inhale to inflate your lungs. Feel your ribs symmetrical and your shoulders level. If you aren't sitting straight, your horse can't balance your weight evenly. As you walk the circle, you have a slight turn to your waist; your right shoulder is slightly back.

Visualize bend like the soft edge of a crescent moon. Bend refers to that sweet *outside* arc of the horse, so counter intuitive as it is, forget your inside hand.

Drop your eyes for a moment and look at your horse's withers between your reins. You want to ask your horse to shift his withers toward the outside rein. *Think withers.* Forget his neck, feel your inside leg at his girth. Each time his barrel swings to the outside, pulse with your inside calf, gently asking his shoulder to release just a hair at a time. There is no force, just a rhythmic swing. It almost feels like a leg yield out on a circle, but again, that inside leg is relaxed and just cuing once per stride. Slow.

Imagine a line from your inside calf that travels diagonally through the horse to his outside shoulder. Ride that line, ask your horse to step into that outside rein. Your outside rein should work like the rail of the arena, containing and supporting the bend, which you remind yourself a million times, refers to the outside arc of the horse. Leave the inside rein alone.

Instead use your leg, and remember the fundamental dressage phrase: Inside leg to outside hand.

Reverse and walk the other way on the circle. Now you are going his stiff way, but his rhythm is still working, so you continue the process. Be slow and quiet. In the beginning, he'll be stiff. Imagine that your inside leg is like a heating pad, gently warming as you ask his withers to shift to the outside. Your inside leg pulses just as softly as the other direction, and the response you get is probably less, but that's fair for a stiff side. If your horse relaxes his neck longer, stretching out and breathing deeply, that's huge. Just walk and ask, let your inside leg pulse to outside rein. Reward him generously for the smallest effort. Massage him soft, and notice that you have some bend but your inside hand is still not pulling. Continue to be patient. If he isn't soft at the walk, nothing will improve at the trot and the canter will be worse.

From here continue to change direction frequently. Rather than naming the bad side, reverse so often that you can't remember which side is which. Then, since you aren't fighting one side, neither is he. Let both bends flow from one to the other walking serpentines and circles until there is no stiff or soft. Feel his balance and fluidity. Feel that same emotional balance in yourself.

Dressage rhymes with massage for a reason.

Mounting Block Conversations

Andante is a Belgian-Thoroughbred cross who likes to have a conversation at the mounting block. He wasn't always like this. In his younger days, he was afraid of most everything. It was fair; he didn't have a great start in life but that isn't the important part. Back then, the mounting block wasn't his favorite thing. Now it is.

He likes to spend a few minutes tapping it with his hoof before his rider has mounted. It makes a pleasing hollow plastic drumming sound. He side-passes over it when asked, because he's tall and it works. It's a sort of groundwork that he and his rider enjoy, kind of a long-winded greeting before the ride. He initiates it now and we all congratulate him. After a few minutes, he's asked to stand still and he does.

Before I get accused of coddling horses, I should add that Andante does challenging work, training up the dressage levels, working on light contact, pushing like a freight train, and dancing like a ballerina. I have great respect for this horse and the training he and his rider have done.

Lately, he's added this twist to his mounting block conversation; he's doing stretches himself. At first only with his left leg, and now it's with both legs. His rider started a touching game years ago to make the mounting block less scary and Andante turned it into an art form.

The whole routine takes extra minutes in the beginning of the ride. You could say these antics mean that his lesson starts late. We think he's started teaching early. This ex-nervous horse reminds us that the art of riding is supposed to be fun because hard work and playfulness are not mutually exclusive. He reminds us to stay in the present moment, in other words, on horse time.

Horses don't much care about our dirty laundry or dinner plans or our riding ambitions. Still, we're busy people who want to ride. We want our hour, so we grab them out of their turnout, do a perfunctory grooming job, and pull them to the arena. That's where our hurry-time for training crashes into horse time. Do we pause long enough to recognize the choice we're making?

(Let's assume that we all use mounting blocks because it's good for horses. Look at a photo of a horse's skeleton and it's easy to understand why equine chiropractors say that the wither area is easy to mangle with ground mounting.)

Does your horse show any calming signals at the mounting block? Does he look away or stretch his head down. Is he fussy? Do you find you have to move the mounting block to him … more than once? Is the mounting block a place where he gets corrected three or four times before you're even in the saddle? Is that how you want to start?

Maybe it's time to see your mounting block in a new light. I like to use mounting blocks as training aids. For people, mainly.

Would you like a total do-over at the mounting block? If you're looking for a partner, whether for dressage competition or for trail riding, it starts here.

With your horse in a halter and lead rope, walk together to the mounting block. The lead must stay slack. Step to the top and stand there. Breathe. Clear your mind. Lay down your thoughts and lists and expectations. Stand still and breathe some more. Let go of your excuses and apologies. Be still mentally and watch your horse take a new interest in you. Then step back to the ground and give yourself a treat. Nice job of changing yourself. Yes, it's just a start but this is how training works.

Go to the arena with your horse again and this time, un-hook the lead. Let your horse run and play. Cheer him on. Cue canters and trots by doing them yourself. Laugh. Remember why you love horses. Then take him back to the barn and curry him till he shines. Now you have his attention.

Go to the arena with your horse, stand on the mounting block and do some light lunging. You'll notice you can't move your feet much while standing there. Good, it will require smaller cues. Ask for different gaits and reverses. Ten minutes, maybe fifteen, and go back to the barn. Confuse him with short work sessions.

Eventually, ask for walk/halt transitions. Take your time, let him think. Trust his answer and find an even better, smaller cue. Let time pass in quiet conversation. You're still on the ground but sometimes his saddle is on and sometimes not. If he's doing halts, in a small circle, both directions around the block, you're almost there.

The lead is still loose and by now, he's starting to forget how much he hated having his head pulled on. It's a miracle. At some point of his choosing, he'll step almost to the perfect spot to mount and halt. Almost but not quite. Here is a chance to be generous. Think successive approximation. Call it good, reward him, and go back to the barn. Yay for you. You didn't nag on toward your idea of perfection while teaching him he's never good enough. Instead, he remembers standing there in the right place with you being happy about it. Win.

The next time, when he comes to the spot sooner, spend a ridiculous amount of time standing on the block, scratching and rubbing his back and neck. Continue until he forgets he had anxiety at the mounting block. Until he wonders if you've taken a mail order course in faith healing. Until he thinks good things happen at the mounting block and he pulls toward the arena.

Reward your horse's stillness with your own. Then congratulate your horse on teaching you patience.

In a perfect world, this mounting block work starts with yearlings, long before saddles and training. In a perfect world, the mounting block is an island of peace and safety in a chaotic world. Let it be your sacred place.

Cultivate the idea that the more you and your horse are together mentally on the ground, the better you will be in the saddle. That affirmative training starts with your mental state. Make your mind a place your horse wants to spend time. When he's comfortable with that, he'll invite you into his.

Calming Signals:
The Dance of the Halter

We're breaking in a new farrier here at Infinity Farm. The new guy is soft-spoken, uses a nice pink hoof-stand, and has an easy laugh that the mares like. But we're like any other herd. We've got some quirks. Not all of us got a great introduction to humans.

The farrier and I trim our way through the pens. The geldings are dependable and the mares tolerant. Lilith, the carbon-dated donkey, turns to face us, lifts her nose level with her ears, and brays like a foghorn. Her feet are fine this visit and all three of us were relieved.

Bhim's next. He came here from a rescue for training a few years back and I'm still working on getting it right. I consider him a bit complicated. He considers me expendable. The farrier waits while I move forward with Bhim's halter. We do a slow-motion dance; two steps this way, a dramatic pause and our shoulders turn. I know we must agree on this part. He continues to think I might go nuts. I continue to out-wait his low opinion of humans. A few more steps of the dance, slow and deliberate, and the halter is on. We walk back to the farrier who says, "Will you teach all my mini clients to do that?"

Funny you should mention that –there's little I like to train more. I love a nuanced greeting, a dance of equals, each of us offering something positive. Haltering Bhim is a process. But that's true for all horses.

Sometimes we chase them till they're out of breath, the predator way. Sometimes we coyote-coax them with treats. Sometimes, (my least favorite), we march right up, pull the halter on snug, and pull them away from breakfast.

All horses give calming signals. Each member of my herd had an individual expression of how their farrier visit went, the horses frequently speaking more eloquently than the humans.

A calming signal is the subtle language of horses. It's a peaceful message to let us know they feel us there, disturbing the Zen, and they are no threat to us. We usually answer by letting them know we are an unpredictable war-like species.

Our haltering method is usually a complacent habit, even with hard to catch horses, and not something we think about much. At the same time, that initial moment of greeting creates a first impression that a horse remembers.

Let me put it another way: How do you like your significant other to greet you? By threatening or bribing or just grabbing you by the hair and pulling you along? It's no surprise when a horse isn't responsive in the saddle if we've already let them know that we're lousy communicators on the ground.

How a horse greets us is his honest expression. He might stretch his neck down to eat almost frantically or look away or maybe his eyes get tense or go dark. If we mistake that for distraction or stupidity or laziness, we are the ones with the problem.

Complacency is your enemy. It makes you dull-headed and lead-footed... not traits horses appreciate. But more than that, it means you're missing the fun.

Before entering the pen or stall, remind yourself of the wild luck and hard work that put you in front of this gate. Take a breath and soften your gaze. Check yourself for anxiety or expectations. Use your peripheral vision and listen to your surroundings. When you're presentable, enter the pen and stop.

Don't "hide" your halter behind your back, horses see that as the first sign something weird is going on. If your horse moves away, you've got some work to do. If your horse runs up to mug you for treats, same thing.

It's that stoic horse who stands where he is with his eyes half-closed that is the most interesting to me. Is he pretending you aren't there? Or is he preparing for a loud advance?

Take just a step or two toward him and say whatever you want because words don't matter. Ask for his eye. Think of it as a greeting more eloquent than words. Ask with your eye and breathe. If he moves away, know that you were too loud. Or it might be that history, either his or yours, is too loud. If he doesn't acknowledge anything at all, know he heard you. Then breathe again and ask even smaller.

If you want to know how you could possibly ask smaller than your eye looking at his eye, then you're on the right path. The horse reads the subtle intention in your body.

We are predators by nature. In comparison to horses, we are loud and obnoxious by accident of birth. Even when we think we're quiet, we roar. Take another breath and empty your mind of the loud jangle of expectations. Quiet the tick-tick-tick of your mental stopwatch. Let your shoulders drop the weight of needing to get it right all the time. Pooch out your belly and trust the ground to hold you.

Then ask for his eye in a lackadaisical way, because you are pretending to be free of expectation. If your horse flicks an ear or blinks an eye, that's your reward. You receive this gift without judgment about its size or expense because you are an adult who's above that kind of spoiled-child behavior. Exhale and let him know that you heard him. Say thank you with a pause of time.

About now, your horse looks right at you. Take another breath and maybe a small step sideways. The dance starts with a subtle invitation. Perhaps he moves a hind leg to re-position himself and so perhaps you take a step back this time. Across the distance of the pen, he looks at you with new eyes, slightly shifting his weight, and pondering the possibility...

The halter was a prop. Something real just happened; he volunteered to meet you in the middle. The world has shifted. Say, "Good boy" and let him watch you leave the pen.

Then feel *your* reward. It's so light, you could be imagining it. If you tried to clutch at it, it would skitter away like seeds from the head of a dandelion. So, you let it be. The best things grow, not with force, but with freedom. It's an invitation to dance beyond ropes and words, and maybe even gravity.

There's No Romance in Rescue.

It's my bi-annual report on the animals fostered here at Infinity Farm. I try to balance on a tightrope when I write about rescue. I want to encourage people to adopt and at the same time, encourage them to not get too romantic about it. I know with bloody certainty than I can't save them all. I just think that the value of animals in our world is worth our inconvenience.

My little farm has always had an open-door policy when it comes to rescues. In the last ten years, thirty-two horses, mules and donkeys have temporarily fostered with us for evaluation or training. Most of them found their way to new homes and happy endings. Some found their way to a larger peace.

We have two fosters now. Seamus is a Welsh Corgi who's been here six months. Sometimes when owners give up their dogs, they give a list of faults that serve as a justification for giving them up. In his case, the faults were worse than described. And I've never met a dog who's such an expert on punishment.

I'd love to say Seamus is happy again, frapping in the yard and cooing in my ear. It would be a lie. It's true he rarely bites anymore but he is not a light-hearted little guy. He believes in evil; a trait you don't often see in his breed. He tries to hide his fear with bravado but it makes him more bi-polar than cute. When he does play, he plays with a vengeance –the dark kind. It's been hard on our other dogs and now the house has a maze of gates between rooms so that the dogs can be separated. It's *inconvenient.*

On a good day, he sleeps on my chest, nearly crushes my lungs, and dreams.

Once Seamus had decompressed a couple of months, I took him to my vet. All of Seamus' work came apart fast. The good news is that the vet didn't get bitten. The good news is that she gave us tranquilizers and told us to come back in a week, under medication. The next visit, with a carefully negotiated muzzle, gave us hard medical answers. He has a bad hip and two bad elbows.

There is a term in rescue: Foster fail. It's a joke that comes with a wink and a nod. It means a foster home has fallen in love. Seamus is the other kind –a literal failure at fostering. He has no place to go from here. He can't be adopted out safely. Euthanizing is probably smart but he's still a few months short of his second birthday. For now, he'll stay. Maybe in a couple of years, he'll age out of his aggression but by then his structural disadvantages will catch up with him. Bittersweet future.

Backyard puppy mills, like his, deserve a special place in hell for their immense cruelty and the waves of damage that follow. Say Seamus out loud and add an "on" in the middle. It wears me down.

It's the one-year and one-month anniversary of Lilith's arrival here. She's probably a hundred years old but we haven't carbon dated her. She has "expired teeth" that, if she'd let you lift her lip up, you don't want to see. She came to rescue from an old ranch where she'd been fighting coyotes for at least a couple of decades. Cantankerous is the charming word for her foul temper.

That extra one-month on her anniversary is because that first month we thought she had come here to die. But that didn't work out.

Now I worry that she's gained so much weight that her frail little legs can't carry it. She has a freight train of a bray that gets a little stronger every day. Her shyness is gone; now when I take strangers into her pen, she strides up for a scratch but the second your hand comes close, she flings her head wildly to the side, ears akimbo, and demands you be cautious with your affection. She's prickly.

Last fall my Grandfather Horse was failing. He was thirty, with a stack of terminal conditions, and the light gone from his eyes. When Lilith rallied it didn't feel fair. Because she was older than he was. Because I just wanted him.

Now on her anniversary, she is pretending to graze. She nibbles dandelions, chews with fierce concentration, and then spits them out. There are no coyotes in her pen but she stays in shape goat wrestling. It's a slow-motion event that involves more ear flinging.

Just yesterday, I was using a hairbrush to thin out the steel wool covering her back. She's itchy so she'll stand for a minute. Then her butt teeters toward me, as her back feet bounce off the ground as a warning, followed by a kick with her knife-like hooves. Then both of us tiptoe quickly in opposite directions. She doesn't love me. I respect that.

Lilith is a failed foster, too. She's alive but she has no place to go. She needs a few bowls of mush a day and between that, and the biting and kicking, she's pretty inconvenient.

Maybe that word is the problem.

Bit or Bitless?
You Won't Like the Answer

Does anyone agree on bits? No. Is riding bitless the perfect solution? No. I've been asked for some bitless information, and I'm not sure I can even do that without talking bits, too. Even then, it's idle chatter if there is no horse in the conversation.

Usually, I rant about the foolish habit of moving to a stronger bit when your horse gets fussy in the "gentle" one he's in now. Like metal on bone is ever gentle. Usually, I'm blunt and say something like:

Using a stronger bit is like winning an argument, not because you're right, but because you're holding a gun.

Then someone chirps up that a bit is only as kind or cruel as the hands on the reins. Truth. We've all seen snaffles used like weapons.

It's just about then that the Amen Choir sings the praises of riding bitless. It feels like they're claiming the moral high ground, riding without a bit, and the rest of us poor riders using snaffles are no better than dominators with gruesome spade bits. Then on the other side, bit-users think bitless riders are incapable of anything but trail riding. Sigh.

Like every bitless bridle is created equal. Like every horse has the same mouth conformation. Like just for this once, an answer could be cut and dried; black and white. No luck.

Now it's my unfortunate task to remind riders of two things:

First, the horse's bit shouldn't matter much because we ride with our seats on their backs, not with our hands in their mouths. We ride back to front. If the horse is forward and balanced, his head will be correct for his conformation, in a bridle or at liberty in the pasture.

Second, but probably more important, it isn't up to you to pick which bit (as long as it's dressage legal) or bitless bridle you use. It's up to your horse.

Back in the dark ages, I thought my two-piece snaffle bit was mild. My trainer recommended it but my horse practically did backflips. I learned that if a horse has a low palate, that middle joint of the bit can be excruciatingly (nutcracker) painful when there is any rein pressure. These days, the market is filled with three-link or French link snaffles that are much kinder and most horses prefer them.

But some horses seem to not like that metallic noise or the taste or hardness, and they prefer Happy Mouth bits. They're the ones with the ivory-colored plastic that's a little like your dog's Nylabone. Or maybe they think links are over-flexible and they prefer something more solid like a one-piece bar, called a Mullen-mouth bit.

All of these bits are dressage legal with no shanks. Each works slightly differently and remains on the light side, as bits go, and are preferable to a more severe bit. I've listened and read, year after year, opinions and reviews of how these bits work and who should use them. I have had success and failure with each of them. People can agree that they are mild bits, but after that, horses will still have their own opinion.

But let's say you want to try something different –no bit at all. There are rope halters with rings tied into knots on the nose band. It's "just a halter" but hard on noses if they fit too loosely and slide around. Those nose band knots put pressure on nerve bundles on the horse's face. Traditional hackamores have no bit but can have shanks and chain curb straps that exert pressure on the horse's nose, use leverage, and can be quite harsh.

There are side pull bridles that have a nose band with rings on either side for the reins, like riding with a rope tied to your halter. If you are critical of nose bands on conventional bridles, this type could cause you concern. Remember that any nose band shouldn't be cranked down tight. A minimum of two fingers should be able to easily slide between the nose band and the horse.

Then there are converter nose bands that have loops to attach the reins. Rather than a buckle that you secure loosely, it's just a slide and the nose band works like a noose. It gets tighter with rein pressure. Be sure it releases when the rein is slacked.

So, maybe a bridle with a nose band that can be buckled loosely and a cross-under attachment to reins, so when you ask with your inside rein, it cues the outside cheek, if that makes sense. I prefer the Barefoot Walnut version. It's made of nice padded leather, has good balance, and a rolled-leather cross-under, with a bit better release.

The traditional bitless attachment favored in Europe is a metal wheel or flower shaped piece attached with adjustable straps for the horse's nose and can be used with any bridle head-stall. Some horses and riders prefer this to a cross-under design.

If you try a bitless bridle, go slow and be safe. Try it in an arena on a good day, after your horse is warmed up. Some horses will lick and chew and love it right away, but the rider will lose confidence. Some horses don't like pressure on their nose even more than a bit in their mouth and will tell you it's uncomfortable for them, preferring the familiarity of a bit. Listen to your horse.

If you think that bitless bridles are necessarily better or easier, sorry. Changing bridles doesn't change a thing about your hands.

When people talk about bits or bitless riding, there is so much passion and hard-felt opinion and I've heard it all from all sides, pro and con. And in my mind, I still see that trainer-who-shall-go-unnamed using a snaffle bit and slamming his fist down and back, while his horse is already inches behind the vertical. The same cruel position is available in a bitless bridle. There is no moral high ground when it comes to aggression against a horse.

If your horse is still fussy with his head and you think your hands are fine, who's right?

I think you know the answer. And this is why so many of us have piles of new but useless bits in our tack boxes. Roughly half of my riders are bitless and the other half are in simple, three-piece snaffles. As a trainer, I have a sweet collection of kind bits and different bitless options that I keep around so my clients can try them without having to buy them immediately. I recommend this try-out method with a knowledgeable trainer and while you're there, sign up for riding lessons.

Instead of conversations about which bit is kinder, I would rather see people actually make the effort to learn kind rein contact with a good trainer. It's the most subtle and challenging work a rider can take on, learning to maintain a neutral seat and working in balance with a horse. Learning to quiet our instinct to control the last four inches of a horse's nose and instead ride the entire horse, relaxed and forward. There is simply nothing more important.

Let your arms be elastic. Let your horse never feel the end of the rein.

Summer Solstice

Teaching Your Horse to Relax

The woman said that her mare had an undeniable "rushiness" and was always tense. The mare was five years old and in their first months together, the mare had good ground manners. She tied and picked up her feet but now, walking out of the barn, she was walking out way ahead or way behind, the woman had to pull the mare all the time. The mare didn't know how to stand still and wanted to walk in circles. Sometimes she got pushy with her muzzle.

The woman got criticism from railbirds at the barn; the mare just needed to work more, she was bored, that all horses need a job, etc. But lunging made the mare even busier and soon frantic. Finally, the woman settled on the goal of teaching her to do nothing. A great idea! And now railbirds suggested sitting in a chair in the mare's pen.

Humans can be such all-or-nothing extremists.

The woman had a good start; she was trying to listen. The mare is very young and moving a horse to a new barn is much more challenging for them than we understand. Settling in with a new owner and a new herd takes time. We can list her bad behaviors but focusing on correcting her mistakes and not dealing with the underlying problem will only have limited success. The mare sounded very anxious.

After such a huge life change, I'd expect this young mare might have a sour stomach, if not full-blown ulcers. First thing is always to make sure the horse is physically okay. Change is hard and these calming signals may also be symptoms of pain.

Some folks would say that mares are always temperamental. They use names to describe mares that we women don't like being called. It's true that mares are more like stallions than they are geldings, they have hormones. In my experience, mares don't enjoy blind repetition of menial work like some geldings can. Mares are smart and want more engagement. I think it speaks well of them to require their riders to be more creative.

And kudos for stopping the frantic lunging. It sounds like this young mare knows all about it. People mistake the purpose of lunging and use it to wear a horse out. It does wear out their bodies, and while exhaustion can pass for obedience, it doesn't teach the horse a thing. Or most riders either, apparently, since it is still common advice.

Sitting with her is harmless enough. It's fun in the pen with horses. Some people bring a book. The mare can tell she isn't being asked to do anything so it's probably peaceful. But be clear; this isn't building relationship either. The stress comes with being handled and that's where the healing will come, too.

Responding to horses doesn't have to be fast and aggressive. Or dull and passive. We can do better than these extremes.

Horses get quick because of anxiety. Every time you see a hint of anxiety, slow down right away. Help the horse feel safe. Rather than punishing her behaviors, find ways to reward her. Affirming good behaviors builds confidence–the opposite of anxiety.

Less correction; more direction.

To get ahead of her behavior curve we must go from being reactive to her problems to proactive to help her past them.

If she is quick, I'd ask her for slow answers. Leading her, I'd ask for a few steps. Start at her speed and then slow your feet. If she gives a tiny hesitation, reward her generously and walk on. Ask for some long strides and then short strides. Eventually, when she is following your stride changes, ask for a halt. Ask with your exhale. Ask with your feet. Leave the lead rope hanging slack between you. If she barely pauses, reward her and walk on. The next time she'll give you more because it went well. Because she can listen to your feet better than your hands.

Be the change you want to see in your horse. If she is hot, you cool your body movements. If she is reluctant to walk, you lighten and lift your body movements. Correct yourself. Ignore what you don't like. Reward her every try.

Do it all in slow motion. Affirm peace. Let your exhale be audible. Lead by example; keep your heart quiet, your breath deep, and your hands soft. Let there be hang time after your cues. If you don't want her to escalate, then don't *you* escalate. Be relentlessly focused and internally slow, even if you are walking quickly.

It won't be perfect. In the beginning, it'll be a hot mess and your only goal is to interrupt your horse's free-fall to panic. If there is a hesitation in her anxiety, reward that.

Think of the words "Good girl" as an affirmation of what will come, rather than a reward for a completed behavior. Eventually the two of you will fluidly shadow each other, but for now, lower your expectations. Nothing kills her try quicker than being told everything she does isn't good enough. Humans understand that feeling, don't we?

Reward anything that looks thoughtful. In the past, cues have escalated to punishment. She's been trained to answer too quickly. Give her time to reason it out. Slow. Down.

Sometimes she'll hesitate too long. She isn't being disrespectful. I think they know when it's been too long and sometimes do a deer-in-headlights response, frozen waiting for the inevitable punishment. On the surface, it looks like disobedience. Take a breath and change the subject. Save her from that dread; start over fresh.

Develop a habit in yourself; demonstrate the behavior you'd like your horse to emulate. The patience you show her today will be returned to you. At some future time, when other horses might quit or panic, she will hold strong. She'll pay it back when it matters.

Good training requires us to go beyond old methods and understand the value of subtlety and finesse. Training is an art. Let it lift both of you.

Learning to Love Negotiation

Rule number one about horses: There will be a high learning curve. Most of us are drawn to horses because we feel some sort of connection. It doesn't matter if we grew up with horses or only saw them in books, eventually, we find our way to a barn.

When we get there, some of us stand in silent awe and some of us are so overwhelmed by emotion that we might as well be screaming for the Beatles in 1964. It doesn't matter where we start on that emotional continuum because as time passes, we'll make every stop. Each of the seven deadly sins will be our own.

There is hardly a lesson where I don't use the word *continuum*. In my mind, I see it as a pendulum on a clock, swinging in an arc from one extreme to the other. We are too afraid or we are too complacent. We punish too much or we sent no boundaries. We try too hard or we quit too soon. We are silent with our cues or we scream bloody murder.

Too much or too little, we understand the extreme edges of the continuum but the subtleties of the sweet spot in the middle can be hard to locate.

Humans aren't great with nuance. We're predators and we want what we want. Now. Our idea of leadership is to get our way. Often, we define success by clawing our way to money or fame. And even that isn't enough; then we worry about how other people will judge us.

Meanwhile, horses are prey animals, that means constantly being aware of what's happening outside their own mind and negotiating their safety. In her life, the best leaders are the ones who keep the herd secure.

It's right about here that I wonder for the umpteenth time, what it is about horses that draw us so strongly. It certainly isn't our similarity.

To make it all a bit more complex, not all humans are created equal. (We make declarations to the contrary, but it's still true.) Some humans, predators by birth, also have the experience of being prey in our own herd. We have experienced the dark side of domination and we know that fear doesn't equal respect. We know what it means to not trust our own kind.

When we want to escape the world, we go to the barn to find that equine connection we crave. But as we begin learning horsemanship, often we're taught to train with intimidation. The irony should not be lost on us.

This is all true before we ever pick up a lead rope, much less ride. Some humans have been negotiating their position in the world forever. What if that was the most valuable asset while working with horses?

And in an age when bullies can be mistaken for strong leaders, being a good negotiator doesn't have much rock star appeal.

Unless, of course, you happen to be a horse. That gift of acceptance over criticism has a huge value to a horse who's fearful. Fear is a wild emotion that doesn't take being cornered well. There is simply no aggressive response that works against fear.

Traditional thought is to push a horse forward and through his anxiety but no matter how exhausted a horse gets from intimidation the result is not going to be positive. That fear becomes internalized, not released.

Instead, let the negotiation begin. Can I ask for his eye? Good, release. May I enter his space? No? Okay, I hear you. Breathe. Step back. He looks at me like I might be unusual. I am making the middle of the continuum look attractive. I linger there, and let him take it in. Moments pass. May I come? Will you consider connecting?

Maybe he turns. His eyes go deep and dark and quietly, he offers me something indescribable. It might be his heart; the vulnerability slams me with awe. Now especially, breathe! If a trainer feels frustration or anger, they should step back and decompress, but I do the same thing when I become besotted. For as much as I do love horses, I respect them more. Any communication that we have with runaway emotions, positive or negative, will cloud the negotiation. I want to be a place of safety, so I choose to stay emotionally level. My inner horse-crazy girl can jump up and down later.

I thrive on the creativity needed when working with horses, especially the ones who have been trained to not trust people. Some of us complain that we aren't as brave as when we were younger. What if that's the trade for better perception in the moment?

What if we let go of that certainty of ego and judgment and learn to honor the skill of negotiation?

Name-calling is a superficial dead-end position to hold. Affirmative training means making confidence easy for a horse. That's setting it up so you can say yes, all the time. It isn't a lack of respect in the horse or the trainer but the exact opposite. When that mutual respect becomes a habit, it turns into trust.

Great trainers of any discipline come to the place of understanding beyond domination. Leadership is a humble service given with kindness. Security exists when both sides truly understand that for trust to exist, there is no place for intimidation.

Calming Signals and
the Aggressive Horse

Just to be clear, calming signals are not something humans do to calm horses. It's the language horses use to calm us because we can be a bit rude and unpredictable.

A rider, who was really enjoying her calming signals work, emailed a question about what to do about an aggressive horse. The rider said that a fancy show mare had come to her barn temporarily and boarders had been told that the mare was fine with horses but not humans; they were warned to not "get in her face."

Our rider was leading her horse in around supper time and that mare was guarding the alley to the gate. The mare tried to get between them, the rider reached out for her horse, and after a couple of warnings, the mare pinned her ears and grabbed the rider's wrist in her teeth. She could have done much worse.

Our rider, demonstrating un-common sense, retreated and took her horse out another gate. This was the right answer because she was in close quarters and it wasn't her horse. She said that several other boarders offered to help bring her horse in next time and show her how to handle this type of situation but she wasn't comfortable with their advice… smart decision.

She added that a few days later, while being led into the barn, the mare attacked a barn-worker who escaped by locking herself in a stall, until the mare eventually sauntered into her own stall. The rider would still like to know how to handle this kind of horse, in this type of situation.

I would be foolish to give advice when I can't literally see the horse; I never substitute someone else's eyes for mine because I usually see the situation differently. And a different perspective can be an opportunity to re-frame everything. That said, I'm thrilled that no one got hurt, and here goes…

Foremost, I wonder if the mare sound? Her health must be the first question. Being a show horse is a stressful life and she's moved to a new barn. I'll ask the usual questions. Does she have ulcers? If she is acting like a stallion, could she have reproductive issues? Ovarian cysts are common and under-diagnosed. It could be her teeth or a million other things. If the horse belonged to me or a client, my first stop would be to call the vet, and in the meantime, rather than warning the boarders, I'd ask the barn owner to not turn the mare out with other horses, for everyone's safety.

I'd bet my truck this mare's in pain, but let's pretend the vet clears her and said her issues aren't physically based. Now what?

Of course, you'll get advice from railbirds and testosterone-junkies of both sexes, but *do not take it.* Too many times, a self-appointed horse expert thinks all the horse needs is to be shown who's boss. And about the time two or three "experts" have had a shot at her and failed, she's worse than when she started. Sounds like this mare may have had a dose of that already.

Aggressive trainers and riders count on getting to a place where their dominating aids and loud emotions intimidate a horse into playing dead or shutting-down. The horse looks like teacher's pet but with flat black eyes. Stoic horses pull inside themselves for a long as they can.

But not all horses are stoic. Some are more expressive, with a bold self-confidence and a fearless heart. The kind of horse who will not be cowed. She proudly looks you in the eye, refuses to submit, and holds her ground. Partnering with a horse who requires a human to be their equal is an amazing opportunity, but most humans take the low road and start a brutal physical battle.

I don't know this mare. My guess is that it wasn't the first time she's been in trouble for behavior; it might be why she was moved. I do know that horses reflect our emotions sometimes, and I know that a horse trained with fear is not dependable. I also know that some horses were never meant to belong to amateur owners –through no one's fault. What about now?

This is where I remind you that affirmative training isn't just a lily-livered game for geriatric geldings on sunny afternoons. It isn't just for decrepit rescue horses or mild-mannered kind souls. Reactive horses who get in trouble need it more than all the "good" horses combined.

I hope the owner hires a competent trainer; someone who understands behavior, human and horse, and sees the big picture. Then, grab a beer, the mare didn't get this way in a day. We know this isn't normal behavior. And we know that she gave calming signals that were not understood. We know that even if she's an alpha mare, she deserved better.

If she came to train with me here, I'd take her back to the beginning. Listening to her calming signals, I might ask quietly for just one step. If she looks away, a calming signal, I'll take a breath. Then I'll ask quieter. If I can tell she considers doing it, I'll exhale and step back. In the process of successive approximation, I'd gradually ask for more, but I'd be slow because she's lost trust. I'd look past her anger and talk to her anxiety.

Don't misunderstand. I don't baby talk and coo. I will use strong body language, I will control my emotions. I won't attack her space, just as I will be very clear about my own. I will not let my guard down for a moment, but I'll have a cool exterior. It will require perception, impeccable timing, and precise response. I won't be perfect; it'll be a work in progress because she will require my very clearest communication and I'll thank her for that. I'll give her "respect" by showing her consistency and focus. I'll let her know that I heard her loud and clear. Then I'll encourage her to quietly continue the conversation.

I will always believe that it's humans who do not understand what respect means. When I see humans teach by demonstrating brutality, to animals or other humans, respect is the last word that comes to my mind. It might be the only thing that this mare and I agree on in the beginning.

What should the rider have done in this situation? She did what she could, she got her horse and herself out safely. I'm glad she didn't encourage people to try to dominate the aggressive behavior; it probably hasn't worked in the past and the mare doesn't belong to you. It's never easy to watch other horses struggle.

This is our mantra. I'm only human. I'll try to do better.

Caring for the Lead Mare

It was a perfect day. There were just enough clouds to soften the heat. The front gate didn't open once all day long. There were no emergency vet calls. Best of all, I had some fence to repair. Perfect.

There was still dew on the grass when I loaded up my yellow wagon with the t-post driver, post hole digger, and a bucket of hand tools, and headed for the north pen. Like usual, I had to go back for the wire cutters. A few days before, I'd come home to find one of the geldings over the fence in my neighbor's pasture. He was banged up and limping, posts bent with chunks of hair hanging off them, and part of the fence pushed over.

I'd been thinking about an incident a friend had related. Some drama that was going on at the barn she kept her horses at; the gossip/nit picking had gotten to her. She said it never seemed to end settle.

I started cutting down the old field fence, laying it down, folding the end piece over, and walking on the edges to flatten it, and then repeating the process. Taking out perimeter fence is always unsettling. I depend on that line of demarcation as much to keep others off my farm as to keep my horses on it.

I know what she means about the gossip. Horse people are a passionate and opinionated crowd. We all have that neighbor whose horses are just too thin or thoughts about the barn that sold to new owners. Who's laid up, who's got a new horse, who's struggling to get by? Those jumpers or reiners or dressage queens or trail riders who make us squint and whisper. The truth is almost all of us have been on both sides; gossip blows in the wind. It's how we know to send a sympathy card and find the best trailer repair. It's how we let people know we're smarter than them.

By now Edgar Rice Burro is snoring. The gelding herd is scattered flat in the morning sun. I sink down on a tire feeder and take a long drink, surveying the work I've done, feeling strong.

Most of my days are over-scheduled with training and lessons and writing. Crossing out days for fence repair is almost like a vacation. The work is simple and I can keep an eye on the pond while wondering what it is about us humans tearing each other down.

There are always tiny flocks of ducklings on the pond but this is the first time there are Canada geese hatchlings –four little ones and two relentlessly protective parents. They move in a tiny gaggle searching for bugs in the prairie grass and then waddling back to the pond. The parents constantly scan the horizon, so aware of the treasure they protect.

Time for new t-posts now. I eyeball the line, lean one way and then the other, and judge it straight enough. It's never perfect, string guide or not. I'm just straight enough.

Some clients of mine have a new fence, professionally built with huge gate posts, tight corners, and as pretty a line of wire as I've ever seen. I've had offers of help, too, but I like to hoard this time for me and my land. The birds are so loud that I can barely hear the fence post driver.

Another hour passes and I go in the house for lunch and a short nap. I've read that countries who practice siesta have better health. Some folks prefer a blanket, but I use a Corgi for that. I nap for my health. Really.

I head back out after the sun has peaked. Nickers follow me, I throw more hay, and then grab my fork. Mucking is a time-honored ritual for true horse lovers. I've got no complaints while pulling the cart from pen to pen, celebrating healthy manure. Never trust a horse person who doesn't muck.

Finally, I make my way to the west pen where the ancient donkey leans into her scratching post, slowly rocking with her neck stretched low and her eyes closed. I almost feel like I should look away; her sublime bliss is too naked. But I keep my wits about me. She'll still kick if I startle her and bray with impatience if I'm late with her mush. This little donkey isn't burdened with the need to be a people pleaser. I'm learning it from her.

I scrub some water tanks and try to fill them without flooding the runs. My mare lets me know it's time to come in from turnout; she wants me to bring her in first, so she can nip at the geldings as they pass her run. I check my watch; I've lost hours tinkering through chores and the afternoon is gone. She's right.

There's something about early summer. The light lingers in pastel color. Hours later, as I carry the last bucket of mush out to the ancient donkey, the grass is cool again and the prairie moon illuminates all the best and worst of the world.

I have no idea what to do about all the negative chatter my friend is struggling to tolerate. It wears me down, too. We're an imperfect species and sometimes we need to build better boundaries to keep our hearts safe. Give ourselves time to rest and time to nurture our hope for the future. And the strength to find a truthful, yet kind, voice to lift the quality of gossip.

Some women have salon days but some of us practice self-care by spending the day with farm tools in horse pens, being part Canada Goose, part Corgi, and part wise old Long Ear.

Common Sense about
Horse Communication

Most of us think our horses are psychic because it's easier to believe than the truth about our own limited senses. The first thing to remember about horses is that their senses are just better than ours.

Trusting them might be easier for me; I've never trusted my own senses. While I was still in grade school, I broke my nose on a sheep. These things happen; he was a big cross-eyed ram by the name of Grandpa. Because of that, I don't have a good sense of smell. But no worries, if I imagine what it might smell like I get by. Not having a sense of smell should impact my taste but you'll never convince me that raspberries taste better to you.

I was born with flimsy eardrums and flunked all my hearing tests in school. Two childhood surgeries did not bring improvement. My parents debated whether I wasn't able to hear or just didn't listen. I do in fact have a hearing loss. It's the lower tone range, so it's mainly men I don't listen to. I mean hear.

My eyes are my strongest sense. I have a spectacular eye for detail. But even on my best day, if I hadn't learned to triangulate llama noses, I'd never be warned about visitors on my farm.

It bears repeating: The first thing to remember about horses is that their senses are better than ours. Every moment.

Horses have a better hearing range with greater frequency than humans. Being flight animals, they use it as an early defense system. We usually decide they're distracted.

Their sense of smell is not as good as a dog, but still much better than ours, as evidenced in the spring when they become besotted with the smell of new grass. We can't tell what grass smells like unless a lawnmower has been by.

Their sense of touch is extremely acute; they can feel a fly on their lower hind leg. Do you think we might over-cue?

And vision. The equine eye is the largest of any land mammal. Like most prey animals, their eyes are set on the sides of their head, allowing them close to a 350-degree range of vision. Horses also have both binocular and monocular vision, which means they can process two separate images at the same time. Go ahead, pause here to push your glasses up your nose.

Compared to prey animals, we're not nearly as aware of our surroundings. We tend to be loud and dominating, especially with our hands. We act like we know everything.

Back in the day on Saturday Night Live, Garrett Morris translated the "News for the Hard of Hearing." He'd stand at the side in a bad parody of an ASL translator, cup his hands to his mouth and yell. Just holler it out. It gave me a deliciously guilty, politically incorrect laugh.

But that's how we are next to horses. We stand and yell, though we think we're speaking a reasonable tone, slowly enunciating each syllable as if the horse is deaf or stupid, or sadly, a child. We repeat ourselves, we escalate our cues. It's what we were taught to do but they "heard" us the first time. It's pretty arrogant for a human to think a horse isn't aware of things that are twice as obvious to them as they are to us.

As the theoretically superior animal, it's up to humans to learn the horse's language. This is where not trusting your senses comes in handy for a horsewoman. It makes it easier to want to listen if you aren't sure what's going on.

I use the word "conversation" when I write about communicating with horses, but I don't mean the verbal kind. It isn't about constantly chattering along, explaining to the horse that his mane is being brushed, that you're going to pick up his feet now, that the saddle is next. He knows all that.

Once we're in the saddle, we sit crooked and our legs flop. Sometimes we kick with each stride. We twist around in the saddle like kids on a school bus. We can't look to the side without flinging our shoulders around. You'd think we didn't have peripheral vision.

We create such a racket to their senses, that horses stop listening, not because they're being disobedient but just to quiet the roar. It's a calming signal to us. The cue that we can do less.

Much of what we do with horses is for ourselves. We use them for comfort and that isn't a bad thing unless we never give back. Unless we always think that it's all about us. If you are looking for a better relationship with horses, then listen more. Strive to understand them more for who they are rather than who we want them to be.

I talk about having a "conversation" with a horse because of what it *doesn't* mean: Lecture. Soliloquy. Pontification. Sermon.

Instead of filling the quiet, let the air rest. It's easier to listen then. Be curious in silence.

Say what you mean and mean what you say. Let the rest go. It's the opportunity your horse is waiting for. He might need a while to trust it but then he'll tell you his side of things. It will make perfect sense.

Sometimes now as a clinician, I find myself speaking to a group while standing next to a demo horse. I'm talking as clearly and audibly as I can for the humans, even as I'm aware that I'm sounding like "News for the Hard of Hearing" to the horse.

They tolerate my noise because of another sense that I think horses have. It's an awareness of intention. It's the sentiment beyond silence.

I think it's the best we can hope for from a horse; to find a bit of grace for our loud and rude ways. Until a time when we are able to still our thinking minds long enough to get past reasoning and let being happen.

Redefining Work Under Saddle.

Should we be riding and working horses? Does training a horse inherently make a horse less "happy. When is it too much? When is it too little? A rider had a previous trainer tell her to not let her horse get away with being lazy because "You work eight hours a day, your horse can give you forty-five minutes."

Not so quick, please. Always first, is the horse sound? I harp on this but it's usually the reason. He can't give you forty-five minutes if his saddle doesn't fit or if his feet aren't trimmed properly. It's too much time if his back is sore or if he has ulcers. If your horse is a mare, is she in her heat cycle? Here is the tricky part: What if you think it's all good but he's still cranky? Who's right? Of course, he is. Keep looking.

If all is well, does working a horse make them inherently less "happy?" Well, horses are all individuals. That's what's fascinating about them. I've known many horses who were unhappy under saddle because of harsh training but also from just being misunderstood.

It's depressing but I think some horses trade that hour under saddle for the rest of their life. Kind of like doing the dishes in exchange for a meal, they make a trade. I'm not critical; I like horses being owned and cared for. Some humans live lives of quiet desperation; I suppose horses could do the same.

It's humans who make training hard work. We're perfectionists and we like drama. We approach every new thing like a potential problem. A problem getting him in the trailer. A problem to get him over cross-rails. Early on, I had a client who moaned endlessly about her horse's problem picking up the canter. (Is it obvious who it was that had the problem?) In the meantime, horses begin to hate arena work, but that doesn't mean that horses want a life loitering in the pasture, eating treats, and waiting for the next farrier visit.

I think the majority of horses don't want either extreme; not vacation and not work. They want a relationship with us. It's a crazy notion. Humans aren't a very emotionally stable species but perhaps they see some potential in us.

Do horses test us? A rider says her mare was stopping at the gate every time they walked/trotted by clearly thinking the increase in physical exertion was unnecessary. The mare wasn't winded, or sweaty or tired in any way. She wonders because she was new to riding and her mare was not.

The rider might be partly right. It doesn't sound like she's tired but that doesn't mean she "clearly" thinks the physical work is too much. It's easy to misread horses by superimposing human thoughts. Perhaps if you are new to riding, she was being patient. She knows more than you, after all. (Mares always do.) Of course, she doesn't like being pushed to work harder. Why would she?

I've never met a horse or rider who's benefited from domination. I'm not necessarily talking bloody whips and spurs. It could be the force of nagging passive aggressive legs and marginally repressed frustration or anger.

It's about now that a rider could feel like giving up on lessons. You could decide that training and competing are cruel and you don't want to fight. So, you think about just wandering the property or sticking to groundwork or even retirement. But I still don't think that's what most horses want.

Stopping at the gate is a clear message from your mare. It isn't a disobedience. You're doing what your trainer suggests but your horse gets an opinion, too. A better question might be, "How can I have a better partnership with my mare?"

In case it isn't obvious, beginning to ride is easy enough. Progressing past that entry-level is the hard part. That's why there are so many long-time novice riders. The reason to hire a trainer and try to push past that point is that horses tolerate us when we ride badly; they routinely save our lives, literally or figuratively, giving us more grace than we deserve. Consider learning better riding skills, like following hands and an independent seat, as a thank-you gift to your horse.

If you are almost overwhelmed, then good. You're starting to understand how challenging it is to ride kindly and well. It may take the lifetime of a horse to become a better rider for the next horse. You have no time to lose.

First, make sure you are laughing in your lessons, even if you throw your hands up at the same time. Horses like us when we laugh and it's an antidote to trying too hard. Take riding seriously but do it with a light heart. Remind yourself that you love your horse. Then trust your horse to tell the truth.

Start here: Is your warm-up effective? If not, it's the deal breaker from the horse's side. Dressage rhymes with massage for a reason. If a horse wants out of the arena, we need to improve their experience there. Done properly, the "work" should make your horse feel strong, supple, and balanced.

If work has become a four-letter word to you and your horse, exchange it for another four-letter word –play. Horses taught me the more we blur the line between work and play, the better we all get along. It's a change in perception.

Defining training as hard work that will only be learned through harsh struggle makes riding feel like a factory job.

Lift the conversation. Training is easier than that. Humans and horses both learn through positive reinforcement. In the end, good training is simply a collection of positive experiences. That's the goal each ride. Warm-up well, ask for a few steps at a time, and reward your horse generously. Be zealous–even ambitious– and have laughter be your music.

Horses are beings of light. And so are we, remember?

How to Relieve Your Horse's Anxiety

Growing up, only one person in our home was allowed to have a temper and the rest of us kept our heads down.

After I left home, I started therapy and tennis lessons. It was the beginning of the age of bad-boy Grand Slam winners. Some of the top players competed without visual emotion, while others blew up on the court. The crazy thing was that the bad-boys played better after their temper tantrum, and if my therapist was right, it had to do with getting the emotion out. Every time I saw a racket slam the ground, I felt a morbid attraction.

I envied their tempers. I knew it was wrong and rude. I'd been taught that the punishment wasn't worth the tantrum. Instead, I was busy holding my stomach in, my feelings in, and silently tending wicked grudges.

The trouble for a human who is stoic, as any stoic horse will tell you, is that you don't have fewer feelings; you just try harder to hide them.

So here in our adult horse world, lots of us don't want to compete because we think it requires emotional hostility and unleashed desire to win. We want nothing to do with it. Horses frequently suffer from our human passion and so it's better to claim the high moral ground and not compete. Because we love horses.

Yay, you. Now you'll never throw a temper tantrum at a show. And all your training challenges dissipate like fog in the sun because you're calm and kind.

Except it doesn't work that way. Our perfect horses have issues. We are quick to blame past owners. It might even be true, but the other thing that's true is that we care about how things go with our horses. We are totally capable of having "show nerves" during an emergency vet call. Sometimes just standing next to our horse in the pasture is enough.

Here is a list of things you are perfectly justified in feeling anxiety about in the horse you love: Spooking unexpectedly. Going too fast. Won't stand still. Has separation anxiety. Doesn't go forward or appreciate your feet telling him to. Won't canter. Doesn't like arenas. Or trailering. Or being nagged to a stupor.

Let's say he's flawless under-saddle. You might resent his chronic vet issues. His constant need for a farrier. Costly supplements. His persistent habit of continuing to get older every year. His eventual need to retire and the unfairness of loving horses in the first place.

For the sake of brevity, I won't add the non-horse angst humans feel about their human relationships, financial dramas, and inevitable mortality. This list is infinitely longer.

Here is a list of who knows about your anxiety no matter how politely you try to hide it: Your horse.

Apparently, the challenges of daily life can rival the stress of competing in the Olympics. But go ahead, make lists and hurry about. Try to tell yourself that you aren't being judged every second, by everyone you see. Then try to tell yourself that you aren't the harshest judge of all.

Maybe now is when you acknowledge that your horse is your therapy. Let me kill that baby, too, while I'm being such a spoilsport. Therapy horses have the hardest job in the horse world. Period. Being a show horse owned by a neurotic overachiever is easier than the being a therapy horse. They are saints. Until they aren't.

Anxiety will win in the end, unless we call it out.

So, how do you deal with "show nerves" even when you're not showing?

First, get lots of sleep. If you can't sleep, lay there deep breathing. When your thoughts turn to the destruction of the world as you know it, kindly go back to deep breathing.

When you get up finally, look in the mirror and smile. Sure, you look like the dog's breakfast, but if you truly can't smile, call a real therapist. Life is too short for excuses. It's time to stop floundering in confusion and acid grudges and good intentions. Set an appointment and do your horse a favor.

Want to know my personal secret weapon? I keep low expectations. Not because of self-doubt; I consider it balance. We all run just a bit hot when it comes to horses. Our dreams scream in a dog whistle pitch that we can't hear. Our love burns like a flame thrower next to a stack of last year's hay. We're not fooling anyone with our obsessive-compulsive passion. It's better to bring it out in broad daylight and do some groundwork with our emotions.

Try the hardest thing and ask for less from yourself. Ignore the problems and celebrate the easy work. Reward the calming signals you give yourself. Just say yes. Sing with the radio, let your belly relax, and leave the dishes for later. Have ridiculously low expectations so you can constantly surprise yourself with your own goodness. Then look in the mirror again. Notice the wrinkles and the stained teeth as you smile and truly mean it when you say thank you.

Now you're ready to go to the barn. Does your horse still have anxiety? Congratulations. You're ready to become part of the solution.

Leadership Percentages
and Confused Horses

Pause, look in his eye. He's sensitive and intelligent and looking for a partner who's his equal. If we're going to agree with scientists that horses are sentient beings, with feelings not unlike our own, when will we start treating them that way?

In riding lessons, I ask number questions a lot, like "What percent of your horse is forward" or "Rate this trot on a scale from one to ten." It's short-hand to quantify where we are compared to where we started and where we'd like to be.

The usual way I hear short-hand numbers talked about in the barn is to quantify leadership. Like most horse things, there is a long continuum of opinion. Some riders demand their horse submits to one hundred percent human leadership. Equine slavery, I'm thrilled to say, is not tolerated here. It's easy to deplore and I doubt it's even possible. We shake our heads and tsk-tsk our tongues. But still, as fantasies come and go, one hundred percent cheerful compliance would be great.

We want a partnership with our horses. And once we really agree to that, the confusion and weird math begins. Should it be a 50-50 balance? Does the human get the deciding vote, 51-49? Or because you have a goal with your horse, 60-40? Or maybe you missed the vote entirely and you just go along for the ride, 90-10, to his favor.

The definition of leadership is the ability to provide another sentient, in this case a horse, the feeling of safety.

Sometimes, in an attempt to evolve and not dominate horses, we just chatter away kindly. We over-cue, carefully introducing their halter for the millionth time and the horse might even politely sniff it. Maybe he thinks he should because we act like it's a brand-new thing each time. We chatter about cleaning his feet and might even think he's listening, when the truth is that it's the same order of hooves every time. A horse would have to be brain-damaged to not learn that pattern and obligingly pick up his foot.

In other words, we think we're training things that they know inside-out. It's like reading a grade school primer in college. Boring at best. At worst they think we aren't all that bright. What would it take to teach up to his level?

I think horses kindly recognize human chatter as a calming signal. Meaning it calms us to chatter away. Maybe they assess what percentage of their rider is stressed out and roles reverse.

The definition of chatter is the rattle and bang of constant noise. Legs and seat and hands and voice that just never stop flapping and nicking and correcting. As annoying as flies buzzing, landing, circling, and buzzing some more. It's the crazy-making babble that any self-respecting horse would shut out to save his sanity.

About this time, since we don't want to dominate or chatter away, we decide to listen. No, really listen. We learn their calming signals and their unique detailed preferences. The more we listen, the more they share, affirmed by the feeling that humans are pulling it together. It's thrilling to have a corner of understanding that didn't start in a human brain, but instead is something you learned from a horse. Listening is pure joy.

We listen to our horses so hard, with such focus and patience... that our horses hear crickets. Silence from us. They revert to doubting our intelligence and worry that they are the only sentients in the room. Horses might wonder if, between the scream of domination and the silence of listening, humans are void of the ability to have a simple conversation.

Let's define conversation as cues that might be body language or movement, or intention; eye contact along with a thought. The least important part is verbal. The most important part is that there are two sides conversing.

The focus is to shape a response on both sides. You give a cue for walking and pause. He considers the request and walks. You release your cue and breathe normally and follow the flow of his walk. In the beginning, it feels stilted like an Intro to French class. *Bonjour, comment vas-tu? Bon, merci et vous?* But don't get impatient and talk over each other.

Any affirmative training conversation starts with rewarding a good basic response. It's one of you giving your best hints until the other guesses the right answer, like a game of equine charades. Creativity! A language between two species is born! Hear the theme from *2001: A Space Odyssey*?

How do you quantify that kind of leadership conversation? 50-50 feels too flat and dull.

Soon, there is not time in the conversation to do any numbers guessing at all. The idea-and-response flip sides between the human and the horse in an instant. It's a flash of intention and a spark of response. A cool breeze of release followed by quicksilver inspiration. So fluid that he finishes the thought before you fully articulate it. And his response was lighter and more beautiful than you imagined. It's a dance that switches leader and follower every few strides.

If a rider complains about a lack of response in their horse, guessing that they only have twenty percent of their horse's attention, I think a better question might be what percentage of their attention is on their horse? Do we think it's his job to hang in suspended animation until our next command? Isn't that how domination works?

What if a better name for an unresponsive horse is a bored horse?

The art of communication with horses means evolving a language of successive approximation to a place of happy response on both sides. It takes a quiet and quick listening mind on the part of the human, along the same amount of physical self-awareness that a horse has. That's the hard part. It would always be easier for a human to dominate or be passive, than find that balance on the middle path.

Pause, look in his eye. He's sensitive and intelligent and looking for a partner who's his equal. The question isn't if he'll meet our expectations. It's what will we need to do to meet his.

How to be a Brilliant Conversationalist: Horse Version

You know how the cat magically goes to the person in the group who has the allergy? Or she goes to the person who happens to agree with Preacher Man, the Corgi, who believes that all cats are agents of the devil? Meanwhile, the person who loves cats is cooing and coaxing with raw fish but the cheeky cat hoists her tail a bit higher and gives us that view as she saunters her way out of the room. Cats think people try too hard. They're suckers for the one who plays hard to get. Corgis are doomed.

How do you catch a cat? Just don't. Don't look, don't talk, and absolutely don't let the thought cross your mind that you'd like to scratch those ears. Then relax and let the cat sneak up on you from behind. Cats can't resist mystery.

Now pretend that a horse is as smart and curious and playful as a cat. And you want to think you are at least as clever as a corgi. This part is much more complicated because we're only human.

Sometimes we let our minds get a little soft. We are prone to thinking we're not predators or prey; instead we act like intellectuals, spending time in our minds and mistaking that for the natural world where cats and horses live. In other words, we're boring.

We debate training technique but then work by rote, busy with opinion and not being fully present with the horse. We unconsciously halter the same way every time. We lead them like they are bricks on the end of a rope.

We agree that riding is an art, but do we hesitate to call ourselves artists? We are a creative species, but we get lazy and use our intellect to doubt ourselves. We let ourselves be ordinary when all we need is a bit of conscious energy. Energy that we can dial up or down like a thermostat on an oven.

Creativity isn't a mystery, it's a habit like brushing your teeth. Or cooking with spices. Or loving someone. Creativity is the cherry on top; it's the extra dollop of energy that adds zing to life. It's a skill, like horsemanship, only with a smile on your face.

When I meet a horse, I start with a simple question like, "Can you please take a step back?" I ask him with the method I least expect the horse to know; no rope, no hands, just my feet. I ask politely and he thinks about it.

His owner wants him to succeed, so she interrupts and tells me how she cues him to back. To be clear, all three of us know he can back. And I could care less if he backs, I am establishing a conversation.

If a horse has just one cue, how do we know he isn't answering by rote, too? Unconscious action might be the first thing we teach horses. I want a fresh response, so I want to engage him. Anyone can back, I want him to be curious about me. Not because I have a stick or a loud voice but because I listen to him. That's how he'll know who I am.

So, I give the horse a minute to up his game. If he looks like he's thinking, then I reward him profusely and it's game on. But if he looks like he isn't thinking, I'm not fooled. Horses are as smart as cats; I reward him, too. Because energy should always be rewarded.

The two things I know more than anything else about horses is that they like consistency. They are like us that way, they like dinner on time and the comfort of knowing they are safe in their home.

And second, horses get bored easily. Just like us. Are you both so used to acting by rote that you think it's normal? Would your horse say that you are?

Here's the secret: Disarm him with unpredictable release.

Be brand new; fluid in your movements, soft in your eye, agile on your feet. Step out of his space when he expects you will ask for more. Unpredictable release.

Go in his pen and actively don't catch him. Hold the halter in your hand and studiously do not try. Unpredictable release.

Go to the mounting block and don't mount. Scratch his withers and go untack him. Unpredictable release.

Work at liberty but trust him. Ride bareback and massage his ribs with your knees. Ride with a neck ring and be patient with the new steering method. Patience is creativity, too.

Instead of warming up with too much contact too soon, along with too much distraction and worry, warm up with too much music and fluidity. Unpredictable release.

Being mentally active means the rider is using less physical strength but keeping her energy up. He mimics you. If he isn't forward, well, wake your-own-self up, change the length of his stride, longer or shorter using just your sit bones. Think with your seat and legs. Still your voice and breathe. Crank up the music.

Ask for a long walk in a soft leg yield, barely asking his withers to the outside. Think inside leg to outside rein while moving in serpentines. Continue reversing direction until neither of you can remember having a stiff side.

Sometimes ask for tiny things and sometimes big. It isn't that you don't train the hard challenges; it's that you train them as if they're fun.

Then ask again, and be ready for a different answer. You don't know what he'll do and that's the best part. It's the call to energy and creativity. Unpredictable release.

I want to be the most interesting thing in the world to my horse. I want our conversation so scintillating that he hangs on my every word, and by that I mean, that I don't cue by rote. I keep my energy percolating.

I want to have the consistency that makes him feel safe and yet still be mysterious and interesting enough to hold his attention. I want him focused on me and I'll train that by focusing on him. I want him to think it's more fun working with me that staring at plastic bags flapping in the wind.

Ride like a cat. Listen, bat some ideas around, then mentally pounce on one and chase it down so you can play with it. Now reward your own creativity for making work feel like play

Helmets: When Complacency and Experience are Killers

"She had a helmet on and she still got hurt," the woman said. It's a common excuse for not wearing a helmet but I have heard too many over the years. If this is solid logic, then I'm missing the point. Staying positive, I answer with a smile, "Well, sure. I take vitamins and I'm still getting older."

A strong helmet awareness movement was sparked in March 2010, by U.S. Olympic dressage rider Courtney King Dye's accident. She fractured her skull and suffered a traumatic brain injury while not wearing a helmet when her horse stumbled and fell.

To be clear, I wasn't born in a helmet. When I was a kid, we didn't have tack, much less helmets. But I'm capable of change. Apparently, that's a bigger deal than I think; the common reason I hear for not using a helmet is that they never wore them in the past. I didn't use a cell phone back then either. I changed.

When I'm able to talk helmets quietly with that helmet-resistant rider, they usually give the same reason. With a self-effacing smile, they admit the reason is probably ego. An uncomfortable silence follows. I disagree with riders who think what's on the outside of their head is more important than protecting what's inside; their intellect, personality, and most important to their horse, the ability to buy hay. Sometimes I stare, wondering if ego is usually the thing that gets in the way of us caring about our loved ones. What does it mean to have concern for horse slaughter or the plight of the mustangs but take your own life for granted? Why not do all you can to be there for your horse (if not your loved ones)?

All the statistics are undeniable. Everyone knows everything. Maybe I should be happy that kids think of helmets as part of their riding/superhero costume and just bite my tongue. I can't because I'm a horse advocate.

The new statistic that caught my eye this year is a study conducted by a team of Alberta researchers who found that riders who reported an injury had an average of twenty-seven years of riding experience. New riders had a relatively small incidence of injury. A sobering idea that more years in the saddle are not an advantage.

It rings true for me. In my extended circle of riders, there were several injuries this past year. Some were quite serious. Some took place on the ground or at the mounting block. All the injured were experienced horse people with many years in the saddle. The beginners were just fine.

So I speculate. I see a lot of complacency in the horse world. It's a luxury I can't afford as a pro. I must keep my focus at all times; I need to see the world with an equine range of vision. Training horses and riders requires awareness. I'm always surprised at the number of times I witness riders unaware of obviously dangerous situations. I'd call it a passive disrespect of their horses. Sometimes they don't know better, even after a life with horses. Sometimes it's laziness. And sometimes we just get bull-headed as we age, set in our ways and unwilling to grow or learn. I suppose there is a certain cosmic balance to getting a head injury from not using your head.

For me, I'm trained to see behavior patterns in both horses and humans. When I see a rider defend their ego, or even just close their minds toward helmets, safety, and common knowledge, how does that reflect on their training methods? Are they willing to learn new methods or just stick to the old ones? Can they change methods to suit the particular horse or is it just one training method for any client? Perhaps closing our minds to opportunities, even for our own safety, is the first stride toward rigidity and retirement.

I understand how difficult it is to change. Looking back, horses have asked me to change everything about myself. I resisted; it was hard and once you start, the learning/changing never ends. But I still see horses through the eyes of that little horse-crazy girl. The rest of me has changed as horses have asked me to. Like most of us who have applied ourselves, I'm a better person for their equine input. It took another species to teach me humanity. If nothing else, I want to be around to enjoy that, sound in mind, for as long as I can.

I'll finish this post with the usual list of important information, in hopes that it might make a difference to the people who can make a difference...

Stats:

Equestrians are 20x more likely to sustain an injury than a motorcycle rider, per hour.

60 number of deaths/year due to head injury (compared with 8 for Football)

60% of riding fatalities occur from head injuries.

15,000 number of ER admissions for equine-related head injuries in 2009.

2 feet number of feet fallen at which head injury can occur.

45% of TBI (traumatic brain injuries) are horse related.

Riding is considered more dangerous than motorcycling or downhill skiing. Approximately twenty percent of accidents which result in head injury happen while the person is on the ground. They are just as common in professionals as amateurs.

If you have a hard impact blow while wearing your helmet, immediately replace it with a new helmet. There may be damage to the helmet that is not visible to the naked eye. Helmet manufacturers generally recommend replacing your helmet every four to five years.

There is no statistical correlation between skill level and injury likelihood. Professional riders are just as at risk to sustain injury due to a fall as less frequent riders.

Head injuries are cumulative. An original head injury can be made much worse by additional concussions. Your injury risk depends on the height from which you fall, as well as the speed at which you're traveling. Even a fall from a standing horse can be catastrophic.

A final note to those riders who refuse a helmet and proudly proclaim that they aren't afraid to die doing what they love. Me either. I am afraid to survive a bad fall and live in a diminished state depending on care from others. I'm afraid of how I would feel if I was alive but unable to ride.

Consider a helmet a kind of generosity. Get yourself a helmet for your family, get yourself a helmet for your horse.

Repetition Vs. Consistency

There is a comfort for both horse and rider in familiarity. It is a cue that they have drilled; a known answer exchanged between partners. Like starting church with a hymn or a ball game with the national anthem, it's hard to say who likes patterns better.

In the beginning, training is a small amount of repetition. We ask for something, the horse tries a few things, and gets a release when he finds the right answer. We cue him, he steps back, and the cue stops. He learns in hindsight and then gives us the right answer when we ask because he likes it when the cue stops. Simple success.

The problem is that we continue to want more. More cues, more obedience, more good feelings. Most horses oblige to a point. Then we want bigger progress and get frustrated when he gets confused or bored. A cue that makes sense to you leaves him blank. Or something changes; the routine gets altered and the two of you lose rhythm. Or the horse is distracted when we ask and we startle him with a correction. Somehow, things come apart. Because they always do.

Or you might want to change things in your training for the very best reason. Maybe you are aware of how hard your horse tries. Aware that he gives you the benefit of the doubt at times you might not entirely deserve it. You see past the surface of obedience, recognize his intelligence, and decide you need to do better because you want to match his kindness. He has inspired you; wonderful.

The two primary training principles that seem to carry across disciplines are these: You must be consistent. You must change things up. This is why so many long-time novice riders get stuck. It's a crazy contradiction so our behaviors go nuts to match.

Repetition isn't a bad thing unless we need perfection. But that's kind of how humans do things, left to our own instinct. We turn the key in the ignition switch, happy that the engine roars. Give it the gas. Push on the brakes. Gas. Brakes. We love that control. It's too bad it doesn't work the same way in a saddle.

One of the ways that learning and understanding sinks deeper, allowing for breakthrough work with horses, is by re-defining old words and taking that new awareness into the present moment. We might evolve from wanting an obedient horse who answers by rote to wanting an engaged horse who is answering spontaneously. The secret to improving your riding is to give up some desire for control to encourage your horse to be more curious and willing to take a guess. It's the kind of counter-intuitive idea that feels just like a stone in your boot.

Riding more often doesn't make a horse better. If that was true, those old, sainted, lesson ponies would be in the Olympics.

Instead think consistency in your time with your horse. Being consistent is more than scheduling rides a certain number of times a week. It's altering the quality of all the time spent with your horse, including conscious haltering and focused grooming. In the saddle, it's being aware of each cue, even the ones you didn't mean to give.

As a rider lifts her awareness, it means that engaging his mind becomes more important than him giving the stock answer. It's the act of having a conversation of cues rather than a command to be obeyed. If the challenge for a rider is to keep a horse interested in the conversation, then we must improve our mental focus. We must stay engaged in each stride if we hope to have a responsive horse.

It can start as simply as asking for longer strides in the walk.

Do it with a subtle cue, using just your sit bones in the saddle. If you feel a tiny difference in his stride, good, reward him with an exhale. Then return to his working walk and in a few strides, ask for some shorter strides, again just with sit bones. Feel his response. He's right there connected in each stride. That part is just as natural as moving together on the ground.

Eventually, the canter. Instead of a hurried jerk-and-kick canter depart, breathe and relax yourself at the trot. Be fluid and quiet, keep your shoulders back, and feel the landing of each stride. Allow him to stay relaxed and you cue in rhythm with his movement, so he can make that transition with balance. Keep your energy in check; you're asking for a change of gait, not a change of speed. Give him time to understand the difference and reward his effort to understand. Let the canter depart have the steady confidence of a jet plane on the runway.

Prepare for the day when you just think the cue, allowing subtle changes in your body, and letting time slow down. You feel a lift in his supple shoulders, his neck is long and soft. His head is on the vertical, not because you are pulling on the reins, but because when he is forward and relaxed, that's his natural head position. On your inhale, he lifts you to a swinging rhythm, your body follows as he glides over the earth. It's a canter that feels like more air than ground. It feels like being weightless and powerful; the peace inside the eye of a hurricane.

Consistency isn't about drilling the same question, judging right and wrong, punishing or rewarding. Consistency is an ever-evolving mentality that stays present with energy and an openness. It's rewarding his curiosity with your creativity; a witty repartee of cues and releases that feels like laughter between equals. It's knowing that he'll give the best answer if you focus on asking the question in the best way.

Trust, first defined as not being afraid of falling, grows into the confidence to fly. Consistency is a rider working toward being the best they can be, allowing their horse to do the same.

Horses reward us for our uplifted consistency, usually with something a little sweeter than what we expect. Generosity.

Sleeping With The Wrong Dog

Warning: This is not an upbeat rescue story. It's a sad story with a sad ending. Proceed with caution. Or don't proceed at all.

I have a habit of writing about the rescue horses and donkeys and dogs that have come through Infinity Farm to be evaluated, fostered, and trained over the years. It's a prickly topic. I hope to encourage people to bring rescues into their homes but at the same time debunk romantic notions about rescue.

Regardless of how it ends, I think an abused pony or a rescue dog deserve to have their story told as much as equine Olympians and beloved family pets from reputable breeders. I write about rescues because I believe their lives matter.

You remember Seamus, given to rescue for aggression, he landed here because there was no other place. We were his last, best chance.

In *Change of Life,* Judith Collas says, "Her life was ok. Sometimes she wished she were sleeping with the right man instead of with her dog, but she never felt she was sleeping with the wrong dog."

I've had this quote tacked up on my wall for as long as I've been sleeping with dogs. It just makes me smile. And I'm grateful for a few generations of dog-piles that helped me find some rest during the rough times in my life. Recently the quote took a different twist.

I've always appreciated challenging dogs. Seamus fit the bill. He had good moments but more commonly, he had a snarling sideways glare. He'd bite at unpredictable times, both dogs and people, and seemed to have no knowledge of his name. Sometimes he could be coaxed with treats and sometimes he attacked us. His extreme destructive behaviors had gotten him crated full-time previously; now he needed to be out to decompress but I wondered how much of the house would survive.

After a few weeks, I thought Seamus was almost leveling out. Not quite improving; there were still dogfights and tense separations and extreme anxiety, but less of a scorched earth policy from him. We'd managed a vet visit by giving him a tranquilizer first. It didn't work well, but with an added muzzle, we managed.

Not surprisingly, his little body was a painful, complicated mess of health questions, lousy joints, and fear... along with the affliction of bad training. Who knows what else?

Then a turning point: Construction workers came to repair hail damage on the farm. I took the time off work, staying with the dogs every minute. A four-day ceiling repair took two weeks. The house was cut in half for asbestos abatement. The tools were loud but the workers were louder and Seamus just came apart. His eyes changed and his anxiety exploded like a virus.

Seamus had loved the boarder who always took the time to talk to him. He'd roll over, asking her to scratch his belly through the fence and it was a happy habit. Until he bit her hard mid-scratch.

The next week, another boarder was talking with me in the house. Her toddler was standing by her chair when Seamus broke down a gate. A strong gate. The boarder picked up her toddler immediately; she knew Seamus' history and didn't hesitate. She was miraculously calm, the right answer as Seamus leaped up, nipping at her little girl. I knew I couldn't correct him without making it worse, so I used treats to try to call him off. It took cheerful coaxing but finally, he turned to me and the aggression stopped long enough to get the little girl out of the house.

It couldn't go on. We all felt like we were living in a war zone. Maybe Seamus most of all.

At night, I'd lay down and he'd leap the edge of the bed, dropping his belly crosswise on mine, and falling immediately asleep. I matched his breath. His weight on my heart was undeniable, as I considered the unthinkable for the millionth time.

My vet wasn't surprised when I called. She'd broached the subject of euthanizing Seamus the previous month when I brought another Corgi, Preacher Man, in with a facial abscess from a bite from Seamus. It's times like this that having an honest vet means the most. We had a complicated conversation about the lack of options and the unfairness of his young life. Finally, we talked about how to euthanize an aggressive dog in the most kind and compassionate way.

On the morning of his final appointment, I gave him a special breakfast. Special because it was his favorite raw meat with a nice fried duck egg on top. Special because it contained an overdose of meds to quiet him. They had the opposite effect.

We did our best for Seamus his last day. Sometimes your best looks ugly-bad. Seamus was one month short of his second birthday.

When things come apart like this, there's some unbalanced equation of physical issues and bad history. Pain and anxiety. I believe that animals can have similar mental health issues as humans. Some find a way through it and some just can't. Again, like humans.

I tried to make sense of backyard puppy mills and shock collars and professionals who give bad advice, as I felt despicable for appreciating the peace. Trust me, I know you can't save 'em all but that's no reason to quit trying.

There's been a horrible quiet in the weeks since Seamus has been gone. It's as if the house got stuck in an exhale. The daily "accidents" inside stopped. The Dude Rancher's dog, Finny eventually trusted the backyard again. My elderly dog came out of her Thundershirt and Preacher Man is trying to be less defensive. I realized that the reverse of that old quote mattered to me just as much. I hoped the dogs always felt they were sleeping with the right human.

And this boy, Seamus. Some of his trouble he was born with, and some of it was done to him. In the end, it doesn't matter how it started. I think he tried his best to fight it but that got turned around, too.

If Seamus finds redemption, I doubt it will be waiting at a mythical rainbow bridge. He might prefer a place that doesn't allow humans.

Reframing Competition as Relationship

A long-time client and I were playing around after a lesson. I was taking photos and we were laughing about she and her horse having the curse of being spokes-models for my blog. She leaned forward and "got" his ears for the photo. Another laugh for the less-than-professional full-hand technique she used. Later we remembered when she first got this horse. He was terribly head shy and worse. Things have changed.

Some of my clients compete and some do not, but when I ask each client about their riding goals, there's just one answer. They all want a better relationship with their horse. Period.

We start by choosing a few specific concrete things they'd like to improve. If you want a responsive horse, change things up. The same dull repetition gets boring and a bored horse is a dangerous horse. It's not to say that everyone needs to become wildly ambitious, but it's smart to keep the conversation interesting.

Start with a horse with a history and a personality. Maybe the horse is a scraggly rescue foal with a halter grown into his head. Or maybe he's a well-trained, bomb-proof dream horse that you spent a fortune on. It's all the same.

Add a human with a history and a personality. It might be their first horse ever or they might be a lifetime horse person. It's all the same.

Something happens to the human the first time they see the horse. It could be watching a video clip or glance into a pen, but intellect and emotions collide. Money changes hands; a horse trailer abduction follows. Horses are not the sort who fall in love at first sight, especially if it means leaving their herd. As much as we wish they'd love us the way we love them, they're prey animals. They put survival first.

Now, it's the two of you, beginning a relationship. You each have a past, not that it matters. It's about the present, with hopes for a future. Let's call the relationship a bubble. In the beginning, it breaks as easily as a gust of wind or a bump on the bit. It's fragile when you're figuring each other out.

Horse training can feel complicated, but this is the simple secret. The more positive experiences you share, the more trust between you, and the stronger the bubble. So, you stay positive, say please and thank you, and let the trust grow. Focus on the relationship; less correction and more direction.

Then later, on the day that the helicopter lands or the fireworks explode or the bear waddles into the barn, life inside the bubble has become so safe and pleasant, that your horse ignores such silly distractions.

It's a universal law that life is change. Nothing stays the same. A sweet ride one day turns into a rodeo the next. The perfect horse comes apart or the rescue finds a way to trust. In my experience, horses are always on a continuum of getting better or getting worse.

We dance between complacency and possibility because both horses and humans resist change and struggle to find trust.

Strengthening the bubble is necessary because maintaining status quo isn't enough. Our job is to provide small challenges that grow confidence. Not being distracted by the random baby stroller or hot air balloon but staying true to each other. During a challenge, a horse learns the bubble is the safe place because you only allow good things to happen there. No punishments, just affirmations.

How many of us mentally abandon our horses when we feel anxiety? And if we doubt them, why shouldn't they doubt us? Now we're getting to the heart of what relationship with a prey animal means. We have to focus on them, no matter what is happening outside the bubble. Outside the bubble is none of your business. Riders must keep the connection inside, regardless of external distractions.

If you're a trail rider and there's a difficult bridge ahead, you stay connected with your horse, giving him confidence and not fear. If you shift priorities and think the bridge is more important than your relationship, things will go badly. A good leader holds their own focus and always puts the horse first, while also pushing the edges to keep the conversation fresh. It's testing the bubble.

Consider competitions the equivalent of a weekend horse camping trip. It's a way to leave home, have adventures that test your bubble in a safe environment, and it's totally legal to love your horse and bring friends. There's even a "bear" in the arena –a scary judge.

Maybe you'll have a flash back to the movies about horse shows, like National Velvet, where there's a miraculous win by an unknown pair? Hey! That's fiction, come back to your horse in real time. It's easy to get distracted by a judge or other competitors but they're none of your business either. They're NOT inside your bubble. If you let those silly distractions cause you to mentally abandon your horse, it's on you. If you allow your emotions to overcome your relationship, whether at a bridge on a trail ride or at a show, you have work to do on your half of the relationship. Sorry.

It's the judge's job to score five minutes of your lifelong relationship. Five lousy minutes. And if their opinion hurts your feelings, that's an opportunity to work on your bubble. Excuse your ego, proud or frail, from the bubble. Showing isn't personal; it's simply a training aid like a bit or saddle.

We can agree that there are bad riders and bad judging.

In dressage, we report abuse to the technical delegate and the show management has judge evaluation sheets. Judges are not ordained by God; they're our employees. Please do rant about abuse and bad judging. It exists in all riding disciplines; it takes no skill to recognize it, but it's up to all of us to support the quality of our sport.

It does take skill to hold to your ethics and ride your own ride. To look past the haters and lighten up. The majority of riders in the competition world are amateurs trying to do their best for their horse. We aren't the minority. We just act that way.

Showing can threaten our sensibilities; we don't like judgment. Even as we judge others. Even though our horses make that call about us every ride. Competition feels like a dirty word for many. Let's petition the USEF to change that word to something more truthful. Like Bubble Challenge.

Horses: Technique and Art

"Shut Up and Dance"

It was written on one of those little tin lapel pins and my friend wore it when we went to bars back in the day. It was like a rebel yell of a Zen mantra; we'd dance with men or women or dogs. It was a rambunctious celebration of being young and alive. We frolicked like colts cantering about a field, snorting and kicking up our hooves. Free.

Then life happened. We got distracted by family and careers. We bought calendars and scribbled appointments and noticed the sound of our parent's voices coming out of our mouths. We learned the attraction of a slow dance because we were hurried all the time.

When we were kids, if we'd had the wild luck to have a horse, we'd climb on and if we wanted to go to the woods, but the horse wanted to go to that patch of tall grass behind the barn, there was no problem. We went to that patch of tall grass behind the barn.

Horses taught us to be spontaneous, but in our new-found maturity, we decided we needed to steer our horses, control their heads, make them do a task. As soon as that happened, we started missing the way it used to be with horses when we were kids.

As the magic escaped us, we searched for what we lost. We asked for help from a neighbor or a local trainer. In my case, I got a book from the library because it was before the time of the Computasaurus.

Some of us found videos put out by trainers who were smart enough to see a need in the market. Technique got seasoned with the sweetness of financial gain... for the trainer. We were desperate to do better for our horses, who had about lost patience with us by now. Which means we had about lost patience with techniques.

We tried our best to find someone who knew the path back to how it was, but there isn't a trainer in the world who holds his hand up and declares, "I train with cruelty and abuse." Still, some do. Each trainer had a different definition of leadership, along with various techniques for picking up feet, doing canter departs, and everything else. Some work and some don't.

Horse people are very opinionated, and everyone is certain their way is absolutely right. This includes me.

We got good advice and we got bad advice, but then we layered that with conflicting advice, and finally on top of that, what worked for your horse one day, probably didn't work on another day. So we ended up with lots of techniques vying for dominance in our minds, and we got more involved with our thoughts than our horses.

Horses keep telling us that they are individuals and we keep trying to squeeze them into a succession of one-size-fits-all training plans that never quite fit.

Some of the horses don't show us much tolerance as we flounder with a new technique. They gave us calming signals because we were abrupt or gave cues louder than we intended. Or we didn't really understand the new technique, so our confidence was a bit frail and the horses responded to that with confusion. Eventually, tired frustration made it feel like nothing worked but aggression, and that only worked if you kept escalating. Pushing blindly on, driven by compulsion and not inspiration.

A plague of doubt settles in, and it doesn't matter if it started with your horse or you. It was contagious.

The secret no one seems to mention is the technique, regardless of whose technique it is, will never be enough. A technique is a noun, a thing like a skeleton or a box. It's dry science until we clothe it with creativity, make it our own, and then allow our horses to discover it for themselves. A technique is hollow until each rider breathes their unique life into it and then introduces it to their unique horse.

It's a Catch-22: The technique won't work unless we are inspired by it but it's hard to be inspired by a flat technique.

The answer is that we have to embrace the art of training. We must believe in the what if. We might need to show our horses more confidence than we have in the beginning.

Shakespeare, the bard of theater, said, "Assume a virtue, if you have it not." It's a much more poetic way of saying "fake it, till you make it," but your horse is reading you right back as you read him. Can you be interesting and mysterious?

Put your doubt on a shelf and let the play begin. Let your serious goals for training take back seat to spontaneity. Lighten up with the science, horses like recess more than books. You were once that way, too, remember? Laugh at yourself. Let him see you try and if you stumble, laugh more. Show him it's more fun to try than to stand back and doubt.

Success depends on not how well you mimic the particular technique you are using, but instead, how well you listen to your horse and engage him in the moment.

Technique is necessary and good. After that, shut up and dance.

Escaping the Death Spiral: Asking For a Step.

Let me begin by defining a death spiral. It's asking a horse to do something he just avoided, by circling around and asking again. It could be as simple as trying to move your horse to a letter on an arena rail. Or repeat an attempted transition to another gait. Or do an obstacle from the ground. Or ask a horse to step into a trailer.

He avoided it, so you circle, pushing him right back. But then you give the inside rein (or lead rope) a hard pull for good measure. It's asking a little louder and a little faster the second time, hoping that you can push him through, but he braces his ribs in response to your sharp heel, planted and pressing, not all that far from his kidneys. His hind end skitters to the side.

Now your brain is running in a fast frustrated circle, too, it's personal, so you circle him one more time pulling your inside rein to the exact degree that he is pulling to the outside, with your seat planted and both legs kicking up a frenzy, along with a tap of the whip.

And did I mention that pulling on the reins during your kicking fit is saying go and stop simultaneously? You're just trying to get him straight, but he has so much tension and resistance from your conflicting cues that now that he won't take a step.

Wait, I forgot the most important part. What makes it a

death spiral isn't the circle or his refusal. It's you. It's your request that gets repeated louder and bigger and faster and never stops. It's the overlapping use of flailing cues that become a rant that accelerates and obliterates your connection with your horse, as if the goal or obstacle was a matter of life or death.

The worst part: You might not have noticed that you cued this pig-fight, but you are the one having a runaway. Not your horse. Stop. Consider yourself in detention. Let your horse breathe.

Ease up, you didn't create the circling back idea and you don't get all the blame. It's somehow become an acceptable training method, you were probably taught to do it. Please forget it now. It's a lousy tactic unless it's your goal to fry your horse's brain.

One calm circle-back might do the trick, but just one. More than that and the circle-back, intended as a way of correcting an evasion, becomes a way for the horse to evade the war of cues, now bigger than the original task ever was. It trains some horses to frantically circle when they get confused. It becomes a hysterical calming signal intended for you; he's forgotten the obstacle and is evading your over-cueing now. You've changed the subject from the original question to letting him know that you're a scary, warlike leader.

Some horses won't go forward at all, preferring to stand and brace for the punishment to come. It can feel like disobedience, but a horse shutting down is a calming signal. It's your horse saying, "I'm no threat to you; you don't have to yell."

Meanwhile, you're still in detention. Take stock in this hindsight moment. Can you tell when your ego kicked in? Can you tell when you went from creating safety and security for your horse to starting a war that you had to win? It's a good question. The line between these extremes is small, especially once you've stopped breathing.

The other side of that line is anxiety. Humans and horses both respond to anxiety the exact same way. We speed up. Then that speed makes us speed up some more.

Most of the time we throw our horses at something scary, pummel them with cues. We might as well yell something ridiculous like, "Brace yourself, this will hurt!" To be abundantly clear, that's why you're in detention.

Back to the beginning. Horses need a moment to think. It doesn't mean they're refusing. Have a little faith. Ask politely.

You may only ask for one thing at a time. Then you wait for an answer. Count to ten, more than once if you need to. It will feel way too slow but that's because you're used to cueing runaways. After he answers, reward him. If the answer was not the one you wanted, then re-phrase the question. Not louder. Not quicker. Ask for something simple that you can both agree on. Cut the task into tiny bite-sized pieces.

Ask for one step. Reward him, pause, and ask for another. Go slow and don't interrupt the conversation. Mounted or on the ground, do you and your horse have this skill? Walk, halt, walk? You won't need your hands for this. He should listen to your seat if you're riding and your feet if you're on the ground. This is fundamental; you should be asking for halts and walk-offs in your warm-up.

Taking one step at a time toward an obstacle, pausing, and rewarding each try, will get the job done in a fraction of the time that jerking and kicking your horse in circles takes. The result will be fewer ulcers and greater partnership.

In dressage, we are constantly returning to the fundamentals and refining them. They are the foundation of good riding and when trained with patience and reward, horses count on the connection and comfort found in these simple conversations. Isn't this the place to learn the finesse to ask more complicated questions? Isn't that the confidence you want to take forward to bigger challenges?

It always seems like we ask for too much or too little. We're too loud and our horse is reactive. We are too confusing and our horse is shut down. It can feel frustrating when you are trying to do right, but sorry, what you think doesn't matter. It's just you talking to yourself.

Talk to your horse instead. Use your body to give clear cues. Practice them in calm situations. Celebrate fundamental connection but more than that, commit yourself to be a leader who never gives up that profound connection with her horse in favor of a silly external distraction. Like a letter on an arena rail or a horse trailer.

Lead with peaceful persistence: Not aggressive. Not conceding. Not emotional.

Making War on Horses:
Is it Leadership?

"Kick him; make him do it right now or you'll ruin him forever."
"He's making a fool out of you –show him who's boss." "You
can't let him win!"

A few weeks ago, a client said something that stopped me in
my tracks. We'd been working on re-habbing her new gelding
who had nothing short of PTSD. Over the weeks, he was slowly
beginning to trust again. She reflected, "He had a trainer like I
had a father."

In a blink, I was fifteen, standing under a tree with my father,
who was spitting mad at me. My filly was nervous about pavement and he thought I'd been too slow coaxing her to step on it.
Now it was his turn to show me how to break a horse. He was
going to teach her to tie and stand quietly. He snubbed her tight
to a tree and spooked her so she would sit back. My filly felt
trapped, naturally, and tried to rear and pull back to get away.
When she did that, my father hit her on the back of her skull
with a two by four, panting with adrenaline. "She won't try that
again, leave her stand there now. She'll learn." He stalked away
and even now, I can see her quivering, trying to stay on her feet.

These were common training practices in our area, for horses
and kids. He just followed tradition. My grandfather was a horse
trader and a hard taskmaster. My father grew up working horses
and farming with teams of mules who (he said) wouldn't work if

you didn't beat them. And me, his daughter-when-he-wanted-a-son, might have been the first one in the family to love horses. Imagine his disappointment.

Truth: Not only do you not have to win every fight; it isn't even a war.

Here's an over-simplified history of humans and horses: Once upon a time there was a culture who saw the world in terms of art and music. Xenophon, a 430 B.C. Greek soldier/philosopher said, "For what the horse does under compulsion … is done without understanding and there is no beauty in it either, any more than if one should whip and spur a dancer." At the same time, the other dominant culture was warlike. The Romans drugged their horses and rode them into battle.

Nothing has changed.

We've always had these two approaches to training horses, raising kids, and generally doing business. It can feel oppositional; men against women, old against young, science-based against traditionally taught, and every other "us versus them" group imaginable.

The most common thing I hear from riders about affirmative training is that it's the opposite of everything they know. They were taught harsh habits, but it never felt right. That being aggressive with horses was never comfortable, but it was required by others. I can understand that. Back then, I wasn't strong enough to stand against my father.

Years ago, I read a scientific paper that described the physical reasons for why a horse can't learn when he's afraid. I held it as sacred proof and quoted it to prove my point about training with kindness.

But that was before a few years of working with various rescue horses, and horses who had been flunked out by other trainers, and the saddest, brilliant young horses who got pushed too fast. Horses who have struggled with violent leadership will be the first to tell you that they learn plenty when they're afraid. But none of it is good.

It makes sense; lots of us have tolerated harsh criticism from family for decades. Some of us rebel and never show the "respect" demanded of us. Some of us just shut down, our dreams broken and our self-worth destroyed. Horses do that, too.

Compassionate training can get some catcalls. I've certainly been criticized for training like a girl. There is that sour feeling that hangs in the air implying that we are cowards. That we just don't have the guts to break a horse. We're too weak to win the fight with a horse and too scared to even take the bait to fight the human taunting you. That we can't sustain a personal attack, insulting our touchy-feely training. Does it all feel like we are still twelve-year-olds?

I recently saw a video of a rider on her young horse. It was their first try at mounted shooting and her horse was confused and extremely frightened. Her "friends" cheered her on, urging her to fight him through it. The rider kept kicking, jerking the reins, and shooting her gun. Her friends kept yelling at her to keep after him. It felt like a death-fight at a Roman Colosseum.

I've also been asked how to deal with railbirds who tell riders they're not tough enough on their horses. How do you defend compassion in the face of criticism? Why is there so much peer pressure to dominate horses? Do the intimidation tactics that they use on their horses work on you, too?

I notice it's as hard to stand up to bullying as it ever was.

In 2016, the FBI raised animal cruelty up to a Class A felony, with murder and arson. Pause. Think about that. It isn't that the FBI thinks kittens and foals are cute. Statistics show a majority of violent crime begins with animal abuse and being able to trace that aids them. We are culturally changing to understand the importance of what this violence toward animals means in a larger sense. It's real progress.

Humans are born predators. We make war but we are also capable of great acts of heart. How we deal with horses, dogs, and even children give us a chance to ask ourselves the hard questions.

This might not be what you expected to hear about the "you can't let him win" philosophy. It's a topic that I take very seriously. I've certainly seen humans declare war, claim dominance using weapons –sticks, whips, and spurs. Only to run horses in circles until they shut down or cripple themselves. And if cruelty was limited to barns, as much as I love horses, I'd be happy with that. But it's a topic that reflects more about who we are than we like to admit.

Are horses who we really hate? Why is it so important for us to label each other victors or victims? Is it possible for our intellect and heart to rise above our predator instinct?

I'm not saying that how we train horses will bring about world peace. It's just one place to start.

Training with Peaceful Persistence

I recently had a spellbinding conversation with a brilliant and beautiful mare.

She was very young, not started under saddle, and her human is doing a fine job with her. They do obstacles in hand, hike a bit, and she has age-appropriate ground manners. Her handler had asked for some advice about the process going forward.

We'd been talking about one of my favorite exercises, leading from behind. It's standing back by the horse's flank, well behind the drive-line, and about four feet to the side. In other words, well out of the horse's space. Once the horse is comfortable moving forward in this position, you can do obstacles, but rather than leading her, you send her from behind. Or more literally, the horse does obstacles in autonomy, volunteering, and out in front like ground driving. The handler walks along, makes suggestions, and cheers.

I asked if I might have her horse's rope. I'm aware that I'm asking for a privilege. I've heard all the trainer horror stories, too. But she trusts her mare to me and I say thank you.

The mare is beautiful and she is quite aware of it. Period. Can I take a moment here and say that if you work with a beautiful mare, it might be more productive to acknowledge your own beauty rather than hers? She already knows, and you will need all your confidence to keep up with her. Says this gray mare with chronic lameness.

We did a few obstacles but she let me know with some sour ears that I was uninteresting. That's fair.

I thought she was answering by rote, meaning the mechanical or habitual repetition of something. You say sit and the dog sits. Yawn. Pretty dull conversation if that's all you do.

The mare had been doing the obstacles in the most obvious way. Not only that, she thought repetition was for dolts. Or that humans might be very slow learners. A conversation by rote is beyond boring. And if we just repeat the obstacle the same way each time, then we deserve a sour ear. Any mare will tell you that.

Time to get creative. I asked her to walk on from behind. There was a pair of arches, and I sent her under. But then I wanted to send her between them. It was wide enough for her but not wide enough for both of us side by side. I sent her out on a curving line, in front of me, and she stopped at that narrow spot between the arches.

She didn't think she could do it. I asked her to hold her own self up.

She was standing right there; she knew what I wanted. She was smart; she didn't need me to "train" her. She needed the confidence to try.

I let her know when she was doing well. I was positioned totally back from her head, she was facing the narrow space between the arches, telling me it might be impossible, and I was just happy. I could tell she's thinking about options, so I exhaled. Good.

This is how obstacles work: She could be standing facing anything: a bridge, a pedestal, or a trailer. It's all the same; I get to say what we do, and she gets to say when. Partnership.

I coaxed her to figure it out. I wasn't going to do it for her and I wasn't going to bully her. I waited. That meant I'd become interesting and mysterious.

I let her know she was on the right path. Good girl. I ignored the rest and I breathed. We were having a conversation. She tried to distract me by suggesting there might be a kangaroo in the bushes. I usually fall for kangaroos but not that time. I told her she was brave with a big inhale.

I was standing to her left with my left hand on a long lead, toward the clip at her chin and my right hand near the end of the rope. I might cue her with the rope end, but if I do, it must be so quiet that she takes only one half-step. I only want small efforts. If she gets over-cued and anxious, things would take longer, and she was paying close attention. No reason to escalate. She wasn't refusing; just trying to figure out how to do it. We're both intelligent people. We whisper and breathe.

Her sour ears had been gone for the last five minutes and I cared less about the obstacle and more about her keen mind. We were focused, enjoying each other.

Would you have upped your aids by now? Circled her or disengaged her? Would you have distracted her from her task or she you? Hold steady; there's time.

Her calming signals were small, with less anxiety than before. She blinked slowly with a large soft eye. She gave me a little lick and chew; she was almost ready. Dialing my energy to balance hers, I asked her to move a bit, and then, with no fanfare, she walked through. Onlookers audibly sighed and gave her a quiet golf-clap and the young mare was positively glowing with pride.

Can we use positive energy to encourage a horse to push her boundaries, in a good way? Can we have the confidence in her to give her time to figure it out? In the saddle, as well as on the ground? And when she volunteers, let's celebrate her new-found courage. Confidence is the most important gift we can give our horses, regardless of our riding discipline.

The primary rule in affirmative training is that you may only say yes to the horse and to yourself. No punishment, just yes. This part is harder than it sounds. Every time you see any calming signal, you listen and go slower or stop. You may not escalate. Keep a friendly tone. Breathe. Acknowledge every tiny try.

Peaceful Persistence:

Not aggressive.

Not conceding.

Not emotional.

We need to pick up our mental game. It's crazy the way we prattle on about how sensitive our horses are, geniuses at reading our minds, and totally capable of learning anything, but then dumb down the training process to learned helplessness, bullying, and answers by rote. It would make my ears go sour, too.

Can We Love Too Much?

Someone wrote to me and said, "I still have questions about how to express love to a horse where it feels good to both you and the horse. I know now for them it is a lot about being calm and not having busy energy in their presence, and sometimes not much touching, while for most humans it's about petting, sweet talking and getting close. Jeez ...seems pretty polar opposite."

This is a question that I want to answer with a question: Why is showing horses physical affection such a big deal to us? Why must we express our love to horses in such noisy needy ways? Tell the truth, doesn't it seem a bit desperate sometimes?

We approach loving horses a little like a bowling ball approaches a triangle of pins.

It's like we're awkward insecure teenagers who want to show the world we can get a date. We coo baby-talk, manipulate horses with treats, and find that itchy spot so we can make them make faces. Perish the thought that a horse might not want our white-hot affection; if he even feigns interest, we pounce. We cannot keep our hands (emotions) to ourselves.

Look at it this way. If you were angry or frustrated with your horse, it would make good sense to take those big ugly feelings and back away. There's no room for anger in training. Is it possible that when our feelings of love and equine addiction become overwhelming, we should do the same?

I'll speak for myself. Sometimes I'll be working with someone's horse in a lesson or clinic, and he will do something that's just spectacular. I'll be gobsmacked; his behavior just pours gasoline on my burning heart. The reason to step back, exhale, and murmur "good" in a moment like this is that my emotional love-fit is as selfish as a temper tantrum would be. It's all about me and I'm the one always lipping off about being an advocate for horses.

Or more importantly, I want to give my horse time to process what has just gone so well, without loading all of my emotions on top of the feelings the horse is having. I step back or get very still, and let it be about him. I give him time. I shut up.

I remember an old self-help book by Gary Chapman, *The 5 Love Languages*. Back in the day, I hated his excruciating explanation of why, if you really wanted your lover to give you flowers but instead, they changed the oil in your truck, it was the same thing. In other words, an act of service is a gift of love, even if it doesn't smell that way. It followed, if you wanted someone to feel your love, you should express it unselfishly, in a way they understood. It's an evolved concept if you lean toward immaturity and really want the damn roses.

I'm a horse trainer but the truth is that I'm a couples therapist. I know a pretty fair amount about riding and training, but more often, I translate language between humans and horses, trying to iron out misunderstandings.

Horses do not thrive on drama. Love and anxiety are contradictions to a horse. I wish humans didn't equate the two either. Emotional runaways, whether it's anger or affection or even extreme confusion, aren't positive input.

When we stand really close to a horse, they frequently look away or partially close their eyes as a calming signal. Close proximity means maybe we'll hug them or maybe push them out of our space, but the conflicting emotions cause them a displacement calming signal, feel anxiety as we would if someone was speaking loudly six inches from your face. When crowded, horses want to shut down and pull inside themselves. If we were farther away, they'd flee, instead they "play dead" passively.

I don't want to be a killjoy. I love a horse hug as much as anyone but more than that, I care that he feels confident and peaceful. Safety means more to a horse than our undying chatter about love.

If it's one of those days when a sideways look might reduce you to tears, consider loving your horse enough to stay away. Just because we feel better around a horse doesn't mean it's our right to dump our hard feelings on them.

The most common miscommunication I see between horses and riders is our apparent unwillingness to recognize anxiety. Years ago, looking at a horse for a client, the mare's face showed every painful ulcer symptom I know; anxiety in the muzzle, busy lips, or tongue chewing. Yet, the sellers stood around laughing about how she liked to make "cute faces." We commonly mistake signs of pain or confusion for affection and end up encouraging their anxiety.

How to tell if your love language is good for your horse? Quiet your mind. No, really. Then be honest and look deeper than what you want to see. Are his eyes soft? His face smooth? Does he show peace? It's a lot less romantic than your horse mugging you but love shouldn't look like insecurity.

How to let your horse know you love him? Develop a quiet mind. Give him a release but then pause. Wait for him to answer. It might be closing his eyes or licking. The huge calming signal response is a stretch and a blow. If you love him, give him time and space. Show him that respect.

Because I don't believe in domination training, I fear that my message will be misconstrued to mean don't ride, don't ask for improvement, and just generally, let your horse walk all over you and call it love. Humans are such extremists; swinging the pendulum from one extreme to the far other is equal dysfunction.

I want clients to ride the middle, to have polite and complicated conversations about willing responses, balanced transitions, and eventually the weirdness of half-pass. Conversations that involve getting one good step, laughing, and taking a break. Conversations without blame, where we ask for the best of each other. The very best.

It isn't that performance horses are trained differently than trail horses, we hold ourselves to clean, clear communication that lifts the relationship in such a way that horses volunteer, feeling strong and confident. That's love in action.

Riding the Middle: My Horse is Lazy.

My horse is lazy. He won't go forward. He doesn't listen to my legs no matter what. Do I need spurs?

If your horse has a problem, look for a resolution in yourself.

Assuming the horse isn't in pain, when I hear this human question, I wonder how the horse would answer. Is the word lazy even in their vocabulary? I mention this because understanding how horses think is much more important than getting our way. Understanding them is how we have a responsive answer to any cue.

If I had to guess, I'd think the horse was shut down. Here's my equine CSI logic: The horse is probably stoic. I know this because a more reactive horse would have bucked his rider off by now. Excessive kicking doesn't go over well with a horse who gets aggravated easily.

Stoic horses don't lie, but they are not forthcoming. They keep their own best council. Think introvert, in human terms. Most horses are conflict avoidant, retreating inside and trying to be invisible. Like me around enthusiastic football fans.

Humans tend to think horses can't hear them, even knowing that each one of his senses is more acute than ours. So, we cue again, louder this time. Or we just nag on with our legs banging their sides each stride. But the more you cue a stoic horse, the more he crouches inside of himself.

Light bulb moment in understanding horses: Less is more.

What do you feel? I don't mean some esoteric theory about

soulmates or an obscure psychological reasoning from possible experiences in his past or even a dispassionate reciting of training aids as described on any of two million articles online. Those are intellectual activities.

Your horse lives in the moment, and to help him, you must escape your over-thinking intellectual mind and join him in the moment. Tune in to your senses. What do you literally feel?

If you are timid in the saddle or if you're not warmed up yet, your thighs might be tight. That means that you are suspended above the saddle. Breathe, imagine an egg under your knee, and let your sit bones settle. A deep seat makes for a connected ride. Not to mention, mounted thigh master exercises are frowned on by horses.

While you're at it, if his poll is tight, do your own slow side-to-side neck roll. If he is clamped on the bit, relax your jaw. In a few moments when your body is looser, see how your horse has changed. Then walk a while longer and let what you thought was relaxed relax some more.

Next, feel your energy level. The rule of thumb is that if your brain is working, your body has gone still, most notably your seat. And that is, after all, the cue to halt. A busy brain can shut a horse down. Too much mental chatter scrutinizing what's happening is not the same thing as feeling it.

See how easy it was to distract you from your energy? I just chattered about brains and your brain couldn't resist hearing its own name. This is what your brain does when you ride. Intellect isn't energy. It distracts you from feeling. Intellect is the enemy of art. Brains think the only worthwhile activity is thinking. Refuse to engage.

Energy is something separate from intellect. It's tuning into your body and listening. It's cultivating an awareness of your muscles and joints, and even your arthritis and old injuries, and then empowering yourself to go beyond. Riding well requires not just an awareness of your body position but also the ability to communicate eloquence in its movement. It's the same thing that makes you gasp when you see a horse gallop in slow motion.

Think of your energy level as a dial that you can adjust. If your horse doesn't have much energy, turn yours up. Do more than breathe, actually smell the air. If you're on the ground, pick up your step, get happy. If you're mounted, fill your lungs and feel your shoulders go broad. Let the sun warm your chest.

Now feel where your body resists the movement of your horse. An example of this kind of resistance would be a rider who braces their legs stiff at the trot, riding like a bundle of two-by-four lumber. No, you don't ride that stiffly, but can you feel small places where you could be resisting your horse's forward motion?

Does your lower back release to the movement of your horse's back? If not, you're giving a constant cue to slow down. If your thighs are tense that counts as a half halt. Are your hands giving or do they drag like a parking brake? And most common, if your intellect kicks in when you notice that your horse isn't doing what you want, does your seat stop following your horse entirely?

Yes, it's natural for us but also not fair to complain that your horse is lazy if you're unable to maintain your energy consistently.

Step one is to notice when it happens. You can't change things that you aren't aware of. To begin, go inside your body and feel the ride. In dressage, we ride the inside of the horse and we do that from deep inside of ourselves. We work to train ourselves to not lose our rhythm to external distractions, even those we make up in our own mind. Rhythm is the foundation of all good with horses.

The challenge of improving your riding, if you are a long-term novice who wants to do better for horses, is that there are usually fairly small things working against you that you might not be aware of. You will need to develop a more focused awareness of your own energy and internal movements in order to communicate nuance to your horse.

The horse world is a place of extremes. Extreme training, extreme use, and extreme love, and finding the path you want can be elusive. Most likely, you'll take a wrong turn from time to time. Learning about horses isn't linear but more of a spherical realization.

Finding balance for you and your horse in the middle of this chaos is an extraordinary feat. Riding the Middle is the path from over-cued and under-inspired work to relaxed and forward brilliance.

Kick less, dance more.

Part One: My Horse Betrayed Me

I hear lots of horror stories in my line of work. "My horse just started bucking, for no good reason." "He was flying like a kite on the end of my lead rope." "One minute he was walking next to me and the next, I had smashed toes, my head knocked sideways, and he was running away."

In that instant, your horse goes from being your soulmate to guilty of conspiracy to commit murder. Slightly less paranoid riders would call his behavior a psychotic break. He became unpredictable. Uncontrollable. Is the term betrayal overly dramatic? He broke your trust.

Lucky for you there are some railbirds ready to dispense training advice. Put a chain over his nose. Run him in the round pen until he gives in. Get a whip and show him who's boss.

Whoa! Slow down. Can we rewind? Tell the lynch mob that you've got this. Because if the only response is hindsight punishment, riders are doomed. Here's a radical thought: How about listening to him in the first place?

Disclaimer: There is the very rare occasion when a pain response forces a horse to explode without warning. Think bee sting. If there is an *extreme* response, look first at his physical condition.

In most cases, the horse runs away just one step at a time. He gives warnings repeatedly, as his anxiety grows. He holds it together as long as he can. If you're listening, you have time. Learning to respond to calming signals from your horse can save both of you.

When I ask riders for the long version of what happened, the story unfolds differently. Maybe he was hard to catch that day, or impatient and a bit barn sour at the gate, or maybe especially girthy during saddling. The rider got complacent. Small details were ignored for expediency. Some of us are so busy in our own heads that we don't even notice the small details. The rest of us were taught to plow on ahead no matter what because we can't let the horse "win."

Then his discomfort got confused with disobedience. Horses just have one way of communicating and it's with their body. If a generally well-behaved horse nips or tosses his head, don't think you can "correct" his anxiety with escalation. When we get resistance from a horse, pause and breathe. Then resolve the anxiety while it is small and manageable. Let your horse see you as worthy of his trust.

The biggest reason to listen to your horse is because you have the awareness equivalency of a blind, deaf, hairless mouse. Horses are prey animals forever; their senses are so much more acute than a human that we literally have no idea what's going on, even if we're paying attention. Let that sink in.

On top of that, science says that a horse's response time is seven times quicker than ours; the fastest response time of any common domestic animal. When things come apart, it happens fast. It makes sense because flight, the instinct to sprint away from perceived danger, is the species' primary defensive behavior.

Is it fair to ask for obedience above instinct? Our safety depends on it, but it's complicated.

Say we're walking to the arena. From the horse's side, they pull their head away and graze because it's their instinct to always eat. Horses are designed for full-time grazing. So we react by jerking the lead-rope. Fighting instinct is a bit like fighting gravity but humans have a plan and a clock ticking, so we get adversarial.

A rider with a greater understanding of her horse's instincts and needs might feed a flake of hay while tacking up and then actively lead her horse to the arena by keeping a good forward rhythm in her feet. He has food in his stomach and she gets to ride within her time constraints. Best of all, there is no fight before the ride even starts. You can tell it's good leadership because everyone "wins."

Most of all, no one betrays anyone. The best reason for a rider to study and understand horse behavior is that learning their logic can keep us from a runaway of our own – an emotional runaway.

Granted, it's a little easier to be logical in a discussion over grazing rights than it is in the middle of a dangerous bucking incident, but we have to start small.

It doesn't hurt to acknowledge that, when you look at it this way, horses and humans aren't that temperamentally well-suited to each other. Still, I don't see either species giving up on the other.

All of this is to say that when your horse appears to overreact to his surroundings, he isn't wrong. And adding our over-reaction on top won't make things better.

At the same time, it's our nature to think we know everything and that our plan is the only thing that matters. It's a good reminder, even if your horses live on your property with you, that you are only a small part of their experience. They have fully dimensional lives, with emotional ups and downs, that have nothing to do with you at all.

If you want an unthinking partner with limited intelligence, dirt bikes are a good option. Otherwise, spend more time understanding and less time wishing horses were different. It takes more than a lifetime to understand horses. You don't have any time to lose.

Yes, you could say that I'm making excuses for horses and, not as sympathetic as I should be toward humans who have been hurt and frightened. I just want to suggest that we be a bit more careful about the words we use to describe horse behaviors.

We must learn to accept and support each other's instincts for self-preservation because that's how both species will flourish.

The words we choose matter, *not* because they give horses a bad name, but because they damage how we think of horses in our own hearts.

Part Two: Now I'm Afraid

Something bad happened. The details don't need to be repeated for me to understand. It doesn't matter whose fault it was; whether it was you or your horse. Excuses don't help and emotions are rarely swayed by logic. Your trust has been broken.

Now you feel fear. Fear in the saddle. Fear about horses in general, but most importantly, fear toward your own horse.

Disclaimer: I am not a therapist; I just act like it when I give riding lessons.

First, can we all admit that a tight feeling in the gut is something we all know well? There is nothing unusual about a feeling of anxiety while climbing on a thousand-pound prey animal with keen senses and a flight response. It's normal human instinct.

The most common thing that good horsewomen tell me is that they don't ride like they did when they were kids–as if that's a bad thing. Kids don't have good hands or clear cues; what I remember most is going where the horse wanted to because I had no steering. Some of us rode fast and bounced when we fell, but the truth remains. Riding wilder is not better. It frightens horses. Bravado or dumb luck will never qualify as good horsemanship.

And worst of all, there is a huge ration of self-loathing that comes along when a rider admits they're timid. It takes up as much room in a rider's heart as the fear does. It's the self-loathing that hurts the most to hear and see in a client. I'm certain horses feel the same.

Well, words matter. I'm going to go back and do some editing before we continue.

Now you feel ~~fear~~ common sense. ~~Fear~~ Common sense in the saddle. ~~Fear~~ Common sense about horses in general, but most importantly, ~~fear~~ common sense toward your own horse.

The problem isn't that we have ~~fear~~ common sense, it's that we love horses and aren't giving them up. Now what?

In my experience, hard feelings grow in the dark. Most of us have some time or place that the bogey man threatens us. I won't say ignore him; there's usually a spark of truth there. You should be cautious about monsters under the bed (lock the house, be careful in parking lots, and yes, monitor the dangers of riding.) Part of that ~~fear~~ common sense is an instinct for self-preservation. It's a good thing and horses have it, too.

At the same time, it's incredibly powerful to drag your bogey man out into the daylight. The first time you admit that you're timid, your voice might quiver a bit but right after that, your heart starts beating again. Your jeans feel like you've lost weight. And you have.

Riders get told to relax because horses can read our emotions. It's true but humans who listen with their eyes read them, too. It doesn't matter what you think intellectually, how much experience you have with horses, or what you should have done. Act timid or act with bravado, but you aren't fooling us, so why not admit it out loud?

Share your feelings. Notice that the rest of us are just like you and let go of the self-loathing part.

Besides, a bogey man doesn't have a chance in the broad daylight with a bunch of middle-aged women glaring at him.

And while we're being honest, here's one more bit of sideways truth. However, it happened that your trust was damaged, it wasn't that you lost control of your horse. You never had control. As a recovering Type-A who thought she could steer her horse, and the rest of her life, to brilliant happiness, I feel qualified to say the sooner we get over thinking we can even control our hair, the better we'll be.

Let it go.

Forgive your horse. He responded by instinct; he didn't betray you or want to hurt you. Forgive him because holding a grudge doesn't work. Breathe and forgive him again. Feels good, doesn't it?

If your ~~fear~~ common sense tells you he isn't the horse for you, then lay down your silly ego and don't be a martyr, owning him forever in purgatory. Confess that he's the perfect horse for someone else. Trade him for a horse who better suits you. It isn't a failure to do what's best for both of you.

Then forgive yourself. We are our own worst enemy and holding a grudge against our own instincts is crazy-making. Show your heart some tolerance and ask your brain to rest. Leave the trash talk to others.

Sit a little taller and remind yourself that you have a noble goal. To collaborate with another species in equality has been the life's work of élite equestrians and children from the beginning of time. You have a rich heritage.

And there's time. Horses are patient teachers and you're lucky to have lifetime tuition. Buy the hay and you're enrolled. On the ground or in the saddle, the lessons will be learned. Horses are perfect that way.

Most of all, count your blessings. ~~Fear~~ Common sense is not a tumor to be cut out. ~~Fear~~ Common sense isn't a weakness, just as bravado isn't courage. Think of it as a training aid.

Fear is common sense trying to get your attention. Say thank you.

Word choice matters. We need to understand each other's instincts for self-preservation because that's how both species–horses and humans–will flourish.

If your fear is truly too big to have a conversation with and you freeze in the saddle and can't breathe, just stop. If your anxiety is debilitating, get help from a real therapist. Do it for your horse, if not yourself. No joke. Having the bogey man with his hands on the reins is a truly dangerous situation.

Short of that, just keep chipping away. Make friends with your instincts. Smile more. Reward yourself for small wins. Breathe. Go slow. Show yourself the kindness that you show your horse. Eventually give him a chance to carry you to a better place, one way or another.

Ever think about where courage comes from? It isn't born of arrogance and success. It's purchased, one drop at a time, by internal moments of persistence in the face of challenge.

You've got that. It's holding to a truth about yourself. And then horses. In the process, keep your love just an inch bigger than your ~~fear~~ common sense and you'll be fine.

Part Three: Riding Above Fear

This is what we knew then: It started with a dream of dancing hooves and a flowing mane. He was strong and fast, and you couldn't tell where he stopped and you started.

This is what we know now: Your horse is frightened, and you know it. Or you're frightened and your horse knows it. And it doesn't matter who started it. You're here now.

If you think this frightened horse is almost within your skill range and you have the time and patience and constant forgiveness, or if you have acquired a huge dose of ~~fear~~ common sense but think your horse would be okay if you relaxed, begin here: Make sure your horse is sound. No, really, have the vet check him over. Call a chiropractor who does acupuncture. If the horse is the problem, he usually has a problem. Then, be safe. Wear a helmet. Remove your watch and work in horse time. Take good and kind care of both of you.

Anxiety is normal on both sides. Pretending it doesn't exist isn't the same thing as releasing it. Acknowledge the weird balance of dread and enthusiasm. Forgive each other again. Then know that this process will take some time.

Words matter. Negative corrections aren't effective. Yelling "NO!" is a dead end. It isn't instructive to horse or human. It's right up there with yelling "Don't be afraid!" or "Quit grabbing the reins!" or "Stop running!" Telling yourself or your horse what to not do is like trying to deny reality. Instead, create a new reality by using simple, clean, positive words like "Walk on." "Breathe." "Well done." In other words:

Less correction. More direction.

Start at the beginning. Is there resistance during haltering? At the first sign of anxiety, pause and breathe. Humans tend to speed up when we get nervous. Before we know it, we're wrestling with a thousand-pound flight animal, when slowing down in the first place could resolve the anxiety on both sides while it was still small and manageable. Go slow.

Then do something mysterious. Take the halter off and leave.

When you both volunteer for the halter, proceed to groundwork. Ask for something small, like walking next to you, but you stay out of his space as much as he stays out of yours. Walk together independently. Take time to get it right; let him test your patience.

Think less about whether he's right or wrong, and more about what your senses are telling you. Practice being less complacent. What are his ears saying? Use all your senses to "listen" to your horse. Soften your visual focus by using peripheral vision to see a wider view of your surroundings. In other words...

Less brain chatter. More physical awareness.

Listen to his calming signals. Cue his movement with your feet instead of your hands. Laugh when he gets it right, and even more when you do. Keep at it until both of you have let go of all the breath you've been holding. Then feel the anxiety begin to shift.

Stay with groundwork for as long as you want. Build confidence by ground driving and doing horse agility. Your horse doesn't care if you ever ride him again. Your relationship isn't defined by proximity; it's defined by trust. If you don't share confidence on the ground, there's no reason to think it will magically appear when you're in the saddle.

When it feels right, groom him and tack up. Go for a walk in the arena and stop at the mounting block. Check the strap on your helmet and climb the steps. Lay a soft hand on his neck and if he's nervous, breathe until his poll releases. Until his eyes relax. Until he is peaceful and your belly is soft.

Only go as far as the beginning of anxiety and stop there. Release it while it's still just a flash of an idea. Then be mysterious again. Step down and go untack him.

Remember where the two of you started and celebrate your progress. Know there will be setbacks ahead and let this time be precious.

Find a good ground coach. Someone who is calm and breathes well. Then take tiny challenges, one after another. Slow and steady, throw your leg over and sit in the saddle at the mounting block. Breathe and feel your thigh muscles. They might need some air, too. Remember you love your horse and melt what is frozen. Dismount without taking a step and call it a win.

Next time, take a few steps. You don't need to feel like you're alone on the high dive. Ask your ground coach to latch on a lead rope and walk beside you and your horse to start. Take baby steps so everyone succeeds. There is no shame in working as a team. Then climb off before you want to.

Think rhythm. All good things for horses happen rhythmically: chewing, walking, breathing. All bad things come with a break in rhythm: bucking, bolting, spooking. Good riding for the horse means rhythm. That's your first concern.

You can count your breath, focus on your sit bones like a metronome, or ride to music. Whatever you like, just so it connects your spine to your horse's movement in a slow, confidence-building rhythm. Then walk on.

When emotions arise, notice them. Refuse to demonize yourself or your horse. Breathe until the feelings get bored and leave.

Remember that science says that a horse's response time is seven times quicker than ours? While they come apart ridiculously fast, they can also come back together quickly, if we ask them. Humans believe in a snowball effect; if the horse shakes his head or any other small infraction, the inevitable end is a train-wreck, but it isn't true. If you take a breath as soon as you feel anxiety in your horse, he will do the same. Other days, your horse might notice you go tense and blow his breath out so loud that you hear it and take his cue.

It's a partnership; sometimes we carry them and sometimes they carry us. It doesn't matter who starts it. Just so we all come home safe.

Then one day you notice that the dark thoughts are rare. Instead, you're distracted by something bright and shiny. It's your childhood dream, balanced with common sense, right here in real life.

Fall Equinox

Horsewoman. Internet. Wine.

It's been a melancholy week at Infinity Farm. I'd call it the dog days of summer but truth is that it's been feeling like fall for a few weeks already. It's getting dark earlier but some days it feels like the sun isn't even up by noon.

It's cool enough that I need a sweatshirt for the night barn check and the season change means mice are starting to move to the house like snowbirds to Tucson. Turns out the cats have all gone vegan or something. Living on a farm isn't what it used to be.

So, I'm sitting in my writing studio with a mouse staring at me from my bookshelf. I wonder if I've fought his ancestors, which makes me spend just a bit too much time considering the big questions: Politics. Religion. Who else would eat the poison before the mouse? Is he too big for a fly swatter? Must I always fumble the Tupperware?

Even more despondent, I give in and do that thing that a certain sort of person does late at night on the internet. I'm not proud of it. It shows a lack of character and if my mother was alive, she would slap my hand away...

First, I get a glass of wine –a thick Cabernet that practically stains my teeth. And some chocolate with almonds because I know where this is going and I'll need some energy in a while. Then I push back in my reclining office chair, put my feet up, and pull the hood of my sweatshirt forward until it nearly covers my eyes. In the dim light, the glow of my computer is as welcoming as a campfire.

A big slow exhale with no need to rush. I'm alone, except for the old dog snoring like someone's weird uncle. I decide to call it ambiance. One finger goes to one key, the "D", and the address line auto-fills. It isn't my first time on this salacious site; Dreamhorse.com. To our kind, it's like a shameless social group where they don't check your income or marital status.

No, I'm not looking for a horse. None of my clients are either. Still, I leer. I ogle, tilting my head to the side as my eyes devour photos of sleek horses for sale in other states. And then I pour over the descriptions. Some sound as if they were written by a used-car salesman and some by horse-crazy girls. They are equally reliable. I know better than to take the words literally: Bombproof. Sixteen hands. Schooling fourth level. And the one that makes me go mushy… Needs experienced rider.

Oh, my heart. Shouldn't horse ads have a literary category of their own, something between Crime Fiction and Romance? After the wine is gone and many pages have been viewed, I doze off to that world where I'm not quite a horse and not quite human. The ad reads:

Available: Mature Gray Mare

Registered name: Shez Gotta Doit Herway

Breed: Grade, DNA test shows some of everything.

First schooled in Pleasure, Reining, and Trail. Currently a dressage schoolmaster with remarkably poor gaits. Not lame really. Just a bit uneven. Big hooves, good teeth, easy keeper. Not exactly uphill.

Classically trained, boss mare skills, and still sits a wicked reining spin. Veteran of all kinds of freestyle; loves to dance. Will tell you how to do it correctly and then stand around breathing until you take her cue. But no exceptions; she won't let you on without a helmet.

Loves trailers, will stand for the right farrier. Will also kick when required but her intolerance for bad manners shouldn't be confused with stubbornness. Prefers body work and a dirt bath to "a cookie." No plans to retire. Dreams of hock injections.

Comes with two donkeys. And a goat. Some ducks that quit laying. A few dogs and some useless cats. And a small herd of horses, all more uneven than her.

Price: Private treaty, of course.

Calming Signals and Pain

First, last, and always, make sure your horse is sound.

I know I'm repetitive but that's the warning every decent equine professional should give before practically anything we do. It's the common disclaimer; we almost skim over it as a formality before getting on to the training issues. In other words, we get complacent to chronic pain messages because it's easier to train sometimes than it is to track down some nebulous pain. We should know better.

It's the first question every rider should ask from the ground every day. Is my horse sound? Learning to read pain takes perception; it's complicated in the beginning. It isn't that we don't care. We might not be sure and that means a vet call. We usually have a plan that day. Even if it's a trail ride, we don't want to cancel. If it's something that involves money or hauling or inconveniencing other people, we usually think it's not so bad and go ahead. We should do better.

There's also a disclaimer that we should hear from horses: First, last and always, they are prey animals. Their instinct is so interwoven into their behavior and personality, that it's inseparable. It isn't safe for prey animals to be forthcoming about pain.

If your horse is stoic, he'll grit his teeth, sometimes literally, and keep trudging on acting like he's fine, until it's too late. If your horse is more reactive than stoic, he'll act aggressively hoping that bravado will pass for strength.

It's common sense if you're a horse. Prey animals hide their pain to survive. They are born knowing that the wolves kill the slow, lame members of the herd. Showing weakness, even within the herd, could mean less access to food. It isn't good or bad; it's nature's plan that the fit survive. We throw a wrench into that cycle when we domesticate animals so, at the very least, we must listen much more carefully.

Most of us can read enough herd dynamics to know that the shy old gelding might need to eat separately. We proudly list each horse's position in the herd as an affirmation that we know our horses. As if it's some kind of equine astrology and now that we know the horse is a Sagittarius that explains everything.

I've been teaching calming signals for the last few years as a way of understanding small messages from our horses before they become huge issues. It's fun to have a non-verbal conversation with a horse. I always give the reminder about soundness but often we'd rather have a conversation about training challenges, like standing still at the mounting block. What if the mounting block represents the beginning of what hurts and your horse resists it because he's smart? That's not a training issue at all.

It's about now that we have to ask the hard questions: Is it my lousy hands or is he in pain for another reason? How is his saddle fit? If you aren't having that checked at the very least once a year, things may have changed. He feels it. Maybe he has a rib out or his withers are a bit jammed and he needs a chiropractic adjustment. Maybe he's in his teens and you have repressed the idea that his back might be getting arthritic.

I don't blame people. Checking for soundness is an affirmation of our horse's mortality. Ick. Lameness can be hard to diagnose, even with radiographs and ultrasound. And I think there are pains that horses feel that we just can't find, even with the best help. Vet science is still an art.

If lameness weren't complicated enough, the existence of ulcers can distract us from questions of soundness. Ulcers are a huge issue for horses. Between sixty percent and ninety percent of horses have them, and worse, they sometimes mask lameness issues. It isn't uncommon to treat a horse for ulcers and then perhaps find a stifle or tendon problem underneath them.

For all our horse's anxiety about pain and not showing it, and for all our anxiety about the same, we have to start by getting past our emotions, fear, and love for a moment. Stand away from your horse, take a breath, and watch with quiet eyes. These are calming signals that could also be signs of pain:

A tense poll, or elevated head.

Ears back or one ear back and one forward.

Tight muscles around the eye.

Exposed white of the eye.

Intense stare or partially closed eyes.

Clenched lips or nostrils.

You're right. Those symptoms are so common. Some are even contradictory. We see them all the time, it's easy to be complacent about them. They could be calming signals to ask you to cue quieter or that they need a moment to think. Or they could be signs of pain.

It's like that experience where you type a couple of your own symptoms into Google trying to self-diagnose something that might be depression, only to find out that depression is a symptom of twenty other terrifying life-threatening issues.

And suddenly playing with calming signals is less fun. If you have a stoic horse, then cut that minimal fun in half. Can we ever trust what a stoic horse relates? Are so many nebulous and negative unknowns looming large enough now that you doubt everything you used to think you knew?

Perfect. You're not supposed to think you know everything.

Instead, work on having an open mind and good intention. We must be willing to see "bad behavior" as a message and not a training issue. Be willing to listen, but also be willing to hear things we don't want to hear. Even embrace the idea that our horses might be in pain. I don't mean that we all become equine hypochondriacs but how can we help them if we don't almost welcome the idea that pain might exist?

Affirmative training, asking a horse to volunteer, is more than kind. It has a distinct advantage for the horse. He gets what he wants from a leader. He gets to be heard when he hurts.

First, last, and always, make sure your horse is sound.

Be the Change Your
Horse Wants to See

Do you ever get the impression that you show up at the barn and your horse is watching you with an expression of "who are you today?"

Most of us have a few different personas. There's the one for work; you watch your language there. The one for your oldest friend from high school; she's the arbiter of honesty. There is a "first" persona, for first dates, job interviews, and meeting strangers formally. We're usually tense and shiny then, from trying too hard while simultaneously hoping to appear totally natural. Whew.

It isn't that we're being dishonest, we're just choosing a version of ourselves for a particular situation. Some of it is following a set of rules that we imagine is required. It's being professional or respectful or nervous. It's being witty and conversational when you're an introvert and you'd rather be mucking the barn.

And sure. Some of us create personas that are dishonest.

We have barn personas, too. Some of us put our horses in our old friend category; we can be whoever we want around them. Some of us want to do the right thing so badly that we show up like a Teacher's pet, reciting rules precisely, wondering if there's a horse making faces behind us. Some of us pick a persona of a little girl around horses, giggling or swooning.

Say you were taught that horses need a strong leader, but you struggle with fear and on top of that, embarrassment. You try for a cool exterior while your stomach churns.

I've got a couple truths for you. First, you can be whoever you want at the barn, any persona at all. It will impact your horse and your riding. It's your choice.

And second, you're probably not fooling anyone. Least of all, your horse. And if you have a mare, she knows the truth about you that day, before you get up in the morning.

Now shift perspective. Pretend it isn't all about us. Gently detach for a moment and see it from your horse's side.

Say you treat your horse like an old friend. You share all your problems, cry in his mane, let him take care of you. He will babysit you, if that's what you want. Maybe you come late, you're in a hurry, swirling a cloud of those sad emotions and a few more, like joy or anger or frustration. How does he cope with our conflicting and changeable emotions? A stoic horse shuts down from the rattle and slam. Horses don't hear pronouns; your stress is now theirs. Stress abides and soon he gives calming signals about his stress. It's okay. We've been using horses this way forever. Be aware there is a cost. Do you want to give your dearest friend your best self or leftovers?

Are you a little Type A? Just to save time, only raise your hand if you aren't. I'm not sure why perfectionists are drawn to horses, but we are. We nit-pick, micro-manage, and fall short of our own ridiculous standards. We create a crust of self-loathing. Horses experience it has never being right. Not you, them. They never feel good enough, like everything they do is partly wrong. Sound familiar? Horses lose confidence. It kills their try and eventually their souls, but we might think they look like push-button horses. (Mares, not so much.)

This last one is touchy. Do you arrive at the mounting block in domination mode? It's the most complex barn persona because it's how most of us were taught: to be the boss and demand respect through fear. We do it with anxiety because it's false bravado, covering up things we'd rather hide from than admit. It's also the false persona that most riders I work with tell me is the one they hate, but it's what is uncomfortable habit.

If I had a nickel for every rider who's told me she gets a lump in her stomach, that it just doesn't feel right to assert harsh leadership, well, I'd have twenty more retired horses in my barn.

What does a horse think about the dominant persona? As prey animals, some will submit in fear to a predator. Flight is their first response. Maybe you can fight through that to something remotely like submission. And since horses don't have social media, they don't know the #metoo hashtag. But fair warning; some mares never get the hang of submission.

What do horses think about personas in general? I think we confuse them with the gap between who we are deep down and this surface behavior that can mean so many things. And more so if we change personas frequently. We confuse horses with our incongruence.

Domination sometimes seems to work because horses are hard to fool, but are fairly easy to intimidate. That kind of training won't make a horse trustworthy, and not surprisingly, they end up learning that we're untrustworthy. There is no trust in domination, on either side. No wonder some riders get a lump in their stomach.

You don't need to change a thing. I'm just suggesting you notice the role your particular persona plays for your horse. How is it working? If you have the perfect partnership, wonderful.

If you think it might be time for a persona upgrade, and you are serious about wanting more and better with your horse, then consider becoming relentlessly, seriously positive.

Take real action in your life. At first spend time just notice what you say and the message your body gives. Be less aware of your horse's behaviors and pay more attention to your own. Begin to focus on being the sort of person horses could respect. The easiest way is to breathe, smile, and say "good" as a cue to your body. When your body follows that cue, so will your horse.

Horses can tell when we fake it too hard but they also seem to understand our intention. They appreciate when we try to do better. That explains why they are so forgiving.

Let's redefine leadership as the one who breathes and smiles the most: Let an inhale relax your body, let an exhale leave soft shoulders and a soft belly. Let a smile give you a soft jaw.

Then be seriously patient and your horse will offer his heart. Be seriously grateful and it will change your heart. Most of all, be seriously light-hearted because horses like us that way.

Horses blossom in behavior and training when we become the best version of ourselves.

Severe Weather Warning

It was 78 degrees yesterday. It's late October so the sun is lower in the sky. There was a slight breeze that would have been perfect for riding, but I was testing the water tank heaters. Then the winds came howling, tearing the last leaves free. The sky turned a sweet apricot color, tinted by a grass fire to the north. Temperatures tonight will drop to 18 degrees with blowing snow. Like they say, 'tis a privilege to live in Colorado.

It's a dry cold here on the high desert prairie but everyone has shelter. Winter coats have grown in dappled and thick. I throw more hay on nights like this to keep their internal heaters working but I don't blanket the horses in my barn as a rule.

Except for this ancient one, Lilith. She came to rescue a couple of years back, not eating or drinking, and so thin that we worried she was dying. But she's a long ear. She outsmarted us.

Last year I bought her a blanket for the wet spring snows that left her shivering. She has expired teeth, so feeding more hay doesn't work. The mush she gets several times a day usually freezes before she finishes it.

This year, she's even more wobbly when she gets stiff, so the blanket came out early. Still, I'm not foolish enough to try blanketing her on my own. I know what you're thinking. She's barely bigger than a goat. Perhaps after you trim that goat's hooves you'll have a better idea where the true danger is on a farm. So, because this isn't my first rodeo, I held off blanketing until help arrived. By midmorning, the temps had dropped ten degrees and the wind was getting stronger. And yes, Lilith may be nearly blind now but not so much as to not see what our plan was.

I stood still while my barn manager did a stilted two-step with Lilith. We go slow, we breathe. We both preach this stuff every day. Then Lilith drags my barn manager, in limping slow-motion, the length of the run as I slowly introduce the blanket. To be clear, the two of us humans outweigh Lilith but she has a kind of lateral gravity to her lean. She's unstoppable. I'm hoping we'll grind to a halt by the end of the run.

Meanwhile, I've managed to get one of the front buckles done on the blanket. That's the easy part. Hooking the belly straps is harder and I'm not wearing a helmet. I try to strike that balance of quickness without jerking, coordination without dawdling. I almost manage it, the blanket is on, and we let her go.

Lilith dodders away indignantly. We can tell because she kicks at each of us as she goes. Sure, we smile but both of us has had hoof contact from this old donkey. It's a bit like being cut by a dull knife.

A few feet away she turns and glares us. She wears her blanket like a bright turquoise muumuu, huge on top with her tiny ankles dangling out below. Just when I am trying to remember which of my mother's sisters she reminds me of, Lilith marches quickly toward me, flopping her ears back to the angle of a jet wing.

She's demanding a forehead rub with the obligatory cleaning of her eye snot. I oblige, being careful to not touch her ears. She's made it clear that they were twitched sometime in the last forty years and I had better pay attention. I just do as I'm told. No hearts and flowers.

She abruptly turns and leaves again with a smaller kick this time. Only marginally dangerous. Another pause with a withering stare before she marches herself over to my barn manager and demands the same homage. Again, given as required and without hesitation.

There is never a shred of doubt what Lilith means. Even if

some of her feelings contradict each other, she has an undeniable clarity. Our other long ear, Edgar Rice Burro, is just as plain. One more time, I recite my fervent wish that people would express themselves as honestly. We bite our tongues until we explode. Donkeys have it right. Bluntness is a virtue.

Spring and fall are rough seasons for elders. Extreme weather changes create problems for equine digestive systems that were poorly designed in the first place. This is colic weather. Beware.

This year I read a scientific article that debunked all the anecdotal things we think we know about colic. Anecdotal evidence is frowned on in the science world, even if they haven't figured out a cure.

Colic is still the number one killer of horses. Treatment hasn't changed much in the last decades. Drugs are better but the condition is still extremely dangerous. The article said colic wasn't tied to heat cycles or getting new hay or changes in barometric pressure (coming storms). Maybe I'm turning into Lilith but I'm cranky and skeptical. I've been schooled by seasons in the barn. If weather change is only superstition and not fact-based, why is the vet always out on a series of colic calls on nights like this?

Do you dread these dark blustering months as much as I do? It's become a habit to make sure horses are doing more than just sniffing their hay, while at the same time casually counting manure piles in their runs.

The equine truth lies somewhere between old wives' tales and hard science.

So, I stay up late for one more feeding. I've got my heavy barn coat and muck boots, and a head light strapped on my wool hat. Leaning into the wind, I drag one more feeding of hay to all the shelters. The old chestnut gelding is struggling with his arthritic knee but the new horse has settled in well. The rest of the herd looks okay for the night.

The Halloween wind howls at my back as I return to the house. There isn't much good to say about the haunted dark and cold months. My Grandfather Horse, gone two months already, won't have to fight the north wind this winter. In a bittersweet way, I'll be glad of that small blessing.

Roo: Letting a Horse Be a Horse

I was doing what I do just before I lay down at night; taking the late-night walk-through, tossing hay for overnight, checking horses one last time. I love my little farm on the flat, windy, treeless prairie of Colorado. It's the first place that ever felt like home to me. I try to pay that forward.

I toss a little extra hay to Roo. He doesn't even belong to me. Roo is a lost horse. That's what his "owner" calls him. She had no intention of owning him and as for him, well, he has low expectations at this point in his life. He failed at his last position, and most likely, a few before that. His history is lost, too.

His name is Rooster, maybe he was that cocky when he was a colt. Now, he's Roo with enough gray hairs that his color looks flat and rough. His withers poke up high and his spine is a bit exposed, even as his belly is round. Roo his mid-teen years, he seems much older. Some chronic joint problems slow him down. On a bad day, he can't always lay down and get up.

That's the problem right now. It's bitter cold in Colorado and he's struggling. He's on my mind, not that he likes me much.

That's the other thing about Roo. He isn't all that friendly. He defends his food aggressively, although he's alone in a pen. His eyes are sunken. He doesn't ask for much and he doesn't say thank you. It's okay. I keep a place for an elder in my barn, in the name of a useless old horse that I loved. I think we all should.

When my friend took Roo on, she thought he was not long for this world. He was in a therapeutic program and when she resigned, she brought him with her. Of his list of issues, it wasn't easy to tell what was mental and what was physical. He was nowhere near sound anymore and had become a bit unpredictable, not entirely safe. He was useless to humans now. Dangerous territory for a horse.

Sometimes I wish horses were as simple as some think; that they were only beasts of burden, here for our use. There's that word again.

My grandmother, a farm woman in the late 1800s, used to say that life was hard if you were useless. She's right still.

My friend's plan for Roo was kind. She planned to let him graze a couple of months, and then, in his sad and painfully diminished state, she'd euthanize him before the icy winter months.

Naturally, he rallied, not that his topline was stronger or that he was able to move any better. He gained some weight but still had the look of a scraggly old stray dog. Then, in the first few weeks here, he got hung up, his hind leg caught through the top of a fence panel. He was fence-fighting with a mare. Who knew he could kick that high? By the time I got him free, it looked like a truck had crashed the fence but miraculously, he limped away not much worse than before. Lame but indestructible.

It isn't that his life on my farm is all that great. I have no green meadow. He's in a dry lot pen with four meals a day, he poops in his water, and he doesn't care much for the donkey.

We hoped he'd have a more romantic outcome than just being a horse. Don't we hope that old horses will all be saved by a little girl's love? Not happening for Roo. He still stumbles, he still has anxiety, and he isn't all that charming. He used to be a bit of a trial to catch. He doesn't really like being petted. You get the feeling he just doesn't care much for people. I'm sure he came to the opinion honestly.

So, we just let him be a horse. We didn't think he needed a faith healing. We didn't think he was a lost soul, only that he was due a safe retirement. One that he didn't have to pay for by pleasing humans.

Sometimes the best advice I give is that we have to let a horse be a horse. It's up to him to find himself. Rescue is all fine and good, if we don't take ourselves too seriously. But sometimes we think being with humans is the healing for every horse. To be blunt, horses need horses more than humans. But Roo didn't want to be with horses and he didn't like us much either. He needed an unconditional place to be.

Roo has been with us a little over a year now, just being a horse. He's got some supplements, not that they help, but his weight is good. It's still heart-stopping to watch him lay down. Winter hurts him.

There has been one small change. He stands closer to the gate when we muck out his pen now. Not offering anything, but not moving away as he had. One day I had to shoo him out of the way and it dawned on me he was passively blocking the gate. Quietly standing in my way. His eye was looking away but a bit softer, too.

It's not much but it's what he could give. It isn't a miraculous healing of his past. We have no expectations and he doesn't owe us a thing. I think he did it because he's remembering what it means to be a horse. It's what they do.

All elder horse stories end the exact same way. Roo will be no different. He'll get to have a safe home between now and then. Most of us have some room to spare in the barn with the memory of a good horse who gave us more than enough. Pay it forward in that horse's name; offer a place to a lost horse. A home where it's safe for an old horse to be useless.

Anthropomorphic Thoughts
About Spaying Mares.

A very well-respected competitor said we don't need to import so many sport horses; we're under-using great mares. He said more people should consider spaying mares and competing them. I read this in an article a year ago and I've been thinking about it ever since.

We have too many horses of all kinds when you look at the rescue numbers and sixty-five percent of those horses are mares. Rescues see quite a few hoarding farms with indiscriminate breeding happening, resulting in horses several years old who aren't even halter broke, making the adoption process expensive since those horses would need training before adoption. It's pretty undeniable, even with the health risks involved, that the spay and neuter programs for dogs and cats have had a huge impact on the number of unwanted pets.

For most colts, it isn't much of a question. Ethical horse people should have extremely high standards for keeping a stallion intact and finding stabling can be challenging if you need to board him. And hopefully by now, we understand that there is an overpopulation problem with horses as well. Beyond that, a gelding can a kind, dependable partner for all kinds of riding, preferred by many riders.

Don't get me wrong; I've known some spectacular mares who are focused, kind partners. I know riders who will always prefer mares for their strength and intelligence. And many mares go through a summer of heat cycles without their owners even being particularly aware. They share pastures with geldings and are all around great horses. Good for them.

I've also known mares that earn the title of alpha through aggression. Mares that become unpredictable, if not un-ride-able, during heat cycles. They flatten their ears threatening all comers–and then there's something about the late fall heat cycle that is particularly strong. I have two mares in my barn right now who have been cranky, spoiling for a fight, and rattling the barn Zen for weeks. Their general attitude is dark and quarrel-some; their nicker sounds like a growl.

Remember the name of Captain Woodrow Call's horse in Larry McMurtry's novel, *Lonesome Dove*? Case in point. The Hell Bitch became a legendary character.

Some mares must be turned out alone, some are eventually asked to leave barns due to behavior issues, for the safety of others. They get retired early or end up as broodmares. We make bad jokes, immortalized as slogans on t-shirts: "You don't scare me, I ride a mare."

Keep in mind, mares are intact. Many experienced horse people, vets included, think that we seriously under-diagnose ovarian cysts in mares. The behavior problems mares show are not a natural part of being a mare but rather a request for help. Beyond that, the connection between this "mare discomfort" and ulcers or colic is well-documented. Why aren't we taking this more seriously?

The ovaries are located just under the fourth or fifth lumbar vertebra, just barely behind the saddle. Yet we name call stereo-typical labels like moody, temperamental, cantankerous. And worst of all, "typical mare."

Generally, we only spay mares who have medical cause, but I've met a few people who have always owned and ridden spayed younger mares and swear by them. Is this a good option for mares who aren't going to be bred? Can a mare become a "smart gelding?" Many say yes.

Years ago, one of my mares struggled with her heat cycles more and more as she aged. I used prescription medications, herbal concoctions, and any other option I heard about. My vet at the time had no better advice. My mare was in her twenties by the time someone suggested ovarian cysts, but that diagnosis came late. By then, my mare wasn't a good candidate because of age and other health conditions. Now I have a young mare who seems to be on the same painful path.

My recent research showed that some surgery methods are complicated and require the mare to be laid down for full anesthesia, frequently resulting in a vet bill over $2000. But I also learned about two different techniques done while the horse is standing. The procedures are only a bit more complicated than gelding, and costs run in the $800. range. It's something to consider.

Seeing these behaviors through the lens of calming signals, shouldn't we acknowledge their pain? Why don't we help mares more?

Maybe I take this hormonal challenge with mares too personally. Back in the day, it was my high school photo next to the definition of PMS in the dictionary. My back ached and if I wasn't crying uncontrollably, I was yelling. Birth control was a godsend; it was like an anti-depressant. It doesn't help me separate my overlapping feelings that the med I took then is also used in horses now.

Am I projecting my experience on mares? The problem with anthropomorphism (attribution of human characteristics or behavior to non-humans) is we dumb it down too much. It isn't about putting a sailor suit on your dog and setting a place at the table. Being at the other extreme, being mechanically scientific without compassion, doesn't work either.

Realistically, the main way us humans have to discern the world around us is through our frame of perception, our human experience. In other words, anthropomorphism. The trick is to find compassion without an over-abundance of sentimentality.

In this case, women innately relate to mare discomfort better. We understand it and should have more compassion for these mares living in purgatory and throwing in the occasional buck. We are the ones who should speak up for mares.

In the male-dominated vet world, there are always those slightly blue jokes about neutering dogs and gelding colts. I am not immune; I usually bring a bottle of champagne to celebrate the event.

In the past there has been no mare equivalent. Most breeders work with vets on reproduction and it's a big part of a vet's business. What if we asked for more birth control? It's a controversial thought traditionally but overpopulation is a more worrisome issue now that so many horses are destroyed and sold for meat every year.

I wonder if there were more female large animal vets, would mare reproductive discomfort get treated more often? Would ovarian cysts be more quickly diagnosed, if for no more reason than personal understanding? Then maybe procedures for spaying would evolve to be easier and safer, and soon, more mares would get to live more comfortable lives.

Less name calling from us, more peaceful autumn days for mares.

Riders Against Bullies

Railbirds. Everyone's a critic, myself included. I'm just no fun anymore.

I can't go to rodeos, a tradition I loved growing up. No dusty old hats, now it's an adrenaline sport with metallic chaps and fringe. Frantic barrel horses, broncs, or rope horses all look miserable, cowboys at odds with horses and livestock, in favor of a faster time. As much as I know Thoroughbreds love to run, I can't watch a race knowing that money will be the priority in every area, over the welfare of the horses. Too many are thrown away or die before they even have their adult teeth.

It's even harder when it gets personal. It's wonderful to have horse-friends who get together and support each other. There you are, cheering someone on, which would be wonderful except that the rider's horse is coming apart. If we're honest, most of us were taught to ride like this when we started, to a milder or more violent degree. The rider pulls her horse to a halt, jerks a rein to pull his head around to her knee, backs him hard with her hand, and gives him a few more kicks for good measure, so he'll know she's mad and he's wrong. It's what she's been taught to do; what her friends expect.

The gelding is frightened, which everyone reads as disobedient. The horse's eyes are wild, his nostrils are huge. Of course, his ears are back. The group shouts to encourage the rider to fight harder, show him who's boss. So they are all cheering her on as she kicks and pulls.

Not long ago you would have been in the middle of the fun. Now you're uncomfortable; you feel the pressure to join the cheering but you're seeing the horse differently than you used to. It's hard to see the bit pull the corners of his mouth, stress wrinkles around his eyes, his nostrils tense with fear and pain. Even the sweet moments between horse and rider look more like tolerance than connection.

You can't look away. You can't continue to pretend you don't see or even blame your friend; you've done versions of this in the past.

Sometimes it cuts closer; it's these same friends giving you training advice because they think you're ruining your horse. You don't want their input but it's habit. Their ideas about leadership contradict yours now. Passion crashes into tradition with hard feelings, followed by judgment on both sides.

The problem is now you're no fun anymore either. Once you can read your horse's body language, it's hard to ignore. Maybe when you look at a video, you turn the sound off. Instead of listening to the sales pitch for the training method, you listen to the calming signals of the horses in the video.

The most frequent question people ask me is what to do when railbirds offer training advice that's "old style?" And what do you do when you see someone being violent with their horse?

Don't attack them. Even with words. No one changes their ways because someone ridicules them in public. Cool down some, even if you feel like screaming. Your emotions will cause more harm than good, especially if the abuser takes their anger toward you out on their horse. Then you'll feel even worse.

The truth is that there is no shortage of ugliness in the horse world these days. It's so common that it takes no special skill to point it out.

If you see it in competition, file a complaint with the organizers. Call the authorities if you see abuse locally. Then follow through and ask for an update on the outcome, or plan to attend the trial. Form a group of like-minded people and get involved in local politics. I seriously believe that if more of us complained less on social media and more to the powers that be, things would change for horses. In other words, it's common sense; you have a voice. If you feel overwhelmed at the cruelty, take your power back. Put your love into action and advocate.

How can we deal with our own emotional response to what we see? We say it breaks our hearts to think of horses being abused. That we love horses, and it all hurts too much. Are you allowing the pain you see in the world to ruin your life at home?

Take an internal survey. Do you languish in the pain? Do you hurt yourself by ruminating on dark topics? Do you let negative emotions be stronger than positive ones? It's crucial to pay attention because you're literally voting with your heart and mind. By passively lingering in those hurtful thoughts, you unintentionally give them power. How you can tell is it feels like slow-release poison.

The sad truth is our tears don't help.

Positive thought isn't just head-in-the-sand foolishness. It's real science; a natural law. The thing we put our attention on is the thing that grows. There is real power in affirmation.

When friends suggest to you that you need to show your horse who's boss, take a breath. Smile and say thank you. If it's hard, let a sideways glint come to your eye, so they wonder if you're crazy. Crazy makes people nervous.

Horse abuse is painful and we need to advocate for horses effectively. But we don't need to fuel that fire by abusing our own hearts.

It's just the easiest thing to get cynical. I might have been born that way, but the more I travel, the more I meet great horse-people who care deeply about horse welfare. People whose passion burns hot for learning and growing and doing better. Sometimes people tell me that I'm preaching to the choir, like it's a bad thing. It looks to me like the choir of people who care about horses is growing by the minute and getting more vocal. If you feel outnumbered and begin to lose hope in the horse world, remember that world belongs to us. Riders against bullies, unite!

There will be bad days, but try to dig deep and see the love in the dark. Instead of feeling sorry for abused rescue horses, be inspired by their resilience. Let your scars heal. Let your heart be as strong as theirs.

Horses Are Pessimists

Your horse is a young horse or a rescue horse or the heart-horse of your life. A mare or a gelding or something oddly in between. He comes in a plain brown wrapper or loud spots. He's fresh as rain or he's an elder with high withers and a slow stride. You stay on the ground, immersed in a simple love of horse breath and mucking. Or he has a canter that makes you feel the way babies feel when their father gently tosses them to the sky, provides a soft landing, and then lobs them up again.

(I stipulate that your horse is beautiful and perfect and the very best horse ever. Just like mine.)

It doesn't matter if you've only just begun with horses or you've been riding forever. It could be an ordinary day or a special day marked by doing something new. It's something beyond your riding discipline or breed or training method. It's so deep in a horse's very fiber that a hundred years after his death it will stay in his distilled essence...

In an instant of overwhelming surprise, he thinks the absolute worst will happen every time. Instinct rules. Fear makes his eyes wide and his poll freezes. His jaw turns to stone and he bolts. You might see it coming or it might hit both of you from behind in a hot blow of furious anxiety. It isn't that he thinks the spooky thing is a matter of life or death. It is most certainly death.

Horses are born pessimists.

Of course, they are. Horses are flight animals, first and foremost. It's an instinct woven into muscle and bone. Bolting away is their best natural defense. Add to that the power of natural selection, at least historically, and the horses here today are the winners of a literal race for survival; the ones who expect the worst and react the quickest.

Horses don't have the luxury of dawdling through a chat with the herd about the spooky thing. It would be crazy. Any extra moment spent wondering if the shadow was a plant or a predator could easily be the end.

In this light, we should be almost grateful for their pessimism instead of correcting them, thinking spooking is a disobedience within their control. We ask so very much from horses and it's easy to get complacent about what we are asking means to them.

Seen from this perspective, fear-based training seems like riding on thin ice by adding anxiety about being corrected on top of the original fear anxiety. Kind, confidence-building training endeavors to encourage a horse to trust his rider with what his instinct tells him is potential death. Shouldn't we humans find that humbling?

Empathy is the word that comes up in quotes from ancient dressage masters and wise old cowboys. Can we try to understand how horses feel without being overly sentimental or overly harsh?

Humans are works in progress, too. Some of us spook every time our horse does. Some of us get mad or frustrated by what we see as their shortcoming. Stoic humans might just get a little tighter deep inside. So, our insecurity shows as timidity or false bravado or perhaps an un-natural stillness, more obvious to our horses sometimes than it is to us. It isn't just that they read our emotions; they're impacted profoundly, even the stoic horses.

In a passive laziness, humans can fall into pessimism quite easily. It's natural for us in a different way; we think too much, so it can feel like common sense in a resting state. No is the easy answer. It's almost sensible to not try rather than make ourselves vulnerable and face failure. Is it just less disappointing to be negative? Ack.

Optimism does take more energy. If the mere idea makes you tired, you might be not just having a rough patch, you might be truly depressed. Give your horse a break, be kind to yourself, and get treatment, please.

If you've just landed in a resting state of pessimism, if you are protecting yourself with cynicism, that's a reasonable behavior. It just doesn't help your horse. Humans are theoretically an advanced animal because we have self-awareness; we think about our thoughts. Positive thought can be as hard to ride as a spooky horse, but we could pick up a good mental trot and head to the barn. Energy spent in positive thought returns at a gallop. Optimism is addictive. What if positive thinking in our own lives was the cue that most helped our horses in theirs?

Let the naysayers make excuses; horses respond to optimism as the confidence-building missing link that bridges the gap between instinct and training. If we want a horse to offer us behavior they've chosen above their natural instinct, then we have to push our own instincts first. Toy with the idea that vulnerability is actually a strength.

Feel your heart soften to empathy. Say the word good with an exhale of warm breath. Let yes be your answer to every question. Remember to say thank you. Practice until praise is your most natural instinct.

Maybe it's humans who need the discipline to lift our optimism to encourage horses, appreciating fully the challenge we pose when asking for their precious trust.

Why Your Horse's Gaits Matter

Let's say you like to jump and so does your Arabian. Let's say you do endurance on an Appaloosa. Let's say you have an expensive, impeccably bred performance horse and you actually use him for the very thing he was bred to do. Or let's say you trail ride your rescue horse. It's all the same.

So, let's say you have a horse you love. He's kind and tries hard. And you always want to do your best. A foundation of dressage would be a real blessing.

Relax. I'm not suggesting that you crank a nose band and then pull on his face; you won't find that written in dressage literature anywhere, even in the small print. You don't have to wear ridiculous white breeches but a helmet would be nice. Just asking that you look past the worst manifestations (after complaining to the ruling boards at least as much as your friends on Facebook) and consider the training fundamentals as a way to help your horse and support his longevity.

Your horse's gaits matter. When I was a fresh baby dressage queen, I hated hearing that. I didn't have spectacularly athletic horses. I didn't want to talk about gaits because watching my horses run at liberty in the pasture, I knew they were not impossibly beautiful to anyone but me. I knew how world-class horses moved and mine were, well, humble versions at best.

It was obvious to me that I loved the horses I had. I knew we were never going to be in the Olympics but being reminded of our less-than-elite movement made me sulky and defensive. I was missing the point of considering my horse's gaits.

Let's all start at the exact same place. Horses are born with gaits. They are wobbly at first. Sometimes they go more upward than forward, sometimes they fall on their faces. In a few days, they find a rhythm moving next to their mothers and not long after that, they have the joy of running circles around their mothers.

In the perfect world, young horses play in pastures until they are four years old or longer, with short stints of learning ground manners and trailer loading before they are started under saddle. They have uneven growth spurts, developing muscles, and search to find balance in their own bodies. Horses live in the moment; they feel the world as it relates to their bodies, so this foundation of balance is very important to their confidence. (Here is where riders committed to their "ordinary" horses should start to think about gaits.)

Horses were never designed to be ridden. Humans asked them to be beasts of burden, and most agree to do it. Horses are social animals; perhaps they are drawn or adapt positively to relationship. At some point, we begin to take the question of their balance for granted but the horse never does. That shows visibly in their gaits.

This is all further complicated by breed, age, and riding disciplines designed by humans. So yes, draft horses can gallop quickly but still couldn't win the Kentucky Derby. Piaffe and passage are advanced dressage movements but any horse can do an untrained, un-cued, and stressed out version of these movements when they get excited; we call it jigging.

So, what is good movement for a horse? Making a study of biomechanics is a good start. As usual, there is no shortage of opinion and science, and then even more opinion. After that our own eyes trick us, people seem to define words differently, and then make things up to suit themselves anyway.

Riding behind the vertical is wrong according to rules and science, but it's common and horses suffer for it. Other riders ride with long reins, thinking it's kind but end up over-correcting and causing more balance trouble than they know.

All horses should be relaxed and forward in their gaits. Most importantly, neither of those may be lost or substituted for the other. They must be balanced together, moving naturally.

Horses should be covering ground freely, with an energetic impulsion and supple fluidity. The physical reason is balance. It's your horse's comfortable place. Going too slow is challenging. Think wobbly bicycle. Think walking on a tightrope. We need to consider the emotional result as well. A horse lacking forward movement falls into a loss of confidence or enough mental confusion to make movement lose rhythm and balance.

Equally important is relaxation, a peaceful mind, free of the crippling effects of resistance and tension. Physically, the most obvious sign is always a horse's poll. There is a natural movement in the head that is the result of the spine's movement at any gait and if that joint is hindered or stopped, there is tension in his body. Think of wearing a neck brace. Think of running forward with lockjaw. The emotional result of tension is fear and doubt. Again, a loss of confidence.

Some horses rebel and act out as a release of tension and even sadder, some shut down and fall into despair. Yes, some horses get depressed. Your horse's gaits matter because his movement defines his balance and his physical expression is akin to his mental health. His mind cannot be separated from his body; it's only humans that do that.

Gaits matter, not because of competition and judging, but for the sense of well-being and strength in the horse.

If you want to know about your horse's real gait, the movement you must aspire to in the saddle, watch him at play in the pasture. That is the true definition of liberty. It isn't forced unnatural movement, delivered with tense, pinned ears. Liberty is not cued with whips.

Pasture gaits include long strides at the walk, with push and swing and rhythmic stride. Think old school *Saturday Night Fever*. Then it's a trot that's effortless and light and fluid. Think of the glide of perpetual motion, think bird on the wing. Most enlightening, it's a canter that's all power and snap and lift. It's more air than dirt. Think freedom. Think true liberty.

The challenge of riding should always be to allow natural movement in a horse. We should never interfere or be an encumbrance to their gaits. The more balanced and rhythmic a horse's gaits are, the happier he is mentally and emotionally. It's our job to figure out how to ride that way.

Calming Signals: Your Response

For those of us who grew up cantering in the living room and then one day heard the term "natural horsemanship" and thought it meant we could be a horse in a real herd, I have some lousy-bad news:

There will never be a day when a horse looks at a human and thinks they see a horse. Give it up. It was just a sales pitch for something else entirely. You don't get to be a horse. Sorry.

The good news is that if we become a slightly more well-mannered version of ourselves and listen in their language, horses will return an in-the-moment relationship so intense, intelligent, and profound, that for the first time in your life, you won't mind *not* being a horse.

I've written about calming signals since 2014. Calming signals are subtle body messages that horses use to let us know they feel anxiety or conflict; that they are no threat and we don't need to act aggressively. The signal demonstrates desired behavior from us at the same time. He might look away, stretching his head down as a way of asking us to relax and go slow.

Just to be clear, calming signals are the language horses use to calm us. We tend to be too loud and bossy.

Think of the barn as a foreign country and decide what kind of tourist you want to be. You can play the part of a privileged elitist throwing alms to the poor or a peace-maker negotiating with heads of state. It's up to you but you don't own this place. You are a visitor. Remember your manners.

Clean yourself up. Take this part very seriously. No, they don't care what you wear. Clean your mind up. Excuse your emotions, you won't need them. Same with expectations and plans; horses don't think about the future. You're the only part of the interchange you can control, so take your time. Square your shoulders and balance your thoughts. Every time you *want* to talk, breathe instead. Get comfortable with silence. Learn to love the peace in waiting because it's real.

If quieting your mind is hard for you, consider a yoga or meditation practice. Do it for your horse. If your emotions rule your life and things feel overwhelming, your horse senses that from you. Sure, you can use your horse as a therapist but why would you want to put those feelings of pain and insecurity on him? (Says the woman who literally went for couple's therapy to talk about her horse.)

Warm up your senses. Tune your eyes to small things. Listen to your surroundings and slow down your perception of time so that you can be fully present. Each of their senses is more acute than ours so we need to start by being sure we are using the marginal senses that we do have to their full potential.

Think more awareness and less intellect. If you wonder if a response is a coincidence or if you might have imagined it, then believe it was real. Considering how limited human senses are, it probably was.

At the same time, be strict not to draw human conclusions. A horse might be giving you welcoming signals but doesn't mean that he's a sweetheart or a caregiver or a Zen master. Just let him be a horse.

You need to learn their language. You probably know the swear words: pinned ears, bared teeth, the threat to kick. We can avoid those by listening sooner, to the smaller messages. Calming signals include looking away, narrowing eyes, stretching his neck to rub his nose on his leg or graze when he isn't hungry. Know that the signals are as varied as there are unique individual horses, there will never be a precise translation.

How to answer back is simple. You let your body demonstrate calm. You breathe. You balance and wait. You put your emotions on him but in a good way. You let him feel safe.

Give him a release by stepping out of his space. Let him know that you heard him, that you understand that he's feeling anxiety and you respect that. Step back. Look for a release in his jaw and mouth, for soft eyes and a relaxed poll.

Nothing good is learned through fear, so let the anxiety pass before doing more. Let him assimilate what happened. Let it rest awhile. Ask again but discipline yourself to ask smaller this time.

If he swings his head back toward you, he's volunteering. It's what you want; give him the reward that he wants. Resist the desire to hug him and baby talk. Instead, give him his space and exhale. You're training him to trust himself. He's been heard. Let him rest in that confidence.

Someone asked me this week, after a particularly communicative session with her horse, "Does it feel as good to them as it does to us?" No. I think it feels even better. Equality is the ultimate freedom. In my experience, some horses are slow to start. It's as if they haven't been listened to for so long that they've given up. Others yell hysterically for the same reason. Hold steady to the calm and peacefully persist.

Once it all shakes out and they trust that line of communication, they become chatterboxes, always mumbling a running commentary. Horses constantly interrupt me in lessons to say the exact thing I'm trying to articulate. I'm humbled by their brevity.

Donkey calming signals are like horse's, but long ears are smarter and hence, more subtle. Are you good enough for donkeys? There's one calming signal that donkeys are particularly famous for using. We call it being stubborn, but I think they see it as not giving in to loud-mouth idiots who don't take time to listen. It certainly doesn't take a donkey more time to answer. They just resent being hurried.

What would happen if humans adopted that particular donkey calming signal? What if we got stubborn about going slow? Stubborn about listening and not fighting. Stubborn about whispering when it's more natural for a human to get louder. Maybe we could convince horses that we are truly no threat to them. Isn't that the calming signal we most want to give horses?

Big Dreams, Low Expectations

I've become a real party-pooper when it comes to talented young horses.

It isn't that I can't see the potential; that my heart doesn't catch in my throat at that fresh brilliance. The beauty of a young sound body, a quick mind, and that total possibility: I know what it feels like to train a horse who catches on fast and offers more than you ask. A horse who seems to not want to stop; who's curious and willing. A horse who really tries to please, so you get caught up in the thrill of progressing quickly. You're sure he's a prodigy, that he will be the exception to every rule.

Horse-people are dreamers. Even the old-timers. Even when we know better.

So, you or your trainer ride him every day. You haul him a few times a month, he'll get used to being alone in the trailer. Sometimes you ride twice a day. You know there are abusive trainers who push young horses too fast, but that's not you. Besides, this beautiful young horse says yes. He asks for it.

I'm going to make a painful comparison now. Doesn't this sound like something they used to say about young girls who dress up on a lark and try to pass for eighteen?

I became a party-pooper about young horses from working with mid-life horses in trouble. Standing next to them, it's easy to imagine them younger. Looking at his eye now, you know he wasn't born this way. That there was a time when he reached out as much as he is tucked inside now. That he was the kind who once gave his body and his heart but has lost the trust to let you stand at his flank. Looking at his stiff body, you can still get a sense of how brilliant his trot used to be. His poll tenses nervously if a human is within ten feet. You don't have to be a professional to see that his face has been ridden hard. His face, that once reached out with curiosity and courage.

The problem with young horses who are over-achievers is that we humans take this period of youthful grace as who they are. We get attached to brilliance and label it their base level work. On a day when he loses confidence, a day when that young horse goes more like a normal, slightly resistant horse, we think they are guilty of a list of failings and we start the fight. Our change is imperceptible at first. Our dream of them is bruised so we lose just a bit of faith.

Maybe some harsher aids will get his brilliance back.

NO! If that previous sentence doesn't make your teeth scream, you're doing it wrong. Not sorry for my bluntness. I've been around horses enough that when I see that broken horse, it's easy to imagine who he once was. The flip-side is that it's also easy to see the perfect youngster, possibly broken by eight or ten.

To be clear, I'm not talking ambitious trainers starting long yearlings to sell before they're four-year-olds, fast and dirty and half-lame. I'm talking about people who love their horses and are enthusiastic about good care and training. It's easy to get caught up in the thrill when things start out so strong.

But young horses start to question training at a certain point. It's normal, not a betrayal but a time of slight rebellion. Consider it a normal stage. It should be seen as a sign of intelligence. The question we ask isn't if our horse will hit a bad stretch in work, but what will I do when he inevitably does?

Because all training, even affirmative training, carries some stress. Because living in a herd, wild or domestic, causes anxiety. Normal stress is caused by being alive.

And it isn't just young horses. You might be re-training a

rescue horse or even just beginning with a new-to-you horse. Progress can start fast and feel great at first. There will be bumps; he will regress. How will we deal with that?

The traditional answer has always been discipline. "Push him through it. Don't let him quit." The reason I'm so against this way of training is the number of horses who flunk out, damaged and frightened. Certainly not all horses but too many.

Horses aren't any closer to perfect than we are. They have bad days but we don't have to turn it into a bad month. Or a bad life. Instead we can stand back to give horses a break. Take time for them, show patience and calm.

Remember the big picture. Most horses live a long life. Not long enough for us loving, greedy humans, but still, a long life. The majority of their lives is spent learning, and then aging. That mid-life sweet spot is comparatively short. Rushing to the sweet spot to make it last longer is the real dream (or fault) most of us share.

Understandable that we might push harder than we intended. It doesn't make us bad riders, just human ones. Forgive yourself. And forgive horses for not living long enough.

Then pretend you have all the time in the world. Keep an eye on the horizon and celebrate how far you've come. Remember how special it is when a horse volunteers. Remember that you sit in a sacred place.

When you do hit a training block, don't fight. Shrug. Exhale. Ride around it and approach it in a different way. Railbirds are notoriously short-sighted, so work for your horse instead. Riding isn't war; it's an art. You and your horse are building a masterpiece.

If you want to work something on contact, keep your expectations on a short rein. Then your dreams can gallop the infinite, where they belong. Learn to tell the difference.

It bears repeating: The arc of a horse's life (or our own) doesn't look like a golden rainbow. It looks more like the jagged readout of a heart monitor. There are ups and downs in each heartbeat. It's how you can tell we're alive.

The Curse of a Self-Aware Mind

We riders think too much. We're mostly introverts with an inclination toward perfection, which means we think even more. Oh, and we like to ride horses.

Let's say you're riding a young horse who is a little quick. You're with your trainer at your first dressage show. You enter the arena, salute the judge, and begin the test. It's great, the new jacket fits well. You begin the trot work. You know people are watching you but you don't smile. You're wearing full-seat white britches you've managed to keep relatively clean, but they don't give much in the saddle. Not that you've had them in the saddle before. Actually, they kind of suspend you above the sadd…. oops. Are you going really fast? You think you're going really fast.

At this point, you look for your trainer on the sideline and she has a furrowed brow. You think, *Okay, he's quick. Let me see. I could half-halt. I don't need a one rein stop, do I? No, not that. I don't want to pull the reins in front of the judge. Oh. I think I might be pulling the reins already. Crap. I think he's pulling back on them, too. Oh, my. Is that slapping sound my backside hitting the saddle? Half-halt, do you think?*

You survive, it's ugly but you're feeling good about staying on when you leave the arena. Your trainer asks you, through a very tense jaw, "Your horse was running away with you. Couldn't you tell your horse was running away?" "Um. Of course," you answer, "I just couldn't decide what to do." And you give your trainer the second deer-in-headlights look of the day.

Meanwhile, your young horse, who lives in the moment, is thinking about noises he hears over by the Porta-Potty.

First, a simple explanation of the difference between us and non-human animals, like horses. Scientists agree that horses have consciousness, defined as being aware of their own body and the surrounding environment. They think. Humans have self-awareness, generally defined as consciousness, as well as the awareness of our existence. We think, and then we think about our thoughts.

This is why humans are considered more evolved but sometimes I wonder. Our senses are not as acute as horses; they hear and smell and see more. Horses live in the moment. We use our brains to override our senses, so we can doubt that horses sense what they sense, and then think about our feelings about that.

Humans have an added dimension; we can read the philosophy of classical horsemanship. Shop online for tack. Get sold methods of training, explained in deceptive terms that may be popular, but don't actually work on horses. Spend hours on DreamHorse.com. Be groupies for previously mentioned training methods, proselytizing to others about the need to punish horses. Think about obscure breeds we'd like to own. Consider different bits to gain more control of our horses. Have a big heart for horse rescue. Plan a trip to Spain.

If humans were on an inter-species dating site, they would not link us up with horses. We're a bad match, but we aren't quitters.

It's important to understand these fundamental differences. If humans want relationships with horses, we must approach it in a non-human way. We need to study technique, but when we're riding, lay down our over-analyzing minds.

Less thought, more feel. In the example at the beginning, the rider stopped breathing, her legs grabbed on, the cue to go faster. Her body got tense, and her horse got scared. Her response was to think more thoughts. She was so busy having a conversation with herself that she abandoned her horse. It isn't a mistake, it's our instinct.

To be partners, we have to quiet our natural instinct, just like horses have to quiet some of theirs. It's why riding well is an art.

Where to begin? Horses live by physical awareness, so first, let your intellectual mind rest. Just feel. Take a deep breath. Did it catch in your throat? Did your shoulders poke up around your ears? Take another breath. Feel it expand your belly. Count to three on the inhale. Hold a count and exhale in three. Continue. Breathe into your knees and let them loosen. Tell your critical voice to breathe with you, but hold her tongue. Do this all day long. Feels good, doesn't it?

When you are breathing deep and soft to your belly, go to the barn and look at your horse's flank. That's how he breathes when he's relaxed, too. About now your brain kicks in with some bright shiny mental distraction. Smile, because it relaxes part of your head. Breathe and smile, stay with your horse. Create a bubble for the two of you to breathe in together.

Try this experiment: Communicate by using the body parts that both you and your horse share. So, no voice and no hands. Become aware of your feet. Become aware of… (I know you're judging yourself. Just stop.) …your senses. Breathe deep and slow. Notice your hands and keep them to yourself again. Give him space to feel confident in; stand square and tall and away. Let him tell you something you don't know. Without interrupting him to make him hurry. Without interrupting yourself with chatter. Takes self-discipline, doesn't it?

In the saddle, warm up on a long rein. Feel your sit bones and note the length of his stride. Now listen to a song or count your breath. In about five minutes, feel the difference in your back and in his stride. Limit yourself to feeling. Don't fix it, just feel it. Go through each of your body parts and introduce yourself. Is your neck tight? Give it a roll and breathe. Notice your horse's poll release but don't talk about it. Feel your elbows and wrists.

Experience your horse, body to body. There is no cleaner or more immediate way to communicate with a horse. Practice acceptance in that exact moment; that's where connection starts.

After you put your horse up, be as obsessed as you like with thoughts. Talk to a horse-friend for hours about your ride. Tell her you fell in love all over again.

Pretending to Be a Horse

There was a time, while I was in junior high school, that I rode my horse on the road. Lots of us did, living on mostly small acreage, just past the city limit. I rode down to the grade school where we raced sometimes. Or over at the holly farm, up and down the rows. It was almost like a maze.

When I was younger, I thought I was fearless because nothing bad had happened. Yet.

There were pastures we'd walk by and if the horses ran up to the fence, my horse got jittery. He'd bounce around on the pavement tossing his head. This might be when I stopped breathing. A hoof would slide out and I'd freeze to a dead pull. The more I wanted him to stand still, the more he was afraid. Or I was, it was hard to tell who started it. I thought if I could keep him from seeing the horses running up, we'd be fine. I kept a tight straight-ahead hold on the reins, and when his neck got stiff, I thought that was good. He couldn't see them that way.

I don't consider this a high point in equine understanding.

Now is a good time to state for the record that horse's range of vision is a large arc covering both flanks, almost a full circle. It's simpler to state what they can't see: Directly in front of their forehead and directly behind their tail. In other words, he saw the horses coming toward his side from a great distance. I was the one with bad peripheral vision, but I did have the big shank bit that came with him and an old saddle.

So, that's when he started bolting.

I was a kid who loved my horse and now I was scared half to death most of the time. The disagreement had to do with me thinking he should pay attention to me. Just me. And him constantly ignoring me. Sure, his excuse was that he needed awareness of his surroundings, being a prey animal, whether I was on his back or not. He claimed it was a matter of life and death. I thought he should just trust me.

He didn't.

In hindsight, I was being quite mature. Meaning lots of adults think a horse should pay attention to them on general principle. Perhaps because we think we're the master species. Perhaps because that's what happens most days when we put the key in the truck ignition. The world is a very logical place, but human logic and horse logic are two very different things. This is the place things start to come apart.

Is your horse distracted?

No. It's impossible for your horse to be distracted. He lives in the world of his immediate senses. His keen eyesight, his acute hearing ability, and his perceptive sense of smell; each of his senses is unimaginably better than ours. Humans use intellectual thoughts to replace physical awareness. It's why we get along so well with cell phones but it makes us tenderfoots in the real world. The disconnect doesn't mean your horse is ignoring you. Your horse is the opposite of distracted. He's hyper-focused.

Should your horse totally focus on you?

Not fair to ask. First, as flight animals, they must always be aware of their surroundings. Instinct does tell them it's life or death. There are brief exceptions, like if you can manage to keep your horse more frightened of you than the natural world through intimidation, then they will focus on you. But not in a good way.

Sometimes when we want a horse to focus, we scare them when we don't know it. If the desire to hold their attention comes packaged in anxiety, if it comes with fear or anger or any other negative thought, our body screams anxiety directly to the horse, even if our mind thinks it's giving a different cue. Our core tightens and our legs grab on. We brace our arms and grab the reins and worst of all, it all happens as quickly as a flinch. Our brain might think we gave a halt cue, but our body gave the OMG-we're-all-gonna-die cue. Your horse picks the loudest cue.

A huge part of the problem we have around horses is a lack of awareness of our own physical reality. Can you feel what your left hand is doing? Can you tell if your calf muscles are tense? Have your lips pulled into a straight hard-line like your mother's used to? Has either you or your horse taken a breath lately?

Your focus has switched from your ride to your impending doom.

About now the idea of leadership enters the scene. As the leader, you might feel your horse doesn't respect your cues. For example, shouldn't he release to the death grip you have on his rein? (No really, it's a death grip, you just haven't noticed.) Your anxiety goes up more, he isn't listening. Your horse's anxiety goes up more, it's metal-on-bone pain. You think you have no control, right before the bolting starts. Your horse thinks he'll die from your heart-stopping control.

"NO!" isn't actually a cue your horse can take.

Just stop. I wouldn't mind if you dismounted right about here. If you're digging a hole with your horse, at this point, it would be a win to just stop digging. Become aware for a moment, beyond your anxiety. Are you frustrated? Are your feelings hurt, for all the love you have for this horse, that he doesn't listen to you? Why does he blow you off? The more you ask, the worse he is. Have you taken a breath yet?

He absolutely listened to you.

About now, it dawns on you that it's true. He did take every lousy cue you gave him. It's amazing the enlightenment that comes with breathing.

What if we had a strong, flexible bubble; a safe place for you and your horse where breathing happened with a life-affirming regularity. It would be a place where leadership meant safety and peace, where we abide in the present moment.

Now for the fun part; we'll build the bubble by pretending to be horses.

Building the Bubble #1. Just Notice

His thought balloon: (hard pavement. head pull, loose gravel. fast car. smell dog-coyotes. she's distracted. breeze picking up. horses in the pasture on right. head pull. pavement. no dog-coyotes close. she's distracted. she kicks. pulls and kicks. need a breath. pulls head, she can't tell she pulls. ignore it. loose gravel. horses coming to share breath. car too close)

Human: Did that man in that car slow down and stare at me? Eeouww.

His thought balloon: (her tense seat. hard pull. feel confused. she's distracted. need to balance. good, horses trotting now. kicks. welcome, herd. she's not breathing. yay, herd. she flinched. jerked. ouch. metal on bone. no escape. ouch. can't move. must move. no air, can't please her. jerked harder. dog-coyotes. held hard, pain. wind. can't breathe. must breathe.)

I'm not proud of my fourteen-year-old self in this ride, but I'm still responsible for causing him to bolt. I punished him for my fear.

People frequently say that their horse just came apart for no good reason. It isn't true. Their horse came apart for a long list of good reasons that the rider either didn't sense or decided to ignore. When we think they're distracted, the truth is that we're finally noticing something they have been following. Humans, having senses that are so much less acute than horses, are perpetually behind. It's like we are forever coming into the movie halfway through yet pretending we know how it ends. Because we're leaders.

We must remind ourselves a horse's senses are better than ours every minute. While we're busy daydreaming, or planning our day, or thinking we're training them something they probably know already, horses are busy being aware of their environment. They are flight animals every moment. Survival depends on it, even in an arena.

It isn't convenient for our agenda. We want them to think what we think. We want cotton in their ears, blinders for their eyes, and the loyalty of a Labrador. We want blind trust from horses who know we are blind, comparatively.

Some of us have been taught that if we cue him loud enough, it will drown out everything else. It's like teaching a horse to trust that we'll make a bad situation worse. Adversity always makes everything worse.

But you can create a bubble, a safe place for you and your horse where breathing happens with a life-affirming regularity. It's a place where leadership means safety and peace, where we both abide in the present moment.

Start now. Learn to love your horse's awareness. Accept this fundamental truth and instead of fighting it, find a way to partner with it. Recognize their intellect; people always tell me that their horse is really smart as if it's a special gift. All horses are that smart, we need to catch up.

Recipe for a Bubble. Step one: Just notice.

Instead of looking at him, look out from him. Stand out of his space, quiet your mind. Breathe. No corrections, no opinions, notice his breath. Match it. Notice what he looks at. Breathe with him. Hold your tongue. Notice the world through his eyes. Let that be enough.

Do you think you should be training something? Good. Start with yourself.

A huge part of the problem we have around horses is a lack of awareness of our own physical reality.

Notice what's going on around you. Look at the small things in the big view. Use your peripheral vision. What do you smell;

is there a breeze? Close your eyes. Is the ground level? Notice. Do you feel anxiety? Breathe. Open your eyes, you're fine.

Let your horse take you for a walk. Let the lead rope be slack, stand behind his drive line or girth area, and let him lead. It's easy to say we put our horses first but let him literally be there. Follow him into the present. This is where the bubble can exist.

Rest in awareness, in the calm recognition that the world is just fine. That your horse will help you stay present. Clear your mind, be true to your intention. Use your senses. Don't think you know what he always does, notice who he is today. Be fresh. Do you listen to him or an inside dialog of your own? Can you perceive without judgment? Now notice the difference between what he actually thinks and what you'd like him to think.

Does he stop to graze? Is it possible that the grazing is a calming signal, not a disobedience? Does your presence distract him? Just notice.

Learning to connect with horses in the present takes mental focus. Notice that. Your brain might be out of shape. It's a kind of meditation for over-thinking humans, it takes a herculean effort to do less; patience is required. Start with two minutes, walk and breathe. Work up to five minutes. Be kind to yourself if you feel like a fidgeting kid in math class. Show yourself tolerance and give your horse a nod. He's doing his best when you see yourself through his eyes.

Say thank you, it's been a good start on the bubble. Head back to the barn. Strolling along, maybe someone calls you from the house. Or maybe you board your horse and you run into a friend on the way to his pen. So you stop and talk. And talk some more. You gesture with the hand holding the lead rope. You talk. Blah, blah, blah.

His thought balloon: (she's gone. she abandoned me. go to the herd. need to eat.)

So, your horse starts fidgeting. Right about now, you notice what you aren't noticing. That's good. This is learning how easy it is to lose focus at the first bright-shiny-thing. How can you be a partner in the saddle when it's this easy to lose focus? And fear isn't even a factor!

Does talking to others teach horses to not listen to us, as we abandon them in favor of human conversation? How about putting your horse first? Value your shared work by making him the priority. Put him up, releasing him with gratitude. You have the rest of the day to over-think and chatter on with friends.

We'll build the bubble by pretending to be horses. If you want your horse's attention, you might have to do some work to earn it.

Building the Bubble #2. Just Converse

One of us flaps our legs while standing still, banging our boots in the stirrups, twisting around in the saddle, then leaning down to throw our arms around his neck. We mean to be funny and child-like and show a certain sort of lazy bravado. We mean to act like there's no special skill involved in riding. Then to get a dramatic response, we jerk the reins hard sideways and pop the gelding with both feet. Oh, and spurs.

His thought balloon: (lost balance. shift. find balance. is that a cue? never mind. not on my neck. sore. re-balance. like a huge boneless chicken. can't balance. ouch! bang! gouge! sour. not stupid. stiffen jaw. brace ribs. ick.)

One of us is holding mane tight, teetering on the mounting block. Then carefully inserting one foot in the stirrup, holding a shallow breath, and slow and soft as a coyote, bringing the other leg over the saddle, careful to not land too hard. Trying to be invisible, thighs are so tight that we're hovering more than sitting. Lurking lightly with our seat, hands, cues, voice. Whoa, not so fast. And constantly apologizing.

His thought balloon: (can feel you. stalk me. vapor for brains. afraid of my back. teeth in her knees. what? please breathe. worry. say again? anxiety. done something wrong. what moved? always wrong. hear that? spook.)

One of us wants to get it just right; reading books, watching videos hour after hour; dressage, reining, eventing. Nuno, Buck, Beezie, Tom, all on a first name basis. There's a plan for each stride, a watch on the wrist, quickly mounting, shortening the reins, going to work. Trying to do our best, each effort judged with blinding perfection, over-cooked passion, and an obsessive desire to ride better each ride.

His thought balloon: (sharpened sit bones. try to breathe. what? don't have to yell. confused. can't go forward. squashed ribs. neck stuck. what? sorry. this? sorry. gripped. pushed. tight. can't. wrong. wrong again.)

It isn't that we're one of these riders; at one time or another, we've been all three. There is such a fine line between bravado and fear, both a lack of confidence. A fine line between caring too little and caring too much, both focus on control. A fine line between being too harsh and being too kind, both are uncomfortable for horses.

Then, there's this one other thing: No one is intentionally communicating with their horse.

Doesn't that seem like a glaring omission? We sit in the saddle, pontificating about this or that in our own minds. It's like we're talking to ourselves about our horse, behind our horse's back, while we're in the saddle. We might as well be folding towels.

Consider building a bubble. It's a safe place for you and your horse where breathing happens with a life-affirming regularity. It's a place where leadership means safety and peace, where we abide in the present moment.

Recipe for a Bubble. Step two: Just converse.

Close the gate to the arena or pen. Please, use a mounting block; your horse's withers don't like lateral pressure. Stand for a moment, take a deep breath, and look at his eye. Is it tense? Dead? Worried? Listen to his calming signals. When he's ready, swing your leg over in one even movement. Breathe, settle, and soften. Pause to feel your sit bones in the saddle, let your horse feel a softness in your legs and shoulders. Keep equal weight in each foot, keep level shoulders aligned with pelvic bones, ribs easy and inflated and your lower back relaxed. Let him hear you exhale. Feel his ribs move as he inhales. The conversation has begun.

Define conversation as communication a in mutual language. Horses have no words, so sing or chatter if you must, but know it might drown out your horse's calming signals. Breath is something you and your horse can share, it'll create connection. Horses listen to your body and answer with theirs. Be aware of what you're asking with your volume, intention, and position. Stay present, focused more on your body awareness than thinking with your brain. Hush.

Breathe and ask him to walk on. Leave his head alone, use a long rein. Let him pick the path. The gate's closed, remember? Experience the movement of your horse as his energy moves through your body. Follow his rhythm. Feel your own movement, sit bones release one at a time, legs follow the sway of his ribs. Take the walk your horse offers and say, "Good boy." Don't correct, don't put hands in his mouth. Find your balance in your seat, the weight of your feet in the stirrups. How does it feel? No words, just feel. That strange thing is your awareness. It could use some exercise. We'll need it to build our bubble.

If you're nervous or bored or over-thinking (and of course you are), count your breath. Match your horse's rhythm and inhale 1-2-3, pause, and exhale, 1-2-3 pause. Repeat. Breath is the antidote to your mind running like a rat on a wheel. Better than that, it's the language of horses. Have you stopped breathing? See how easily you're distracted? Smile and start counting again. Count your breath for five minutes. Finally, a good use for that wristwatch. It'll feel like forever. Impatient? You're not breathing.

This is silence. Your horse loves it.

Allow him to walk in arcs. Turn your waist until your shoulders are at the angle you want your horse's shoulders to be. Feel him bend between your legs in response. Acknowledge his try, say thank you.

Now, using just your sit bones, ask for a longer stride. Not faster, longer. Feel that? Now back to your working walk, big breath. Stride on. Then ask for smaller steps, using only your sit bones. Good boy, thank you.

That's your horse connected with you in a bubble. It isn't mystical. It's natural communication.

Think situational awareness. No escalating, just feel and stay present. Do you fidget? Are your shoulders still up by your ears? Could you hold an egg under your knee without cracking it? Do you fiddle with the reins? Still counting? Okay, start again.

Peace in the bubble: Just you and him, moving in unison, sharing breath, and covering ground. Just so you know, you're also working on your canter depart, tempi changes, reining spins, negotiating an oxer.

This is you riding the inside of your horse. You're riding him with the inside of your body. Allow yourself to be lifted and carried. Say thank you in every exhale. Feels great, doesn't it?

Building the Bubble #3. Just Move

Morning turnout just after breakfast. Once he's released, he bolts to a soft spot and rolls, and then gallop happens. No, his tail isn't groomed, and he could certainly use a bath, but who cares?

Is there anything more beautiful and inspiring than watching a horse move at liberty? To see a horse feel the glory of his own body, strong and powerful? We're horse people, so no, there isn't. Unless it's a foal's first steps, but really, that's the same thing. We're the ones who can't pull our eyes away from horses moving in pastures as we drive by. We get choked up in horse movies during the galloping-in-slow-motion part. Every time.

In our own barns, we scrutinize each stride for beauty and its evil twin, lameness. Our hearts soar with young athletic horses at play and we feel our own mortality when we watch elders in a head-bobbing stroll. And we love their movement so much, we want to feel it. Most of us want to ride.

Alas. We're humans, and as such, lousy dancers. It's just true. We've lost our wildness; we move in small spaces, have sedentary jobs, struggle with our own balance, physical and otherwise. We think too much.

And we were never flight animals to begin with.

Humans have been "borrowing" strength and athleticism from horses forever and for the most part, horses have paid the beast-of-burden price for that. But there have always been humans who want to get it right. Who will always see riding horses as an art. Who say thank you for each brush with grace and lightness.

Your horse's thought balloon: (must run, run strong and go far. run with others. be fast. pounding hoof beat music. calming balance in my body. settle into consistent rhythm: trotting, chewing, breathing very good. muscle pull warm. rider pulls, holds back. Too slow, leaning, give me my head, twisting. Can't breathe, bucking, bolting, spooking. Human, your choice, predator or partner?)

Sure, some humans are magically graceful and some horses are clumsy. Some horses move with a rhythm like a metronome and some have been so dominated by over-correction and fear that they can't remember how to walk naturally. I notice few of us have the confidence to strut down the street to the music in our heads. We live with fear and restriction as well.

Can we make a pact to lay all the whining down while we're with horses? Can we stop telling stories of their victimization and weakness? Can we accept our own frailty as well as theirs, let it be okay, and make some rhythm of our own?

Consider building a bubble. It's a safe place for you and your horse where breathing happens with a life-affirming regularity. It's a place where leadership means safety and peace, where we abide in the present moment.

Our partnership, our bubble, is made stronger by communicating in their language. Their language is rhythm.

Some training methods seem to thrive on the disruption of a horse's rhythmic movement. Western pleasure is the obvious example, as the horses move in an un-natural human-taught rhythm. Other riding disciplines depend more on developing that flight response in a positive way like jumping or endurance riding. But not all of us are up to loving that amount of forward. Where to start?

Rhythm is the foundation of the dressage training pyramid, meaning they must be allowed to move in a relaxed ground-covering gait. It's tricky because you can't sacrifice forward for relaxation or vice versa. Think about that.

This isn't about a judge or competition, it's because it's natural, right for the horse. Rhythm is the place that their instinct can allow them to join with us. The more peaceful fluid rhythm we give them in our bubble, the more connected they are to us because the leader is the one who provides safety, in a way that they understand, that makes them feel good.

The rider's dream goal is that the horse moves as freely under-saddle as he does at liberty.

Start in an arena, mount up and have a neck ring on your horse. You can buy them, but you can also make them out of old reins or a rope (sixty to seventy inches depending on horse size). It should be a loop going around the base of his neck long enough to hold with both hands, along with your reins, in a good position: hands in front of the saddle and just a couple of inches above the withers. Adjust so the rope touches the horse's chest long before they feel the reins or bit in their mouth. His head is free.

Now, crank up the music and ride. Feel his walk rhythm. This is the warm-up part of the ride, the most important part. This is where you and your horse connect through rhythm. Just feel his stride. No corrections, just movement. Here's the first thing you notice:

Over-thinking kills the dance.

Breathe, feel the sway of his flanks, and cue him in rhythm. Not faster or slower or harder. A leg cue in rhythm with his flank is irresistible. If he's slow or quick, you go meet him there. He leads this part of the dance, but once the two of you are dancing, then you can suggest a movement, you can lead. Then the song changes and it begins again. Let him lead. Feel your body move with his. Experiment. Say thank you.

By now you've noticed that it feels like you have no steering. Most folks hate the neck-ring to the exact degree that they oversteer. It seriously limits the amount you can micromanage and correct him. Focusing on rhythm is the quickest, smartest way to pretend you're a horse.

After twenty minutes of this, he's relaxed and forward, his muscles are soft, and you eventually reminded yourself that you have a seat and legs and that turning your waist is all you needed in the first place. Both of you are loose and happy. His neck is gloriously long. A bubble of bliss.

So, you pick up the reins and in an instant, his poll is tense, your sit bones are frozen, and your beautiful bubble feels more like a wet sheet. Dance over.

Did your cue disturb his rhythm? Did it contradict his movement or support the flow? Did it make him feel wrong and weak, or strong and balanced?

Riding is hard, doing it well is an art. Remember the foundation for horses and riders: All riding questions are answered with relaxed and forward rhythm. (And one of you might need dance lessons.)

Building the Bubble #4.
Just Train Less

It's an obstacle course, by golly. And there's a pedestal, by golly. We both see it, but one of us acts like it's a meteor from Krypton. It's a big step up. The lead gets tight, the human doesn't notice because the world has fallen away. Now the human is nothing but pedestal, pedestal, pedestal.

Horse thought balloon: (something wrong. no breath. she says scary. where, that thing? Squeeze bad. we go slower. blow. blow. can you breathe, too? your backside hard, calm please.)

One of us has a problem with a canter depart. There's head tossing, counter-bend, and a wrong lead. The first eight departures were pretty good, but now it's come apart and we need a good place to stop, like five or six perfect departs in a row. Damn, he knows how to do this, he's just being bad.

Horse thought balloon: (confused. no rhythm. scared. you make me tired. can't tell what you want. leaning and pulling. are you falling? it can't be a canter, been doin' that since birth. what? you're mad? stop. quit.)

Day's end and time to go home. One of us has a lunge line, a long stick with a flag, and a shorter whip. The human starts getting loud anxiety in her body, hand tighter, shoulders tense, throat-breathing every step closer to the trailer and then...

Horse thought balloon: (behind the trailer. you're mad. tired. could you think I don't know what to do? your anxiety big. going some place bad. stiff like you, fight like you.)

The thing that drives me craziest about humans is our arrogant belief that we are the super-species, the only intelligent animals on the planet. Our scientists are just now getting smart enough to figure out what other species have known forever.

We admit that horses seem to read our minds about emotions, but then when it comes to training, suddenly we're like Wile E. Coyote strangling Roadrunner. Maybe horses and dogs tolerate it because of our good intentions, even if we aren't very bright. Donkeys and cats are not burdened with the same restraint.

We think every instant is a training opportunity; not trusting that they can remember, we "train" every obstacle or trailer, or mounting block, even if they have been done previously. We get serious and loud, we repeat ourselves, and when we get an answer we don't like, we discipline them because it's easier than being creative enough to ask in a better way.

Then if something does get a good response, we over-repeat the lesson. How many horses had been over-disengaged until they won't let us stand next to their flank? How many of us are so sick of over-discipline that we develop a new habit of kindly over-nagging, over-whispering, or over-treating?

Just stop. And if you are doing the same groundwork you were a year ago, just stop that, too.

When children are potty-training, it's appropriate to cheer and congratulate them for using the toilet. But if you are calling your son at college and asking if he has "done his business" you're letting him know you're an idiot. At some point, we trust children to use the bathroom.

If we continue to train the obvious, we are encouraging horses to a state of learned helplessness. Killing any spark of spontaneity, brilliance, and even their spirit. Killing the thing we loved in the first place.

In the beginning, we don't know what we don't know, humans and horses, but when we know better, we must evolve. At one point, western pleasure might look inspiring and at another, you might consider flunking out of western pleasure a riding achievement.

Start building a bubble. It's a safe place for you and your horse where breathing happens with a life-affirming regularity. It's a place where leadership means safety and peace, where we abide in the present moment.

Have you been using the wrong definition for training all this time?

Training is defined as the action of teaching a person or animal a particular skill or type of behavior. (synonyms: teaching, coaching, schooling.) Training is also defined as the action of undertaking a course of exercise and diet in preparation for a sporting event. (synonyms: exercises, working out, conditioning.)

Stop training discipline. Start training strength.

Let the concept of training be illustrated by an iceberg. The training of movements is only the small tip visible. The vast majority of training is the other definition. In an hour's ride, spend forty-five minutes riding forward, on a long rein, to warm muscles slowly, to strengthen and supple the horse. Riding exercises that encourage balanced movement and lightness. You are training for longevity and soundness.

The rider stays engaged and positive, always looking for ways to communicate clearly and letting the horse know how much each try is appreciated. You are training for confidence and trust.

There was a reason your mother taught you to say thank-you.

By the way, this definition of training also results in a horse who is focused, brilliant, and wins at shows.

Now he's warmed up and you start the actual work. The first canter transition or first lateral movement won't be his best, just get through it and go on. If you start correcting his first try.... Do I need to explain why it's silly to correct a horse's first try? Because you kill his courageous heart.

Remember successive approximation.

The first of any movement isn't the best. Did he toss his head in an upward transition? Make a note; you weren't forward enough. Maybe you pulled back as you asked. Tell him good boy and prepare him better for the second try. Then he'll be the one to say thank you.

If you still are just not quite okay with the lack of discipline, if the training doesn't feel serious enough, or isn't result-oriented enough, there's an answer for that: Train yourself to breathe and notice the color of the sky. Train yourself to be an artist; sculpt a horse under-saddle depicting all the traits you respect and love. Train your heart to feel empathy, acknowledge the teamwork and effort that you and your horse share. Let it be enough for today.

How can you tell this approach to training is working?

Instead of pretending to be a horse, you're becoming more of a horse: Tolerant. Forgiving. Willing to try.

Building the Bubble #5.
Just Honor Them

Some of us value horses for their physical working ability on ranches, we "use 'em hard." Decent care, no frills. Some of us think horses were put on the earth to be spiritual healers and therapists; we use them emotionally. Some of us commit to a lifestyle, we call ourselves horsewomen and horsemen, with the accent on the first syllable. We are evolving.

Horse thought balloon: (they're confusing. they're confused. about who they are. who I am. some leaders are too hard. some frail, almost invisible. some are all noise. some just crowd me. some hold fear close, others anger. some have peace. some listen. some accept me. most want to change me. feeling their expectations. anxiety. emotions. good intentions. confusion. loud. shut down or explode. it's too much busy. just a horse. always be just a horse.)

I believe with every fiber that horses were created to be a part of the natural world, and like all animals, express their lives in their unique way, for their own reasons. If we manage to learn from them, it's our luck and not their job. They owe us nothing.

We do owe horses a debt historically. The distance we've traveled using of horse-power would have been so much slower on our own feet, with our own muscles. Horses have been a part of the human story for centuries and as civilization has brought benefits to us, domestication has been a challenge for horses.

In the U.K., researchers have recently identified four primary areas of horse welfare issues:

Unresolved stress and/or pain;

Inappropriate nutrition;

Inappropriate stabling/turnout;

Delayed death (i.e., not euthanizing when appropriate).

I agree with this list; it looks about right. When I ask vets and equine professionals what percentage of horses are sound, the optimistic answer is fifteen percent. Most say lower. Your vet might say he didn't find anything wrong with your horse, but those are carefully chosen words. The nutrition issues are obesity-related mostly, along with a list of related chronic illnesses. With more urban sprawl, ranches get sold for housing developments. The less grazing and turn out for boarded horses, the more horses live in stalls and runs, for our convenience. And that last one on the list; we struggle talking about it, much less doing it.

Notice the problems are all related to living with humans. Depressing, isn't it?

Horses carry more of our baggage than we admit. The weight of our emotions, past and present. Our daily stress outside the barn is as heavy as our physical bodies, whether we're old cowboys or horse-crazy girls. Horses don't have a choice but to notice our sharp baggage, being prey animals with keen senses. It's written all over us.

It's up to us to learn their language, the calming signals that tell us how they feel. After that, it's up to us to make it better.

Notice the difference between what he thinks and what you want him to think.

When riders ask me about a training issue, my first question is about the horse's soundness. A change in behavior is usually pain and an unwilling attitude is a dead giveaway. We can't discipline the pain away, and for a species like us, brought to our knees by a paper cut, you'd think we'd understand.

Consider building a bubble. It's a safe place for you and your horse where breathing happens with a life-affirming regularity. It's a place where leadership means safety and peace, where we abide in the present moment.

I've described a bubble as a place that we find connection while riding but it's more than that. It's the place we live with horses. It's their safe haven, even more than ours.

Horses need a home as close to natural as possible, rather than trying to fit into ours. For the handful of us who don't own two thousand acres of forest and meadows, we do the best we can. Horses are social, they need friends. They need to graze, free choice hay even if it's a dry lot. They need space to move around, take dirt baths, and see the natural world. It means we commit to the constant challenge to do better with their care. It will be ironically inconvenient and expensive to do the natural thing.

We need to let them be horses. No more or less.

Humans tend to define equine relationships by work under saddle, but horses see the whole picture. Sometimes doctoring an injury and changing bandages can do more to bring a horse to you than any training method. And for all the right reasons.

Maybe if we paid more attention to the quality of our own feelings and behaviors, horses could deal with their stress better.

If harsh training can cause injuries and ulcers, then affirmative training can heal them.

Their calming signals are telling us they're not a threat. Can we let go of our predator ways and listen? Can we raise the quality of conversation with horses beyond punishment, proving we can become trustworthy?

Rather than asking horses to fit into our world, we'll build the bubble by pretending to be horses ourselves. No, as much as we might try, horses never mistake us for herd members, but we can gain more situational awareness around horses and learn to see the world as they do. We can shift our perspective to caring more about what we give them than what they give us.

Breathe. No, I mean it. Match your breath to his, deep and

slow. Clear your mind. That's the bubble, now make it as big as the barn. Listen to the words you use, be honest about your intention, do you need him to listen or are you offering? Don't say what he always does, notice who he is today. Be fresh. Now, be the leader that you always wanted. Say thank you. Acknowledgment is all any of us wants.

Train less, "relationship" more.

It takes no special skill to fall in love with horses. Standing next to a horse and feeling their breath is a wildly intoxicating thing. Every single time. But don't confuse that with having some mystical bond. That's just them being ordinary, everyday horses. We have to work for a true connection, over time and through honest effort.

It's mucking, doctoring, and laying down our worst instincts and lower selves that earn us a place in the saddle, and the right to share their bubble.

Equine Retirement Planning

First, I watched Brentina's retirement ceremony. Then Secretariat's last race and Valegro's final Olympic freestyle. Who doesn't need to watch Aldrich's one-tempi victory lap one more time? Olympic horses and famous running horses are one thing. This part is embarrassing. I searched for a ridiculously sappy scene from that old movie, *The Electric Horseman,* where Redford sets the stallion free. It's a kind of retirement, too, and the camera slo-mos his gallop toward a herd of mustangs. He's got a gallon of baby oil slathered on him (the stallion of course, who cares about Redford) and his muscles ripple and flex as his stride lengthens. Slow motion photography was made for this and they milk it, changing camera angles in a way that doesn't make sense but shows more skin. You know in the real world, he'll be muddy, scraped up, and half-lame in a day, if a varmint hole doesn't kill him sooner, but the music swells...

I hate thinking about it, but retirement conversations have come up a lot these last months and it's never too soon to start planning.

The thing I like about retirement ceremonies is that the horses are sound and fit and bright, mugging for the crowd, who love them like their own. We celebrate them at the top of their game and wave from our chairs. Real life is more complicated.

How did retirement get such a bad name in our own barns? There's someone who'll comment that she's riding her thirty-five-year-old horse, and another who bites her lip because her horse retired at nineteen. Can we set our emotions aside for a moment and talk reality?

Comparing horses never works. A lanky long-backed Thoroughbred ages differently than a compact round Arabian because of accident of birth. A performance horse might have more miles on him than a backyard grade horse, but he also might have gotten a higher standard of care. Add in the wild cards: injuries, being a kid's horse, your location. No one denies that horses live longer these days, long enough to suffer chronic issues for even longer.

Comparing people is even harder. Some aren't the best riders. Some say they "only" trail ride but that means packing in for a week in mountain terrain, while other's trail ride in their two-acre pasture. Some compete their horses, trying to improve their riding skills to progress farther in their discipline, while making their horses stronger and steadier. Some happily stay at entry levels of jumping or pleasure riding or dressage forever.

One thing riders have in common is that we like to think our horses love being ridden. I'm not going to be popular for saying this, but I doubt it. Not every rider, not forever. Some of us understand and work hard to ride better for the horse. Then some of our horses are stoic and it's easier to think it's all good than listen to their quiet signals about things we don't want to hear.

At some point, we need to stop valuing what they *do* for us and shift to being grateful for what they've *done*.

I don't know what's right for your horse. I do know that I want my horses to get to stop work at some point. Considering his retirement is good planning for his old age.

If you have a young horse, know that you have time. Go slow and build a solid foundation for your horse's future. Train with compassion.

If you have a midlife horse, recognize that these are precious days. His prime is finite and the view from the top is beautiful. Work him with kindness, to keep him strong and supple. Be aware in the moment. Be gobsmacked.

And if you have an elder, listen to him closely. Remind him of his golden days and respect what it must feel like to be a flight animal whose body is losing strength as years pass. Then try to be as generous as he has been.

I want to share two elder stories because my clients inspire me.

There is a gooney-sweet chestnut gelding grazing in a pasture today. I met him and his rider a few years ago. He was as undone a horse as I've seen, not quite sound and not quite young. His owner was an accomplished rider but we spent months on a lunge line, letting him find the ground. Convincing him that nothing bad was going to happen until finally his poll relaxed, finally he exhaled. There was a glorious summer when he competed at intro dressage. His tests were not brilliant. Instead he was steady and relaxed, making round circles and gliding across the diagonals. I was in awe that he was capable of a free walk.

These last months have been up and down. No expense was spared, but his back has still dropped some. We worked to make him stronger, but gravity might be winning. With sadness and no fanfare, his owner took him back to his home barn. We miss him here, but he's been reunited with an old one-eyed mare and the grass is green. Writing about him is my version of a retirement celebration. I imagine thousands cheering him from the stands.

My other story is about a lesson I gave recently to a rider with a fine gaited mare of a certain age. It's taken some time to get her checked out; she's had the full run of vet help for her stiff body and an ulcer supplement is working. The lesson started at the walk, but the mare stopped from time to time. We didn't rush her. The rider was generous with wither scratches while I talked about rhythm to relax her topline and leg cues to supple her barrel. Her walk became more fluid. We did a couple of exercises that released her shoulders a fraction and finally, an exercise to ask her stiff hind legs to step under a tiny bit. She tried a tiny bit. She was thoughtful, feeling her old body soften, you know, a tiny bit.

A spectator might not have noticed her effort and left in ten minutes. We noticed. In the end, the rider found a rhythm that helped the mare feel a little better in her body–a mounted massage of sorts. We never did more than a walk. The lesson ended early and the mare licked and chewed. Her eyes were soft, and I might have kissed her nose. Dressage is a gift for older horses if you do it right.

Thinking of retirement takes some getting used to; we'd be smart to start when they're young. I think the thing we are mad at, the thing we want to control, is time. We are never satisfied in the moment because a good horse will always make us greedy for more. Living in that slo-mo shot of our horses getting old, in front of our own eyes, strangles our hearts even worse than a sappy scene in an old movie.

Sometimes we forget that horses belong to the stars and moon; they were never ours in the first place.

A Serenity Prayer for Both of You

The seasons are changing and the air feels cooler. That's what you notice, but your horse seems just a bit more interested in his surroundings than usual. You feel his tension, so you push ahead. Maybe if you put him to work right away, he'll pay more attention.

You ask him to do the first thing that occurs to you; you turn him toward the rail. He's sticky. So the reins get shorter as you insist. He steps slower, and your inside leg goes to work pushing. Then pushing harder. He's stuck, so you pull the reins over his withers, hard to the outside. Then his shoulder falls to the outside as he tries to find relief from that impossible pull on the inside rein. Now the two of you look like you are trying out for roller derby, but not on the same team.

It's a war of wills; more passive-aggressive than an out-and-out fight, but just as adversarial. The resistance is undeniable and you just got on. Fighting resistance comes naturally to humans. Meanwhile, the ride feels like one long correction to your horse and he can either get stoic and shut down, or get so compressed that he needs to explode. His anxiety is even higher than when you got on.

Both you and the horse bear down, it's a grudge match. Probably better than whips-and-spurs violence, but is it any kinder? Now, what?

Well, first, your horse is right. That doesn't mean that you are wrong, it just means that his vote counts. He's on the defensive because everything he does is wrong. The conversation between the two of you escalated. Somewhere in those first steps, you felt a need to control him and he resisted. Because that's the answer every horse gives when you pull on the reins.

Reins give us an illusion of control. And by illusion, I mean it isn't true.

But the heart of the problem is that rather than being in the moment moving forward, every action is a reaction to what just happened. It's like a downward spiral and the tone of the partnership changes completely. You stop being a leader and become a passive-aggressive bully, but we only notice that in hindsight. And was either of you even breathing?

Another way of saying it is that *the correction was bigger than the mistake*. The fight over what they did in the first place is out of proportion to the initial action. Think about it. It's like we're a court judge that decides to make an example of a kid by giving him twenty years for shoplifting a sandwich, rather than finding out why he was hungry.

Gaining good judgment about over-correcting is crucial for a rider to improve because constant over-correcting makes a horse dull. It kills his try. Eventually, he becomes broken. It's the flip side of the adage Less is More.

Ray Hunt says, "You need to do less sooner; you're always doing too much, late."

I smile every time I read this nearly unintelligible quote. You have to have had the experience of being tied up in a knot with a horse for it to even make sense. Here's the good news; if the quote does make sense, you're half-way there.

Go back, let's start the same ride over. The air feels cooler and your horse seems just a bit more interested in his surroundings than usual. You feel his tension, so you let him look around, as he walks on a long rein. His tension cues you to take deep breaths and blow them out. You're going to put him to work, but you'll show him the respect of allowing him to get comfortable first. Take that first walk he offers you, and exhale a thank you.

Feel your sit bones unite with his movement. A few strides later, your waist feels looser. That's how you can tell his stride is lengthening.

If you want to move to the rail, that's great. Let your legs follow his barrel as it moves back and forth, and begin to pulse with your inside leg, asking him to step to the outside. The rein is still long. Give him all day to figure out his answer. It's an attitude of a leg yield, in a way, but you are massaging his ribs, so the outside bend is a stretch. It might take the length of the arena to get to the rail, but your horse is more relaxed when you get there. There has been no fight. You have used time as an aid to release his distraction and anxiety. You and your horse are together in the present moment, partners at the beginning of a great ride.

Making corrections that are bigger than the original mistake can be habit-forming. You can't remember the first wrong step, but now it feels like you're always correcting. You aren't a malicious rider; you love your horse. It might be nothing more than letting your mind run off to a default position, but even as it's happening, you wish it was different.

Do you ever have that moment when things are beginning to spin out of control, and almost as a joke, through gritted teeth, you hiss the Serenity Prayer? But the words work, even said sarcastically, because the anxiety has to take a breath. You can stop this sad behavior that you never meant to start. Next time you're having a mental runaway in the saddle, try this:

Horse, grant me the serenity to breathe, the patience to give a small, quiet cue, and the wisdom to listen for the answer with gratitude.

Then in that stillness, perhaps you'll hear a message back:

Rider, grant me the time to understand what you ask, the confidence to try without fear, and the grateful release of giving you my trust.

Circling Back: How We Became One.

We were hooked and it was written all over us. The first weird looks passed between our parents. We were too young to know anyone else. It didn't matter if there were horses close by; some of us were in the country but just as many of us were in city apartments. We squealed at "horsies!" from car windows or stared at pictures in books we were too little to read. We cantered in the house when horses only lived inside our TV.

Eventually we turned into old women with squint-wrinkles around our eyes and some sort of chronic lameness. Through decades of life, we might have changed homes and changed jobs and changed spouses… but our feelings about horses never changed. Some would say that we're past our riding prime, but I'm confident that the residue of those crazy young rides has made us better with horses now. Probably better with our own species as well.

Horses are like a beautiful water-color rinse washed over top of the ink drawing of our lives. It's the water we swim in while living on dry land. It's the herd we belong to before and through and beyond our other connections. It isn't just that we were born this horse-crazy way. Much to the chagrin of those around us, we stay that way. I think we take it with us when we walk on from this world.

What is this hook that horses have in us? It's the question I've asked as long as I've known horses. Unless I was busy actually grooming or riding or training at the moment. Then it was only in the back of my mind.

Of course, we love all animals, but horses are different. We play favorites. They have similar emotions to us, so they feel familiar, but at the same time, horses hold an edge of wild. They are more honest and true. Is love even the right word? It feels a bit shallow.

When philosophers consider the nature of God and the metaphysics of the universe, surely they must consider the central position that horses hold. If they don't, we know they've fallen short of the thing artists have known since the time of cave paintings; it was always about humans and horses.

We began this journey before there was choice or reason; before we knew the word for how we would feel. We rode when there were no horses. It was a prehistoric promise, sealed with horse dander and spit. Or things that would evolve into that eventually.

Maybe back then some DNA got mixed up in the primordial mush and we're actually a slightly different species. That would explain a lot of misfit behavior over the centuries and all the way to our mother's kitchen tables.

But somewhere in the middle of everything, life happened. Plans went sideways. Some of us gave up horses for a while and some of us gave up everything but horses. Some of us finally got our first pony fifty years later. All of us stayed true to that prehistoric promise with horses; we always circle back.

Now that I'm older, I've laid down some of my wild. I'm more conservative about safety. There are days that it breaks my heart to be cautious, but I have a herd that depends on me. It's lead mare logic; I wasn't born knowing it. I do all the barn work my body allows and then remember the kindness that all past-prime horses have shown me. I try to practice that same kindness on myself but never quite feel deserving.

Perhaps younger riders look at me like I'm a crazy old nag. I smile and wave, stubborn as a pony, working to show them the patience that my first horse had for me, back when I fell short of my horse's withers and wisdom.

We're the sort who never quite settle the struggle to find our balance, drunk with horses and gasping with rude want. We've been loud, crying or pouting if we can't ride. There is nothing polite about passion. Other times, while making the tough choices, we felt as old as sticks and dirt with the bitter maturity of our decisions. Still horses never change for us.

We have a secret that others don't know. While other women dream of romance novel lovers or foreign shores, we dream of a horse who comes to us with an invitation. Personally, I think it's a white horse –like my Grandfather Horse. He was perfectly ordinary. We all had one just like him. The one that we knew before we were born. Even now, he continues to circle back. The one who never leaves us.

ABOUT THE AUTHOR

Anna Blake was born in Cavalier County, North Dakota, in 1954, the youngest daughter of a farm family. Blake is a horse advocate, international clinician, equine pro, and award-winning author, living on the Colorado prairie. Infinity Farm is home to a multi-species herd of horses, llamas, goats, dogs, cats, and everyone's moral compass, Edgar Rice Burro.

Her books include:

Stable Relation, a Memoir of One Woman's Spirited Journey Home, by Way of the Barn, a Peoples' Choice Gold Medal Winner.

Relaxed & Forward: Relationship Advice from Your Horse.

Barn Dance, Nickers, brays, bleats, howls, and quacks: Tales from the herd.

Horse Prayers, Poems from the Prairie.

Available online everywhere with signed copies at
www.annablake.com

Made in the USA
Lexington, KY
23 October 2019